John Shen
619-243-5013

School Choice 2000
What's Happening in the States

By Nina Shokraii Rees

The Heritage Foundation

The Heritage Foundation
214 Massachusetts Avenue, NE
Washington, DC 20002–4999
www.heritage.org

Copyright © 2000 The Heritage Foundation

ISBN 0–89195–089–3

TABLE OF CONTENTS

FOREWORD

CHOICE LEAVES NO CHILD BEHIND

The Honorable Jeb Bush

Ideas really do have consequences, and if you stick with them and you believe in trying them, and you are creative—not just in the ideas themselves, but in how to implement them—good things can happen.

When I first became governor of the great state of Florida, I set out to implement one such idea that has been near and dear to my heart for a long while: educational choice. I, like many concerned Americans, believe that not enough children in our state or in our country get a year's worth of knowledge in a year's time; and so, over time, in increments not necessarily discernible to everybody, kids fall behind in school. They lose interest in learning. They don't connect what they do at school with the potential it offers their lives. And we have quiet little tragedies unfolding across our country.

So we decided to do something dramatic in the state of Florida last year. Our A+ Education Plan is based upon some guiding principles.

First, we have implemented measures for meaningful and undiluted accountability. For the public education system, there are now different consequences for success and failure. That must be one of the standard principles for any reform effort.

Second, we have zero tolerance for failure. Not only do we have the honesty to admit it, but we also are creating a system in which we are going to roll up our sleeves to ensure that every child gains a year's worth of knowledge in a year's time. We're not going to excuse it away, as sadly happens so often.

Finally, and most importantly, the education system in Florida is becoming child-centered. How many times do you hear the term "public school system," with the focus on the word "system" and not on whether children are learning or not. We don't want a school-centered system or a public education-centered system. We want a child-centered system, where the whole objective is that our children gain a year's worth of knowledge in a year's time.

Now, the elements of our plan are fairly simple. Our students will now be tested in grades three through ten. Until now, we could not measure how one student did compared to another, but starting this school year we will be able to measure how children have progressed. We have created high standards, and our test is a rigorous assessment of those standards. This year, in Florida, we will clearly communicate how schools perform based on student achievement. Schools are graded on an A through F grading system. We have also aligned the schools based upon how they perform in student achievement: We graded all schools; and we moved back to that principle of imposing different consequences for success and failure in some very meaningful ways. Here is how:

- We will reward the schools that show improvement. Three hundred schools are A-rated and others have shown improvement by moving up at least one grade. These schools all will get an additional $100 per student. They will be able to use that money for anything they want, with no strings attached.

- As for those that fail, we now have a different consequence. When schools are rated F for two years running (to be rated F in the state of Florida today requires that 60 percent of the students taking the standardized test are below the basic level in reading, math, and writing) parents are given other choices. They can send their child to any public school in their school district; send their child to any private school that opts into our system; or send their child to the same school—but that school is going to be dramatically changed because it will have to come to the State Board of Education with a dramatic plan of action to rectify its problems.

During the first year, 78 schools in Florida received an F grade. They serve a total of 61,000 students. So this fall the A+ Program will expand dramatically if there is not marked improvement in these schools. This school year, 134 children in two schools opted out of their current school. Seventy-six moved to another public school; 53 of the students' parents chose to send their children to five participating private schools in Pensacola, Florida: a Montessori School, and four parochial schools.

The advocacy of ideas is more difficult when the issue is abstract. It is easier when you put a human face on it; and now, there is a human face on parental choice in our state. And that is helping to erase the myths about education that have been built up over time.

Myth #1: The Brain Drain.

You have undoubtedly heard about how only the smart students, only the really committed parents, will accept the choice of a scholarship to send their child to another school. This myth is constantly used by the advocates of the status quo who don't want to change any systems anywhere.

A study was conducted of the 53 children that have gone to the private schools and the 70-plus students who are going to public schools, and the several hundred students who have remained in the two elementary schools I mentioned earlier. The study shows that their aptitudes are the same, their family income is basically the same, and their family structures are basically the same. I might add, 95 percent of these children are African–American, and about 90 percent qualify for the reduced-price or free school lunch program.

So, the myth of the brain drain has been shattered, at least in the case of our experiment, and I believe we will continue to see that parents will make these choices in their own interest no matter what level of income they have, no matter what their family structure is, no matter what the aptitude of their child may be. That is exactly how it should be. We should not be mandating and demanding that parents adapt to our model of behavior. These are their children. They should have the power to make those choices.

Myth #2: Only the wealthy and elite will benefit.

A myth often repeated by the advocates of the status quo is that only high-income families will benefit. In fact, of the 61,000 students in schools that were graded F, 85 percent are minorities, and 81 percent are eligible for free and reduced-price lunches.

Don't let people tell you this program only helps people in the suburbs. It's not true. It is going to advance student achievement across the board. It is not geared to the wealthy in our state; and I believe that it is the appropriate thing to do. We should, and will, focus our energies where learning achievement has been deficient.

The public school system in the state of Florida will always be there. It will always be the principal choice for most Floridians. It needs to be improved, and it needs to be reinvigorated, and that is our objective. Because of that, people like Andrew Young, speaking to the NAACP Freedom Dinner in Tallahassee, supported our Opportunity Scholarships. The NAACP is suing us, but Young had the courage to step up to the plate and say he is for Opportunity Scholarships because he knows it will help the kids that have been left behind. I applaud him for his courage.

Bob Butterworth, Florida's Attorney General, one of the highest ranking Democrats in the state, has to support the A+ plan as Attorney General because the state is being sued left and right. But, while he was not a personal supporter of this plan as I proposed it during the campaign, he personally supports it now because he has seen the benefits of focusing our efforts where the effort needs to be made: in schools where kids have not been given a proper quality education. We are beginning to see movement among the traditional advocates of the status quo, who are now recognizing that this plan is going to improve public schools across the board.

Myth #3: Schools that are failing will be left behind.

Our whole approach, the whole point of this reform is to achieve the exact opposite result. I wish you all could have been at the cabinet meeting where the State Board of Education heard from the principals of the two schools that I mentioned previously about their mitigation plans, their plans to improve the quality of education at their schools.

First, the state offered support for additional reading programs. Second, the state and the local school district supported and approved their idea of expanding the school year from 180 days to 210 days. Third, the school district said that it was going to give the power to the principals to select and retain teachers. They could remove teachers they did not want to retain, they could hire any teacher they wanted who wanted to come to work there. Trust me, this is a big deal in public schools across the state of Florida.

Schools focused on after-school programs because they wanted to extend not only the school year, but also the school day. They showed us a plan that would have 70 volunteers in each school to provide mentoring and tutoring opportunities for these young people. They explained how they were going to use direct instruction to ensure that kids in the early grades begin to learn to read at an appropriate level.

It was exciting: more money and a more focused approach to ensure that children learn. I'm not a big gambling man, but I can almost guarantee that these schools are going to see improvement, and that the children are going to get a year's worth of knowledge in a year's time.

So, the myth that somehow the schools will be left behind because parents are pulling their children out, that they will languish, and that we're going to "destroy" public education is not becoming a reality. What this attitude reflects is pessimism about the condition of public schools. Virtually every parent would have to remove their child from a public school in order for them to be "destroyed." In fact, the exact opposite will happen if reform is done the right way, and, in Florida, we are committed to doing it the right way.

I wish you could see the reaction across the state to this plan. The folks in the system who are most protective of it were probably a little more angry at first than anything else when they saw the law pass that allows us to do this. But now we are beginning to see a very positive reaction to our plan. There are smaller class sizes now in Broward County in the 104 low-performing schools, the schools that were graded D and F. In Jacksonville, the School Board decided to expand summer school and after-school programs for the low-performing schools. In Tampa, Earl Leonard, the superintendent of the Hillsborough County School District, made a public statement that he would take a 5 percent pay cut in his salary, and all of his top administrators would do the same, if any of the schools in Hillsborough County were given a grade of F. A quote from a teacher says it all:

> I've seen principals eat worms. I've seen vice-principals kiss pigs to get students to read a certain number of pages. But I have never seen a superintendent put his salary on the line.

At the end of this process, in a decade perhaps, we will see rising test scores across the board; each and every year we will see more significant improvements in test scores among students at the 25th percentile and below. We're going to see more resources go to the classroom and less to the bureaucracy; and we're going to see a renaissance of involvement by in public education.

I hope other governors will use the Florida model as they set to reform education in their states. With education a high priority among voters, one could fairly say now is the time we must act to ensure that all children receive the best possible education.

ACKNOWLEDGMENTS

School Choice 2000: What's Happening in the States is the product of many years of painstaking research by education analysts and others at The Heritage Foundation, working closely with many school choice supporters at the national, state, and local levels. The author wishes to thank all those who have contributed to this ongoing effort over the years, especially our national and state contacts.

In addition, the author wishes to thank the many individuals at Heritage who have contributed to this year's edition, including Angela Antonelli, Director, Thomas A. Roe Institute for Economic Policy Studies; Devin Brown, Domestic Policy Administrative Assistant; Adam Condo, former Domestic Policy Research Assistant; Jennifer Garrett, Domestic Policy Research Assistant; Erin Hymel, Domestic Policy Administrative Assistant; Philippe Lacoude, Senior Database Programmer, Center for Data Analysis; William Rasmussen, Center for Data Analysis Intern; Amber Williams, Domestic Policy Research Intern; and Sarah Youssef, former Domestic Policy Research Assistant.

Special thanks to William T. Poole, Senior Copy Editor, for his diligent editing of the entire book. The author also thanks John H. Dickson, Deputy Director of Online Services; Richard Odermatt, Senior Editor; Janice A. Smith, Managing Editor; and the following members of the Publishing Services staff: Ann Klucsarits, Director of Publishing Services; Anne C. Gartland, Design and Layout Specialist; and Thomas J. Timmons, Deputy Director of Publishing Services.

A NOTE ON UPDATING THIS EDITION

School Choice: What's Happening in the States is published in book form early each year and posted in its entirety on the World Wide Web at *http://www.heritage.org/schools/*. To make sure that users of this resource enjoy ready access to the latest developments in this rapidly changing field, we also post new, updated information on our Web site. Readers who access the Web site will find a note on the home page calling their attention to all recent updates.

Previous editions of *School Choice* are available for those who wish to make their own comparisons of progress in the states on the school choice front. Links to the 1999, 1998, 1997, and 1996 editions may be found on the school choice home page.

We encourage all readers, school choice advocates, teachers, and parents to keep us abreast of what's happening in their states by e-mailing the author at *nina.rees@heritage.org*. We also encourage you to call us at (202) 546-4400, as well as our state contacts at the phone numbers listed, for additional information on particular state laws.

AN EXPLANATION OF THE STATE PROFILE CATEGORIES

School Choice Status

- Public school choice: Status of public school choice in the state

  Statewide: Students can choose to enroll in any public school within the state.

  Limited: Students can choose only from schools in their own districts or where it is voluntary for districts to have local choice programs.

  Source: "Choice of Schools: State Actions," Education Commission of the States *Clearinghouse Notes*, March 7, 2000, and state contacts.

- Charter schools: Year a charter school law was enacted in the state.

  Strength of law: Strong or weak as determined by the Center for Education Reform, a free-market public policy organization.

  Also reflects the number of charter schools and their enrollment.

  Source: Center for Education Reform, "Charter School Legislation and Laws," downloaded October 29, 1999, available at *http://www.edreform.com/charter_schools/laws/chlaws.htm*, and various state contacts.

- Publicly funded private school choice: Describes state programs that offer parents additional choices among private or religious schools through vouchers, tax credits, or deductions.

  Source: Author's summary of state profile.

K–12 Public and Private School Students and Schools

- Public school enrollment (fall 1998) and number of schools (1997–1998)

  Sources: National Education Association, "Rankings and Estimates: Rankings of States 1999 and Estimates of School Statistics 2000," October 1999 (enrollment); U.S. Department of Education, National Center for Education Statistics, "Overview of Public Elementary and Secondary Schools and Districts: School Year 1997–98," May 1999 (number of schools).

- Private school enrollment and number of schools (1997–1998)

  Source: U.S. Department of Education, National Center for Education Statistics, "Private School Universe Survey, 1997–1998," August 31, 1999.

K–12 Public and Private School Student Academic Performance

- Table provides percentage of students at each performance level on the National Assessment of Educational Progress test for both public and private schools, with national percentages in parentheses.

  Source: Business Roundtable, *Transforming Education Policy—Assessing 10 Years of Progress in the States*, June 1999, and National Assessment of Educational Progress Report Cards at *http://nces.ed.gov/nationsreportcard/*.

- SAT and ACT weighted ranks (1999): The state's ranking based on the 1999 average test scores on the college entrance exams. States are ranked according to the predominant test (the SAT or ACT) administered to students.

    Source: American Legislative Council, *Report Card on American Education 1999*, forthcoming.

K–12 Public School Expenditures

- Current expenditures (1999–2000)

- Amount of revenue from the federal government (1998–1999)

- Current per-pupil expenditures (1999–2000)

    Source: National Education Association, "Rankings and Estimates: Rankings of States 1999 and Estimates of School Statistics 2000," October 1999.

K–12 Public School Teachers (1998–1999)

- Number of schools

- Average salary

- Students enrolled per teacher

    Source: National Education Association, "Rankings and Estimates: Rankings of States 1999 and Estimates of School Statistics 2000," October 1999.

- Leading teachers union

    Source: Information obtained by calling the United States Department of Education in October 1999 and from Mike Antonucci, Education Intelligence Agency.

A SCHOOL CHOICE GLOSSARY OF TERMS

Charter school: A public school that agrees to meet certain performance standards in exchange for exemptions from public school regulations other than those governing health, safety, and civil rights; accepts accountability for results in exchange for autonomy in the choice of methods for achieving those results. States determine further specificity of the law. Depending on the state law, parents, a group of teachers, or businesses may create charter schools and design the curriculum.

Child-centered funding: A school financing plan that would allow a single dollar amount, representing both operations and capital funding costs, to follow each student to the school of his or her choice.

Controlled choice: Choice of school that is limited by court-ordered desegregation guidelines. In Missouri, for example, Kansas City and St. Louis must observe strict racial guidelines for the placement of students in city schools. Parents are limited to choices that will not upset the racial balance of a particular school.

Education savings accounts: Accounts, similar to individual retirement accounts (IRAs), in which individuals save a certain amount of post-tax dollars each year for the educational benefit of a student. The amount in the account, with the interest it has accrued, can be withdrawn tax-free to pay a student's education-related expenses in grades K–16 at a school of choice.

Full choice: Choice that includes public, private, and parochial or religious schools.

Inter-district choice: Choice that allows students to cross district lines. Some states, such as Alabama, allow inter-district choice among only a limited number of districts.

Intra-district choice: Open enrollment among schools within a particular district. Also known as transfers.

Magnet schools: Public schools that offer specialized programs. Sometimes used as a voluntary method to achieve racial balance when districts are under court order to desegregate. Magnet schools offer students an option or a substitute for their own location-based school assignments.

Mandatory statewide choice: See open enrollment.

Open enrollment: System that allows parents to decide which public school their children will attend anywhere in the state, rather than having children assigned to a school based on home location. With voluntary open enrollment, the district is not required to offer a choice, but may allow parents to choose the schools their children attend. With mandatory open enrollment, the district must allow parents this option.

Post-secondary enrollment options: Choice of enrollment that allows high school students (usually juniors or seniors) to enroll in courses at state universities or community colleges at government expense and receive high school and college credits for those courses. The money allocated for the student's education pays for the courses selected, thus forcing high schools to compete with colleges for students.

Private voucher programs: Programs supported by individuals, businesses, and other groups that give vouchers directly to low-income children to enable them to attend private schools. Programs differ by the types of support they give to families and the types of schools that are eligible.

Public school choice: Choice only among public schools.

Site-based management: System under which responsibility for decisions affecting the personnel and educational policies of a school is shifted from a central administration or school board to committees of teachers and the principal of that school (and perhaps to parents).

Tax credits and/or deductions: Funding method that facilitates choice by granting parents a credit or deduction against income or property taxes for money they spend on private school tuition, books, or other expenses. The United States Supreme Court has ruled that education tax credits and deductions are constitutional.

Tuitioning town: A town that does not have a public school and allows per-pupil funds to follow students to the nearest public or independent school of choice. Currently, Maine and Vermont have tuitioning towns.

Voluntary choice: See open enrollment.

Vouchers: Certificates with a designated dollar value that may be applied toward tuition or fees at the public or private educational institution of the parents' choice. Used in much the same way that food stamps are used to buy food and housing vouchers are used to offset rent.

SCHOOL CHOICE 2000 ANNUAL REPORT

Nina Shokraii Rees

"If you're in an...under-achieving school, then you have a right to seek a voucher to go to a school where you can be guaranteed some level of achievement."

—*Andrew Young, former mayor of Atlanta and top aide to Dr. Martin Luther King, Jr.*

The school choice movement ended the millennium on a high note. In 1999, it secured the enactment of a sweeping school choice plan in Florida, an education tax credit program in Illinois, and two new charter school laws. Perhaps most impressive, the Children's Scholarship Fund found that 1.25 million low-income parents would take advantage of scholarships to attend a better private or religious school if given a choice.

Michigan and California are up next: Choice initiatives are on each state's ballot this November. Also, two governors have pledged to push for school choice in the coming year. Governor Gary Johnson of New Mexico plans to offer all students a voucher to attend a school of choice, and Governor John Rowland of Connecticut wants to offer the parents of private and religious school students a $500 tax credit.

Regardless of what happens at the state level, however, one development could significantly alter the course of school choice in 2000: the presidential elections. The next President will decide the composition of the U.S. Supreme Court and determine who fills the vacancies on the lower federal courts. Most legal scholars expect that the Supreme Court could decide, once and for all, the constitutionality of school choice in the near future.

Growth of Publicly Financed Private School Choice Programs

Florida and Illinois led the way in school reform last year. Thanks to the hard work of Florida Governor Jeb Bush and allies such as T. Willard

Fair of the Urban League of Greater Miami, Florida is now the first state in the nation to allow a "money back guarantee" for students trapped in failing schools. This statewide school choice plan allows students who have been trapped for two out of four years in a failing school an opportunity to attend a better public, private, or religious school of choice. In the first year (1999–2000), 134 families from two elementary schools in Pensacola were offered scholarships, of which 78 were for attendance at public schools. Students in as many as 50 schools could qualify in 2000–2001.

Faced with the prospect of a mass exodus from poorly performing public schools, public school officials are responding quickly. The Superintendent of the Hillsborough County School District (in Tampa) even said that he and all of his top administrators would take a 5 percent pay cut if any of the schools in Hillsborough County were given a grade of "F." The leaders of the teachers unions and their allies, as expected, already have filed two lawsuits against the Florida plan. On March 14, 2000, a state judge struck down the program. An appeal has been filed.

Florida may have been in the spotlight this year, but other states have taken positive action as well. Last year, for example, Illinois enacted an educational expenses tax credit, which would provide parents a tax credit of up to 25 percent of education-related expenses (tuition, book fees, lab fees) exceeding $250, for a maximum of $500 per family. This program has been challenged in two separate lawsuits even though its key beneficiaries are public school students.

New Mexico, Pennsylvania, and Texas were the other states in the school choice spotlight.

- **In New Mexico,** thanks to Governor Gary Johnson, a bill to award each of the state's 316,000 schoolchildren a voucher worth $3,500 a year gained momentum; after being scaled back, however, it was killed by the opposition.

- **In Pennsylvania,** Governor Tom Ridge introduced a plan that would offer, among other things, a voucher to parents in struggling districts to send their children to the public, private, or religious school of choice. After being scaled back, the plan was withdrawn from consideration.

- **In Texas,** several bills were introduced with the backing of both Governor George Bush and Lieutenant Governor Rick Perry, but none passed the legislature.

Nevertheless, Johnson, Ridge, Bush, and Perry have vowed to continue pushing for these reforms in the future.

Charter Schools on the Rise

In the waning hours of the 1999 legislative session, the legislatures of Oklahoma and Oregon passed two bipartisan charter school measures that later were signed into law.

Meanwhile, for the third year in a row, Hugh Price, president of the National Urban League, has implored his members to think like real reformers, urging that all the nation's urban schools be turned into independently run charter schools.

In February 2000, the U.S. Department of Education released *The State of Charter Schools—2000,* the fourth-year report of a national study on charter schools.[1] The report finds that:

- During 1999, 421 new charter schools opened, bringing the total to 1,484 as of September. (If multiple branches of a school operating under the same charter are taken into account, the total number of charter school sites operating was 1,605.)

- The number of students in charter schools increased during the 1998–1999 school year by nearly 90,000, bringing the total to more than 250,000 students.

- Of the 36 states with charter laws, 11 allow private schools to convert to charter schools.

- Most charter schools are small, with an average enrollment of 137 students.

- White students made up about 48 percent of charter school enrollment in 1998 compared to about 59 percent of public school enrollment in 1997–1998.

Another report by Professor Scott Milliman of James Madison University, Fredrick Hess and Robert Maranto of the University of Virginia, and Charlottesville, Virginia, social psychologist April Gresham reveals that the establishment of charter schools has spurred noticeable differences in the public school system.[2] Based on a March 1998 survey of Arizona public school teachers, the researchers concluded that the power of choice and market competition from charter schools led to the following changes between the 1994–1995 and 1997–1998 school years:

- Districts made greater attempts to inform parents about school programs and options.

- Districts placed greater emphasis on promoting professional development for teachers.

- School principals increased consultation with teaching staff.

The authors also found that charter schools do not replace district schools, but rather push district schools to compete, primarily because state subsidies follow the students.

Growth of the Private Scholarship Movement

Perhaps the most interesting and encouraging phenomenon in education reform during the past decade has been the creation of the Children's Scholarship Fund. The CSF is a $100 million foundation underwritten by entrepreneurs Ted Forstmann and John Walton. The plan initially offered 43 cities and three states matching funds to allow poor students trapped in failing schools an opportunity to attend a school of choice. Later, because of an overwhelming number of applications for CSF challenge grants, the program expanded to offer vouchers to all low-income students entering kindergarten through 8th grade, not just those in the 43 cities and three states originally selected as partners.

By the March 31, 1999, deadline for applications, the CSF had received responses from all 50 states—from 22,000 communities and 90 percent of all counties across America. In some cities, a remarkable percentage of the eligible population applied: 29 percent in New York; 33 percent in Washington, D.C.; and a stunning 44 percent in Baltimore.

In all, the CSF received a total of 1,250,000 applications—*30 times the number of scholarships available*. This response is even more remarkable because to qualify for these partial scholarships, applicants must be from low-income families willing to contribute an average of $1,000 per year. This $1,000-per-year contribution for four years from parents of 1.25 million children adds up to $5 billion from families who have very little to give. These parents are willing to sacrifice in order to give their children the chance to escape bad schools and, through choice, gain access to greater educational opportunities.

Altogether, the CSF has awarded nearly 40,000 four-year partial scholarships, totaling $170 million, to enable thousands of low-income students across the country to attend the school of their choice. Recipients are selected randomly by a computer-generated lottery.

The CSF board includes civil rights leaders like Andrew Young, Martin Luther King III, and Dorothy Height, and such national leaders as General Colin Powell, Barbara Bush, and the majority and minority leaders of the U.S. Senate—Trent Lott (R–MS) and Thomas Daschle (D–SD). Other members include baseball legend Sammy Sosa and actor Will Smith; Disney president Michael Ovitz, Black Entertainment Television founder Robert Johnson, and MTV president Tom Freston; and prominent business leaders like news magnate Rupert Murdoch and America Online founder Jim Kimsey.

Although school choice is strongly opposed by the leadership of the teachers unions, the idea is clearly winning the hearts and minds of many Americans on all sides of the political spectrum, particularly those who want all children to get the best education available.

School Choice's Topsy-Turvy Year in the Courts

Although a May 1999 ruling by the Ohio Supreme Court upheld the constitutionality of the Cleveland scholarship program, the court also ruled that the program violated the state constitution's single-subject rule because it had been attached to the state's biennial budget. The court stayed the effect of its ruling until June 30 to allow the legislature time to reenact the program in a proper manner.

The legislature did so, and Governor Robert Taft signed the bill into law. Shortly thereafter, however, the same parties that had filed the first lawsuit against the program filed another suit. They repeated their claim that the program violated the Establishment Clause of the U.S. Constitution and asked the court to issue a preliminary injunction, halting the program before the start of the school year.[3]

One day before the Cleveland public schools opened in August 1999, Judge Solomon Oliver granted the plaintiffs' request for a preliminary injunction. Three days later, in reaction to the nationwide outcry over his decision displacing 3,800 students, Judge Oliver modified his order, allowing those students who had participated in the program last year to continue in the program for one semester while the litigation proceeded. In early November, the U.S. Supreme Court stayed the preliminary injunction, allowing the program to resume operation in its entirety.

Then, in December 1999, Judge Oliver ruled that the program violated the First Amendment's Establishment Clause. He stayed the injunction, however, pending appellate review. An appeal has been filed, and the Ohio Supreme Court should consider this appeal sometime this spring. At present, the Ohio case is considered the best candidate for review by the U.S. Supreme Court.[4]

The U.S. Supreme Court declined to take up the question of whether the Vermont and Maine Supreme Courts' decisions to exclude religious schools in their tuitioning program violated parents' First Amendment rights under the Free Exercise Clause. The two states currently provide private and public school tuition for children in rural school districts that do not have their own public schools.[5]

On a more positive note, the Supreme Court also declined to review an Arizona Supreme Court decision to allow a $500 tax credit to individuals who contribute money to private scholarship organizations. As a result, the legal status of the Arizona tax credit is now secure.[6]

School Choice Works: What the Research Shows

Social science researchers offered several promising findings for school choice last year.

• A study released in September 1999 by Dr. Kim Metcalf of Indiana University found that Cleveland scholarship students show a small but statistically significant improvement in achievement scores in language and science. The researchers found that the program effectively serves the population of families and children for which it was intended and developed, and that the majority of the children who participate in the program were not likely to have enrolled in a private school without a scholarship. The study also found that scholarship parents' perceptions of and satisfaction with their children's schools were substantially improved.[7]

• Similarly, a June 1999 survey conducted by Professor Paul Peterson of Harvard University's John F. Kennedy School of Government reveals that parents participating in Cleveland's voucher program are more satisfied with many aspects of the schools they chose than are parents with children still in public schools.[8] A study released by the Columbus-based Buckeye Institute argues that school choice in Cleveland also has provided better racial integration than the Cleveland public school system.[9]

• In March, the Children's Educational Opportunities Foundation (CEO America) released its findings on San Antonio's Horizon program, the nation's first fully funded private voucher program offered to all parents in an entire district. The study, also conducted by Harvard's Paul Peterson, found that the program did not lead to an exodus from the public schools: Only 800 students left the public schools, reducing the district's budget by only 3.5 percent. However, after the inception of the Horizon program, the Edgewood Independent School District implemented an inter-district choice program which allowed 200 students from other districts to transfer to Edgewood Schools, bringing with them $775,000 that otherwise would have gone to their home districts.

In addition, nearly every scholarship applicant was accepted at a school of choice, thus refuting arguments that private schools would "cherry pick" the best students. In September 1999, Peterson concluded that the program does not "cream" the best students out of the public school system. The multiyear study found that there was no significant academic or economic difference between the students who entered the Horizon program and those who remained in the public school system.[10]

Perhaps the most promising development in school choice research, however, is a new book by the official evaluator of the Milwaukee school choice program, John Witte. Witte's previous reports have been used to show that school choice does not work; but in a new book released in early 2000, *The Market Approach to Education: An Analysis of America's First Voucher Program*, he finds choice to be a "useful tool to aid low-income families."[11]

Similarly, a report released in early 2000 by Wisconsin's Legislative Audit Bureau finds that despite fears of "creaming" and segregation, school choice is serving a student population identical to that of the Milwaukee public school system. The report also finds that most of the schools participating in the Milwaukee parental choice program provide high-quality academic programs and tests.[12]

And to the pleasant surprise of many school reformers, the National Research Council (NRC) proposed a "large and ambitious" school choice research experiment to determine whether the program might benefit students. The NRC, a federally financed arm of the National Academy of Sciences (NAS), has called for a multi-district, 10-year voucher experiment.[13]

Winning in the Court of Public Opinion

Choice continues to gain acceptance among some of the nation's most prominent African–American leaders, such as former Atlanta Mayor Andrew Young, once a prominent aide to the Reverend Doctor Martin Luther King, and former Colorado NAACP President Willie Breazell, who was asked to leave his post recently after publicly voicing his support for school choice. Breaking with the educational establishment and its liberal allies can be costly. However, the most powerful support for the school choice movement among African–Americans is found at the grass roots, particularly among African–American parents. The Joint Center for Political and Economic Studies, a leading black think tank, found in its 1999 annual poll that support for choice among blacks is at an all-time high: 60 percent. This includes two-thirds of black baby boomers and over 70 percent of blacks under 35.[14]

Support is also growing among educators. An annual poll by Phi Delta Kappa, a professional association of educators, recently revealed that support for vouchers rose from 45 percent in 1994 to 51 percent this past year.[15] Similarly, among parents of public school students, the number has risen from 51 percent in 1994 to 60 percent today.

Nevertheless, confusion about school choice and what it can do for children's education also abounds. For example, in spite of the widespread debate on the issue, a recent report by Public Agenda, a public opinion research organization, found among other things that 60 percent of parents in Milwaukee and Cleveland either know very little or nothing about school choice programs.[16]

The Challenges Ahead

The three states to watch during the coming year are Connecticut, Michigan, and California.

- **In Connecticut,** Governor John Rowland has called for a $500 tax break for parents with children in private and religious schools. "School choice increases competition and raises expectations," Governor Rowland said in his February 9 state of the state address.[17]

- **In Michigan,** school choice advocates have collected the 302,711 signatures required by the state to place a school choice initiative on this November's ballot. The proposed constitutional amendment would repeal a prohibition against K–12 vouchers and tuition tax credits while leaving in place a ban against direct aid to non-public schools. It also would award children in the state's worst-performing school districts a $3,100 "opportunity scholarship" to help them transfer to private schools. Philanthropist Richard DeVos and leaders of Detroit's black community have been leading the way to promote this initiative, called "Kids First! Yes!"

- **In California,** Tim Draper, a Silicon Valley venture capitalist and former Republican-appointed member of the state board of education, is promoting another initiative for this fall. The initiative would amend the state constitution, setting funding for support of public schools at a "national average dollar per pupil

funding amount" and providing a scholarship of $4,000 to parents who wish to enroll their children in non-public schools. For parents with children already in private schools, the full scholarship amount would be phased in over three years.[18]

In addition, Congress may resurrect a school choice plan for the District of Columbia when it begins debating the District's appropriations. Proposed by House Majority Leader Richard Armey (R–TX), the plan would provide scholarships of up to $3,200 each for approximately 1,800 of D.C.'s poorest students in kindergarten through 12th grade to attend a public, private, or religious school of choice in the D.C. metropolitan area. A plan to expand existing education savings accounts to students in K–12 and allow the funding in Title I (a federal program designed to close the achievement gap between rich and poor students by offering additional funding to needy school districts) to follow poor students to a provider of choice also will be debated this year.

In New Mexico, Governor Gary Johnson is back and ready to fight for choice. In his recent state of the state address, he said that "What is missing from public education is not money; what is missing is competition and choice. I call on you to support the heart and soul of real educational reform, which is school vouchers." Governor Johnson believes the 2000 elections in his state will bring in a crop of pro-voucher legislators, making it easier for him to pass school choice in 2001.

Finally, conservative lawmakers and minority activists in Colorado plan to promote a Milwaukee-style pilot program for Denver during the 2001 legislative session. Other states to watch in 2001 are Texas and Virginia.

Conclusion

With the introduction of the first statewide "money back guarantee" program in Florida and the rising demand for private scholarship programs offered by groups like the Children's Scholarship Fund, the entrenched opposition to school choice is not only losing in the court of public opinion, but also slowly losing its bureaucratic stranglehold over the nation's schools and students.

School choice advocates continue to gain support from thoughtful leaders on the left and in the civil rights community while powerful special interests, led by the leaders of the teachers unions and groups like People for the American Way

(PAW), continue to fight the parents of poor students who want a better education for their children. PAW's leaders, for example, rejoiced over a federal judge's ruling in Ohio that prevented poor students from attending a school of choice three days before the start of the new school year.

But the evidence shows that the education establishment and its political allies are now playing defense. The new millennium is sure to bring more victories, and 2000 will be a pivotal year for the school choice movement.

Endnotes

1 See U.S. Department of Education Web site at *http://www.ed.gov/pubs/charter4thyear/*.

2 Scott Milliman *et al.*, "Coping With Competition: How School Systems Respond to School Choice," May 1999.

3 Clint Bolick, *School Choice Litigation Status,* as of January 21, 2000, e-mail correspondence from Institute for Justice.

4 *Ibid.*

5 *Ibid.*

6 *Ibid.*

7 Dr. Kim K. Metcalf, "Evaluation of the Cleveland Scholarship and Tutoring Grant Program, 1996–99," Indiana Center for Evaluation, Indiana University, September 1999.

8 See John F. Kennedy School of Government Web site at *http://data.fas.harvard.edu/PEPG/*

9 Jay Greene, Ph.D., "The Racial, Economic, and Religious Context of Parental Choice in Cleveland," Buckeye Institute, November 17, 1999.

10 See John F. Kennedy School of Government Web site at *http://data.fas.harvard.edu/PEPG/*.

11 Joe Williams, "Ex-Milwaukee Evaluator Endorses School Choice," *The Sunday Journal Sentinel*, January 9, 2000, p. 1.

12 See Wisconsin Legislative Audit Bureau Web site at *www.legis.state.wi.us/lab/windex.htm*.

13 Kerry A. White, "NRC Report Calls for Voucher Experiment," *Education Week*, September 15, 1999.

14 See Joint Center for Political and Economic Studies Web site at *http://www.jointcenter.org/selpaper/poll_edu99.htm*.

15 See Phi Delta Kappa Web site at *http://www.pdkintl.org/kappan/kpol9909.htm*

16 See Public Agenda Web site at *http://www.publicagenda.org/*

17 Jeff Archer, "Rowland Proposing Tuition Tax Credits for Connecticut," *Education Week*, February 16, 2000.

18 See Draper Initiative Web site at *www.localchoice.com*.

Governor Support of School Vouchers and Composition of State Legislatures

	Governor	Pro Voucher?	Legislative Majority Party House	Senate
Alabama	Don Siegelman (D)	No	Democrat	Democrat
Alaska	Tony Knowles (D)	No	Republican	Republican
Arizona	Jane Dee Hull (R)	Yes	Republican	Republican
Arkansas	Mike Huckabee (R)	"Skeptical"	Democrat	Democrat
California	Gray Davis (D)	No	Democrat	Democrat
Colorado	Bill Owens (R)	Yes	Republican	Republican
Connecticut	John Rowland (R)	Yes	Democrat	Democrat
Delaware	Thomas Carper (D)	No	Republican	Democrat
District of Columbia	Mayor Anthony Williams (D)	No	N/A	N/A
Florida	Jeb Bush (R)	Yes	Republican	Republican
Georgia	Roy Barnes (D)	Possible yes	Democrat	Democrat
Hawaii	Ben Cayetano (D)	No	Democrat	Democrat
Idaho	Dirk Kempthorne (R)	Possible yes	Republican	Republican
Illinois	George Ryan (R)	Possible yes	Democrat	Republican
Indiana	Frank O'Bannon (D)	No	Democrat	Republican
Iowa	Tom Vilsack (D)	No	Republican	Republican
Kansas	Bill Graves (R)	No position	Republican	Republican
Kentucky	Paul Patton (D)	No position	Democrat	Republican
Louisiana	Mike Foster (D)	No position	Democrat	Democrat
Maine	Angus King, Jr. (I)	No	Democrat	Democrat
Maryland	Parris Glendening (D)	No	Democrat	Democrat
Massachusetts	A. Paul Cellucci (R)	Possible yes	Democrat	Democrat
Michigan	John Engler (R)	Yes, qualified	Republican	Republican
Minnesota	Jesse Ventura (I)	No	Republican	Democrat
Mississippi	Ronnie Musgrove (D)	No	Democrat	Democrat
Missouri	Mel Carnahan (D)	No	Democrat	Democrat
Montana	Marc Racicot (R)	No interest	Republican	Republican
Nebraska	Mike Johanns (R)	Yes	Unicameral, nonpartisan legislature	
Nevada	Kenny Guinn (R)	Yes, qualified	Democrat	Republican
New Hampshire	Jeanne Shaheen (D)	No	Republican	Democrat
New Jersey	Christine Whitman (R)	Yes, qualified	Republican	Republican
New Mexico	Gary Johnson (R)	Yes	Democrat	Democrat
New York	George Pataki (R)	Possible yes	Democrat	Republican
North Carolina	James Hunt, Jr. (D)	No	Democrat	Democrat
North Dakota	Edward Schafer (R)	No	Republican	Republican
Ohio	Robert Taft (R)	Yes	Republican	Republican
Oklahoma	Frank Keating (R)	Yes	Democrat	Democrat
Oregon	John Kitzhaber (D)	No	Republican	Republican
Pennsylvania	Tom Ridge (R)	Yes	Republican	Republican
Rhode Island	Lincoln Almond (R)	Yes	Democrat	Democrat
South Carolina	Jim Hodges (D)	No	Republican	Democrat
South Dakota	William Janklow (R)	No position	Republican	Republican
Tennessee	Don Sundquist (R)	No position	Democrat	Democrat
Texas	George W. Bush (R)	Yes	Democrat	Republican
Utah	Michael Leavitt (R)	No	Republican	Republican
Vermont	Howard Dean (D)	No	Democrat	Democrat
Virginia	James Gilmore (R)	Yes	Republican	Republican
Washington	Gary Locke (D)	No	Tie	Democrat
West Virginia	Cecil Underwood (R)	No position	Democrat	Democrat
Wisconsin	Tommy Thompson (R)	Yes	Republican	Democrat
Wyoming	Jim Geringer (R)	No interest	Republican	Republican

Note: Highlighted states currently have a publicly funded private school choice program.
Sources: The Heritage Foundation and the American Education Reform Foundation.

School Choice and Charter School Programs at a Glance

	Public School Choice	Charter Schools	Vouchers	Tax Credits and/or Deductions
Alabama	Limited	N/A	N/A	N/A
Alaska	N/A	Weak	N/A	N/A
Arizona	Statewide	Strong	N/A	Tax credits
Arkansas	Statewide	Weak	N/A	N/A
California	Limited	Strong	N/A	N/A
Colorado	Statewide	Strong	N/A	N/A
Connecticut	Statewide	Strong	N/A	N/A
Delaware	Statewide	Strong	N/A	N/A
District of Columbia	Citywide	Strong	N/A	N/A
Florida	Limited	Strong	Statewide for students in failing schools*	N/A
Georgia	N/A	Strong	N/A	N/A
Hawaii	N/A	Weak	N/A	N/A
Idaho	Statewide	Strong	N/A	N/A
Illinois	N/A	Strong	N/A	Tax credits
Indiana	Limited	N/A	N/A	N/A
Iowa	Statewide	N/A	N/A	Tax credits
Kansas	N/A	Weak	N/A	N/A
Kentucky	N/A	N/A	N/A	N/A
Louisiana	Limited	Strong	N/A	N/A
Maine	Limited	N/A	Statewide/does not include religious schools	N/A
Maryland	N/A	N/A	N/A	N/A
Massachusetts	Limited	Strong	N/A	N/A
Michigan	Statewide	Strong	N/A	N/A
Minnesota	Statewide	Strong	N/A	Tax credits and deductions
Mississippi	Limited	Weak	N/A	N/A
Missouri	Limited	Strong	N/A	N/A
Montana	N/A	N/A	N/A	N/A
Nebraska	Statewide	N/A	N/A	N/A
Nevada	Limited	Weak	N/A	N/A
New Hampshire	Limited	Strong	N/A	N/A
New Jersey	Limited	Strong	N/A	N/A
New Mexico	Limited	Weak	N/A	N/A
New York	Limited	Strong	N/A	N/A
North Carolina	N/A	Strong	N/A	N/A
North Dakota	Statewide	N/A	N/A	N/A
Ohio	Limited	Strong	Means-tested pilot for Cleveland*	N/A
Oklahoma	Statewide	Strong	N/A	N/A
Oregon	Limited	Strong	N/A	N/A
Pennsylvania	N/A	Strong	N/A	N/A
Rhode Island	N/A	Weak	N/A	N/A
South Carolina	N/A	Strong	N/A	N/A
South Dakota	Statewide	N/A	N/A	N/A
Tennessee	Statewide	N/A	N/A	N/A
Texas	Limited	Strong	N/A	N/A
Utah	Statewide	Weak	N/A	N/A
Vermont	N/A	N/A	Statewide/does not include religious schools	N/A
Virginia	N/A	Weak	N/A	N/A
Washington	Statewide	N/A	N/A	N/A
West Virginia	Limited	N/A	N/A	N/A
Wisconsin	Statewide	Strong	Means-tested pilot for Milwaukee	N/A
Wyoming	Limited	Weak	N/A	N/A

Note: The Ohio and Florida voucher programs have been struck down. They are both on appeal. The Florida program will continue until the end of the 1999–2000 school year and the Ohio plan will continue until an appellate ruling.
Sources: The Heritage Foundation, the Center for Education Reform, and the Education Commission of the States.

School Choice and Charter School Programs: 2000

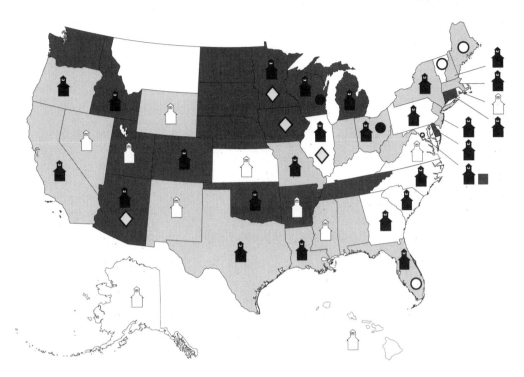

■ Public School Choice Statewide (18)	● Cities with Publicly Sponsored Full School Choice (2)
▨ Public School Choice Limited to Some or All Districts (19)	○ States with Publicly Sponsored Full School Choice (3)
Medium to Strong Charter School Laws (26)	◇ States with Education Tax Deductions or Credits (4)
Weak Charter School Laws (11)	

Note: Information is current as of March 15, 2000. In Maine and Vermont, publicly sponsored full school choice is limited to non-religious private schools.

Sources: The Heritage Foundation, the Center for Education Reform, and the Education Commission of the States.

STATE BY STATE ANALYSIS

Alabama

State Profile[1]

School Choice Status
- Public school choice: Limited
- Charter schools: N/A
- Publicly funded private school choice: N/A

K–12 Public and Private School Students and Schools
- Public school enrollment (fall 1998) and number of schools (1997–1998): 739,956 in 1,345 schools
- Private school enrollment and number of schools (1997–1998): 72,486 in 333 schools

K–12 Public and Private School Student Academic Performance
NAEP Test Results—percentage of students at each performance level for both public and private schools, with national percentages in parentheses

Performance Level	Reading 4th grade 1998	Reading 8th grade 1998	Math 4th grade 1996	Math 8th grade 1996	Science 8th grade 1996
Advanced	5% (6%)	1% (2%)	1% (2%)	1% (4%)	1% (3%)
Proficient	19 (23)	20 (28)	10 (18)	11 (19)	17 (24)
Basic	32 (31)	45 (41)	37 (42)	33 (38)	29 (33)
Below Basic	44 (39)	34 (28)	52 (38)	55 (39)	53 (40)

- SAT weighted rank (1999): N/A
- ACT weighted rank (1999): 20 out of 26 states

K–12 Public School Expenditures
- Current expenditures (1999–2000): $3,581,430,000
- Amount of revenue from the federal government (1998–1999): 9.1%
- Current per-pupil expenditures (1999–2000): $4,832

K–12 Public School Teachers (1998–1999)
- Number of teachers: 46,177
- Average salary: $35,820
- Students enrolled per teacher: 16.0
- Leading teachers union: NEA

Background

Beginning in the fall of 1998, a new private scholarship program, Students First, provided half tuition scholarships of up to $1,000 for 50 to 100 low-income students in the Birmingham five-county region. Eligible students entering kindergarten through 8th grade were selected by lottery.

On September 28, 1998, Birmingham was named a "partner city" to receive a Children's Scholarship Fund (CSF) challenge grant.[2] The CSF is a $100 million foundation underwritten by entrepreneurs Ted Forstmann and John Walton. It will match funds raised by residents of Birmingham to fund approximately 375 private scholarships for low-income students to attend a school of choice.

Developments in 1999

On April 22, 1999, the CSF announced the winners of its private scholarships. The recipients were selected randomly by computer-generated lottery. In Birmingham, 375 scholarship recipients were chosen from 9,172 applicants. Students First will administer the program.

Position of the Governor/Composition of State Legislature

Governor Don Siegelman, a Democrat, does not support school choice. Both houses of the legislature are led by Democrats.

State Contacts

Alabama Family Alliance
Gary Palmer, President
402 Office Park Drive, Suite 300
Birmingham, AL 35223
Phone: (205) 870-9900
Fax: (205) 870-4407
Web site: http://www.alabamafamily.org
E-mail: alfamily@bellsouth.net

Alabama Department of Education
Dr. Ed Richardson, Superintendent of Education
50 North Ripley Street
P.O. Box 302101
Montgomery, AL 36130-2101
Phone: (334) 242-9700
Web site: http://www.alsde.edu

Eagle Forum of Alabama
Eunice Smith, President
4200 Stone River Circle
Birmingham, AL 35213
Phone: (205) 879-7096
Fax: (205) 871-2859
E-mail: Ala eagles@aol.com

Students First
Terrell Kennedy, President
Vernard Gant
1204 4th Avenue West
Birmingham, AL 35208
Phone: (205) 786-8400
Fax: (205) 992-6691
E-mail: clarkecw@aol.com

Endnotes

1 For sources, see "An Explanation of the State Profile Categories."

2 See Children's Scholarship Fund Web site at *http://www.scholarshipfund.org*.

Alaska

State Profile[1]

School Choice Status
- Public school choice: N/A
- Charter schools: Established 1995
    - Strength of law: Weak
    - Number of charter schools in operation (fall 1999): 18
    - Number of students enrolled in charter schools (1998–1999): 1,388
- Publicly funded private school choice: N/A

K–12 Public and Private School Students and Schools
- Public school enrollment (fall 1998) and number of schools (1997–1998): 135,373 in 497 schools
- Private school enrollment and number of schools (1997–1998): 6,253 in 70 schools

K–12 Public and Private School Student Academic Performance
NAEP Test Results—percentage of students at each performance level for both public and private schools, with national percentages in parentheses

Performance Level	Reading 4th grade 1998	Reading 8th grade 1998	Math 4th grade 1996	Math 8th grade 1996	Science 8th grade 1996
Advanced	n/a	n/a	2% (2%)	7% (4%)	3% (3%)
Proficient	n/a	n/a	19 (18)	23 (19)	28 (24)
Basic	n/a	n/a	44 (42)	38 (38)	34 (33)
Below Basic	n/a	n/a	35 (38)	32 (39)	35 (40)

- SAT weighted rank (1999): 5 out of 24 states and the District of Columbia
- ACT weighted rank (1999): N/A

K–12 Public School Expenditures
- Current expenditures (1999–2000): $1,217,365,000
- Amount of revenue from the federal government (1998–1999): 12.6%
- Current per-pupil expenditures (1999–2000): $8,834

K–12 Public School Teachers (1998–1999)
- Number of teachers: 7,696
- Average salary: $46,845
- Students enrolled per teacher: 17.6
- Leading teachers union: NEA

Background

In 1991, then-Governor Wally Hickel, an Independent, appointed a special commission to examine the issue of school choice. The commission's report, released in 1992, fell short of advocating full choice. It favored experimenting with charter schools, magnet schools, and other types of public school choice.

As of June 1995, pursuant to a state Board of Education regulation, school districts were allowed to accept part-time enrollment in public school by students who were enrolled in private schools, home schools, and correspondence schools. State funding follows the students.

CSSB 88 (FIN), a restrictive charter school bill establishing a pilot program, was signed by Governor Tony Knowles, a Democrat, and took effect on July 1, 1995. The plan capped the number of charter schools at 30 and mandated that they be geographically balanced. It included such restrictions as requiring approval of an application by the local school board and the state Board of Education and imposed a five-year limit on each charter. The law exempts charter schools from the requirements of local school districts on textbooks, programs, curricula, and scheduling.

Developments in 1999

A constitutional amendment (HJR 6) to allow the spending of public funds "for the direct benefit of religious or other private educational institution(s)" in Alaska was approved by the House Judiciary Committee on May 3, 1999. This resolution could come to the House for a vote during the legislative session of 2000. If the House and Senate approve it, the measure would then need to be approved by the voters before becoming law.

State Representative Vic Kohring (R–26) introduced a voucher bill (HB 5) that would have established a voucher equivalent in value to the per-pupil spending of the student's local school district, to be used at private schools, for children whose family incomes fall below 200 percent of the federal poverty line. No action was taken on this bill.

Position of the Governor/Composition of State Legislature

Governor Tony Knowles, a Democrat, supports charter schools but does not support school choice programs that include private and religious schools. Both houses of the legislature are led by Republicans.

State Contacts

Alaska Department of Education
Shirley J. Holloway, Commissioner
801 West 10th Street
Juneau, AK 99801
Phone: (907) 465-2800
Charter schools
   Marjorie Menzi: (907) 465-8720
Private schools (1997–1998)
   Julie Orsborn: (907) 465-2026
Web site: http://www.educ.state.ak.us/

Alaskans for Educational Choice
P.O. Box 1900–51
Anchorage, AK 99519-0051
Phone: (907) 245-5501
Fax: (907) 245-5502

Endnote

1   For sources, see "An Explanation of the State Profile Categories."

Arizona

State Profile[1]

School Choice Status
- Public school choice: Statewide
- Charter schools: Established 1994
  Strength of law: Strong
  Number of charter schools in operation (fall 1999): 348
  Number of students enrolled in charter schools (1998–1999): 31,063
- Publicly funded private school choice: School tuition organization (STO) tax credit
  Program description: Enacted in 1997, the plan allows taxpayers to take a credit against state income taxes of up to $500 for donations that provide scholarships for children attending K–12 private schools. During the 1998–1999 school year, more than 500 students received tuition assistance from 18 tuition organizations.

K–12 Public and Private School Students and Schools
- Public school enrollment (fall 1998) and number of schools (1997–1998): 823,040 in 1,384 schools
- Private school enrollment and number of schools (1997–1998): 44,991 in 283 schools

K–12 Public and Private School Student Academic Performance
NAEP Test Results—percentage of students at each performance level for both public and private schools, with national percentages in parentheses

Performance Level	Reading 4th grade 1998	Reading 8th grade 1998	Math 4th grade 1996	Math 8th grade 1996	Science 8th grade 1996
Advanced	5% (6%)	2% (2%)	1% (2%)	2% (4%)	2% (3%)
Proficient	17 (23)	26 (28)	14 (18)	16 (19)	21 (24)
Basic	31 (31)	45 (41)	42 (42)	39 (38)	32 (33)
Below Basic	47 (39)	27 (28)	43 (38)	43 (39)	45 (40)

- SAT weighted rank (1999): 3 out of 24 states and the District of Columbia
- ACT weighted rank (1999): N/A

K–12 Public School Expenditures
- Current expenditures (1999–2000): $3,869,440,000
- Amount of revenue from the federal government (1998–1999): 7.6%
- Current per-pupil expenditures (1999–2000): $4,634

K–12 Public School Teachers (1998–1999)
- Number of teachers: 43,219
- Average salary: $35,025

K–12 Public School Teachers (1998–1999) cont.

- Students enrolled per teacher: 19.0
- Leading teachers union: NEA

Background

Arizona has one of the strongest charter school laws in the United States and more charter schools in operation than any other state: nearly 350 as of September 1999.[2]

In 1994, the legislature passed the Arizona School Improvement Act to allow charter schools to be created as alternatives to traditional public schools and to establish a State Board for Charter Schools to grant the charters. Any public group or private citizen or organization may apply for a charter. Applications for the 15-year charters (with five-year reviews) may be submitted to the charter school board or the state school board, which may grant a maximum of 25 charters per year, or to the local school boards, which are not subject to a limit.

The legislation gives charter schools vast fiscal and legal autonomy. Charter schools sponsored by the charter school board or the state school board are mostly independent and exempt from some state regulations in such areas as teacher certification, compliance reviews, and mandated classes. To be approved, a charter school must comply with civil rights as well as insurance and special education laws. No charter school may deny admission to students on grounds of academic ability or physical handicap.

Funding for charter schools is simple: For state-sponsored charter schools, state funds flow from the state to the school. If a district sponsors the charter school, federal, state, and local funds flow through the district to the school. The amount of funding available to the school must be equal to or greater than the minimum per-pupil expenditure within the district.

More than one-third of Arizona's charter schools have programs designed to serve at-risk students. Contrary to claims that charter schools are just publicly funded elite schools for students already enrolled in private schools, a 1996 study by the Arizona-based Goldwater Institute shows that more than 69 percent of the charter school students that year had attended public school the previous year; 16 percent had attended private schools; 9 percent had not begun school, had dropped out, or had been expelled; and 6 percent had been home schooled.

In 1997, the legislature passed H.B. 2162 to clarify several provisions of the state's charter school law.

The state also has a sweeping open enrollment law so that some public school districts can accommodate student requests for transfers to different schools. Arizona law permits special education students and students designated as "unable to profit from public schools" to use state funding to attend private schools. During the 1996–1997 school year, 4,000 children—twice the number of students served by the program during the 1995–1996 school year—used the allocated student funds to attend private education programs.[3]

On April 7, 1997, then-Governor Fife Symington, a Republican, signed legislation to allow residents to claim an income tax credit of up to $500 for donations to charitable organizations providing scholarships to children to attend private or religious schools. The tax credits will also apply to up to $200 of activity fees at public schools in Arizona. This is the first law of its kind in the country. In protest, the Arizona Education Association tried to gather signatures to place a referendum on the ballot opposing the tax credit. Having gathered only 10,000 of the 60,000 signatures needed to place the measure on the ballot, the union decided to file a lawsuit challenging the constitutionality of the tax credit.

On September 29, 1997, the Arizona Education Association, Arizona School Boards Association, and American Federation of Teachers filed the lawsuit. The Institute for Justice, representing State Superintendent of Public Instruction Lisa Graham Keegan, the taxpayers, and low-income parents and students, led the defense to preserve the credit. The program eventually was found to be constitutional by the Arizona Supreme Court, but it has been challenged again by the ACLU on February 15, 2000.

Meanwhile, a survey conducted between February 26 and March 6, 1998, by the Goldwater Institute found that 73 percent of Arizona voters think parents should have the right to send their children to any public school that has room for them, regardless of school attendance boundaries. The same survey also found that 72 percent favor tax-deductible donations as a mechanism to allow communities to raise additional funds for local education.[4]

On April 10, 1998, the Arizona legislature passed the nation's first child-centered school finance reform package. The plan equalizes funding for all students in the state and replaces the current local property tax-based finance system with existing sales taxes. The Arizona Supreme Court had declared the school financing formula based on local property resources to be unconstitutional because it caused inequities in funding for school construction and vast disparities among school districts. In order to secure passage, the final version of the plan was modified to allow school districts to opt out of the financing plan if they wished to exceed state standards. The plan also offers charter schools an additional $300 per student to offset capital costs.[5]

The state currently has several private tuition scholarship programs, including the Arizona School CHOICE Trust, which was launched in 1992. On September 28, 1998, Phoenix was named one of the 40 "partner cities" for the Children's Scholarship Fund (CSF) challenge grant. The CSF is a $100 million foundation underwritten by entrepreneurs Ted Forstmann and John Walton. It will match funds raised by Phoenix residents to fund approximately 500 private scholarships for low-income students to attend a school of choice.[6]

Developments in 1999

On January 26, 1999, by a vote of 3 to 2, the Arizona Supreme Court upheld the state's income tax credit for contributions to private scholarship programs. The tax credit bill, which was signed into law on April 7, 1997, allows tax deductions of $500 for taxpayers who contribute to programs that provide private scholarships for students attending private schools in grades K–12 and $200 for contributions to public school extracurricular activities. In a majority opinion written by Chief Justice Thomas A. Zlaket, the court held that the program does not violate the First Amendment, partly because the "primary beneficiaries of this credit are taxpayers who contribute to the [school tuition organizations], parents who might otherwise be deprived of an opportunity to make meaningful decisions about their children's education, and the students themselves."[7] Citing the U.S. Supreme Court's decision to uphold tuition tax credits in *Mueller* v. *Allen* and the Wisconsin Supreme Court's recent ruling on the Milwaukee school choice program in *Jackson* v. *Benson*, the majority stated that "Arizona's tax credit achieves a higher degree of parity by making private schools more accessible and providing alternatives to public education."[8]

With respect to the claim that the plan also violated the state constitution by using public funds to aid religious schools, Justice Stanley Feldman admonished in his dissenting opinion that if the tuition plan were upheld, "this state and every other will be able to use the taxing power to direct unrestricted aid to support religious instruction and observance, thus destroying any pretense of separation of church and state." The majority, however, held that tax credits are not public funds; therefore, the plan does not violate the state's constitution. The Arizona Education Association later appealed the case to the U.S. Supreme Court, which in October refused to consider the case, thus letting the Arizona Supreme Court decision stand.

On January 11, 1999, the office of State Superintendent of Public Instruction Lisa Graham Keegan submitted legislation proposing a statewide school choice program. The program would have enabled the parents of children who qualify for free or reduced-price lunches to send their children to the public, private, or religious school of choice. Payments would be equivalent to the amount the child would generate in a public charter school or the cost of tuition at the receiving choice school, whichever is less. The receiving school would be required to administer to the child the statewide norm-referenced achievement test and the Arizona Instrument to Measure Standards (AIMS) criterion referenced test to ensure that the child is receiving a quality education.[9]

On March 15, by a vote of 31–27, the Arizona House passed a bill to establish Keegan's plan by offering Parental Choice Grants to low-income parents. The grants would have been worth either $4,800 or the cost of tuition, whichever is less, and would have allowed low-income parents to send their children to local private or parochial schools. H.B. 2279 was approved on March 25 by the Senate Education Committee; but even though both Governor Jane Hull and Superintendent of Public Instruction Keegan supported it, the bill was killed by Senate inaction.

On the charter school front, a report by Scott Milliman of James Madison University, Fredrick Hess and Robert Maranto of the University of Virginia, and social psychologist April Gresham of Charlottesville, Virginia, on a March 1998 survey of Arizona public school teachers reveals that the establishment of charter schools has spurred noticeable differences in the public school system.[10] Based on teacher surveys, which had a 79 percent response rate, the researchers concluded that competition from charter schools led to the following changes between the 1994–1995 and 1997–1998 school years:

- Districts made greater attempts to inform parents about school programs and options;

- Districts placed greater emphasis on promoting professional development for teachers; and

- School principals increased their consultation with teaching staff.

The researchers also found that charter schools, instead of replacing district schools, actually push district schools to compete, primarily because state subsidies follow the students. To help parents choose schools, the Arizona Department of Education posts report cards for all public schools on the Internet. So far, around 20 charter schools have had to shut down, either because they were not able to attract enough students or because state regulators closed the schools.

On April 22, 1999, the Children's Scholarship Fund announced the winners of its private voucher program. The recipients were selected randomly by computer-generated lottery. In Phoenix and Tuscon, 320 scholarship recipients were chosen from 12,637 applicants.[11]

Developments in 2000

Efforts to build protections against fraudulent or financially unsound charter schools are underway. The ACLU filed a lawsuit against the Arizona tax credit plan on February 15, 2000, in federal court in Phoenix.

Position of the Governor/Composition of State Legislature

Governor Jane Dee Hull, a Republican, is an advocate of publicly funded private school choice and charter schools. Both houses of the legislature are led by Republicans.

State Contacts

Arizona Charter Schools Association
Gary Richardson, Executive Director
P.O. Box 27235
Tempe, AZ 85285-7235
Phone: (480) 775-6237
Fax: (480) 820- 8277

Arizona Department of Public Instruction
Lisa Graham Keegan, Superintendent
1535 West Jefferson Street
Phoenix, AZ 85007
Phone: (602) 542-4361
Fax: (602) 542-5440
Web site: http://www.ade.state.az.us/

Arizona School Choice Trust
Tom Patterson, Chairman
Lynn Short, Executive Director
3737 East Broadway Road
Phoenix, AZ 85040-2966
Phone: (602) 454-1360
Fax: (602) 454-1362
Web site: www.asct.org
E-mail: info@asct.org

Arizona Scholarship Fund
ChamBria Henderson, Executive Director
P.O. Box 2576
Mesa, AZ 85214-2576
Phone: (480) 497-4564
Fax: (480) 832-8853
E-mail: AZScholarships@juno.com

Arizona State Board for Charter Schools
Cassandra Larsen, Executive Director
4105 North 20th Street, Suite 280
Phoenix, AZ 85016
Phone: (602) 468-6369
Fax: (602) 468-1682
E-mail: larsen_cassandra@pop.state.az.us

Arizona State Board of Education
Bonnie Barclay
Charter School Division
1535 West Jefferson Street
Phoenix, AZ 85007
Phone: (602) 542-5968
Fax: (602) 542-3590
Web site: http://www.ade.state.az.us
E-mail: bbarcla@mail1.ade.state.az.us

Benjamin Franklin Charter School
Edwin W. Farnsworth, Executive Director
13732 East Warner Road
Gilbert, AZ 85296
Phone: (602) 632-0722
Fax: (602) 632-8716

Goldwater Institute
Christopher Smith, Executive Director
Mary Gifford, Director, Center for Market-Based Education
201 North Central Avenue
Phoenix, AZ 85004
Phone: (602) 256-7018
Fax: (602) 256-7045
Web site: http://www.goldwaterinstitute.org;
www.cmbe.org
E-mail: info@goldwaterinstitute.org;
cmbe@usa.net

Morrison Institute for Public Policy
Mary Joe Waits, Acting Director
Arizona State University
Box 874405
Tempe, AZ 85287-4405
Phone: (602) 965-4525
Fax: (602) 965-9219
Web site: www.asu.edu/copp/morrison

Endnotes

1 For sources, see "An Explanation of the State Profile Categories."

2 Center for Education Reform at *http://www.edreform.com/pubs/chglance.htm.* Updates as of October 24, 1998. See also Angela Dale and Dave DeSchryver, eds., *The Charter School Workbook: Your Roadmap to the Charter School Movement* (Washington, D.C.: Center for Education Reform, 1997).

3 *Ibid.*

4 "Education Ranks as No. 1 Concern Among Arizona Voters," *School Reform News*, May 1998, p. 12. According to information from Office of the State Superintendent of Education in the Arizona Department of Public Instruction.

5 Education Leaders Council, press release, Washington, D.C., April 14, 1998.

6 See Children's Scholarship Fund Web site at *http://www.scholarshipfund.org.*

7 Correspondence from the Institute for Justice, April 22, 1999. All quotes in this section are taken from *Kotterman* v. *Killian*, CV–1997–0412–SA, January 26, 1999, at *http://www.supreme.state.az.us/opin/opinidx.htm.*

8 *Ibid.*

9 According to information from Office of the State Superintendent of Education in the Arizona Department of Public Instruction.

10 Scott Milliman *et al.*, "Coping with Competition: How School Systems Respond to School Choice," May 1999.

11 See Children's Scholarship Fund Web site at *http://www.scholarshipfund.org.*

Arkansas

State Profile[1]

School Choice Status
- Public school choice: Statewide
- Charter schools: Established 1995
    Strength of law: Weak
    Number of charter schools in operation (fall 1999): 0
    Number of students enrolled in charter schools (1998–1999): 0
- Publicly funded private school choice: N/A

K–12 Public and Private School Students and Schools
- Public school enrollment (fall 1998) and number of schools (1997–1998): 456,710 in 1,112 schools
- Private school enrollment and number of schools (1997–1998): 26,645 in 196 schools

K–12 Public and Private School Student Academic Performance
NAEP Test Results—percentage of students at each performance level for both public and private schools, with national percentages in parentheses

Performance Level	Reading 4th grade 1998	Reading 8th grade 1998	Math 4th grade 1996	Math 8th grade 1996	Science 8th grade 1996
Advanced	4% (6%)	1% (2%)	1% (2%)	2% (4%)	1% (3%)
Proficient	19 (23)	22 (28)	12 (18)	11 (19)	21 (24)
Basic	32 (31)	45 (41)	41 (42)	39 (38)	33 (33)
Below Basic	45 (39)	32 (28)	46 (38)	48 (39)	45 (40)

- SAT weighted rank (1999): N/A
- ACT weighted rank (1999): 19 out of 26 states

K–12 Public School Expenditures
- Current expenditures (1999–2000): $2,548,001,000
- Amount of revenue from the federal government (1998–1999): 8.1%
- Current per-pupil expenditures (1999–2000): $5,566

K–12 Public School Teachers (1998–1999)
- Number of teachers: 28,108
- Average salary: $32,350
- Students enrolled per teacher: 16.2
- Leading teachers union: NEA

Background

In 1990, a statewide open enrollment law permitting parents to enroll their children in public schools outside their school districts went into effect. It included an outreach program to help parents decide where to send their children. Although transportation is the responsibility of the transferring student, state aid covers a student's transfer costs.

On April 10, 1995, then-Governor Jim Guy Tucker, a Democrat, signed a weak charter school bill (Act 1126) into law. It allowed any local school to become a charter school, provided the charter proposal does not infringe upon or remove any existing collective bargaining requirements and the school is approved by the local board of education; has the support of two-thirds of the employees of the petitioning public school and two-thirds of the parents of the students of the petitioning school; establishes a plan to meet pre-established state and national education goals; and accepts the established rules and regulations imposed by the state Board of Education.

Because of these strict bureaucratic requirements, the regulatory hoops discouraged teachers and parents, including those committed to reform, from seeking to obtain a charter. In March 1999, however, Governor Mike Huckabee, a Republican, signed the Charter Schools Act of 1999 (Act 890), which allows any university, private non-sectarian institution, or government entity to open one of 12 open enrollment charter schools. The new law also allows an unlimited number of conversions from public to charter schools. Each congressional district is limited to 3 open enrollment charter schools. This new and improved law allows charter applicants that have been denied a charter by the local school board to appeal to the state board of education. (Conversions are allowed only at the local school board level.) The law also allows charter school principals to hire "qualified" teachers who may not be certified by the state.

A May 1997 survey by the Arkansas Policy Foundation's Murphy Commission[2] found that 44 percent of Arkansas parents believe their children's education is not equal to or greater than the education afforded children in other states; 63 percent believe the state's public schools need at least some improvement; 88 percent favor school choice in principle; and 61 percent endorse school choice for any school, whether public, private, or religious. African–Americans are even more pro-school choice: 90 percent of those surveyed favor school choice.

Those who responded to the survey blamed inefficient administrators or inefficient use of resources, not teachers, for the state's education woes. In fact, a majority of Arkansans rated their children's teachers either "good" or "exceptional."

During the 1997 session, legislators passed a bill to ease regulatory requirements on parents who home school their children. The new law requires these parents to register their children once a year rather than each semester, and to have their children tested only in 5th, 7th, and 10th grades with their peers in public school instead of every academic year.

On September 28, 1998, the entire state of Arkansas was named a partner for the Children's Scholarship Fund (CSF) challenge grant and CEO of Central Arkansas (the state's existing private scholarship program) was renamed CSF Arkansas, serving students in the entire state. The CSF is a $100 million foundation underwritten by entrepreneurs Ted Forstmann and John Walton. It will match funds raised by Arkansans to underwrite approximately 1,250 private scholarships to enable low-income children entering kindergarten through 8th grade to attend a school of choice for at least four years.[3]

Developments in 1999

On April 22, 1999, the CSF announced the winners of the largest private scholarship program in the country. The recipients were selected randomly by computer-generated lottery. In Arkansas, 1,250 scholarship recipients were chosen from 12,210 applicants.

The Arkansas House Education Committee failed to take up HB 2275, a voucher bill that would have provided scholarships equal to the public school expenditure per pupil to allow students to attend a school of choice. In addition, a bill to offer tuition tax credits of up to $500 was introduced in the House Revenue and Taxation Committee but did not pass.[4]

Position of the Governor/Composition of State Legislature

Governor Mike Huckabee, a Republican, supported strengthening the state's charter school law. He has not initiated any school choice efforts and is skeptical of the success of a state-wide voucher system in his predominantly rural state. According to the Center for Education Reform, however, the governor has stated that choice might be possible in urban areas such as Little Rock.[5] Both houses of the legislature are led by Democrats.

State Contacts

Arkansans for School Choice
Oscar Stilley, Chairman
Central Mall, Suite 516
5111 Rogers Avenue
Fort Smith, AR 72903-2041
Phone: (501) 452-3714
Fax: (501) 452-5387
Web site: http://www.ostilley.com
E-mail: oscar@ostilley.com

Arkansas Family Council
Jerry Cox, Executive Director
414 South Pulaski, Suite 2
Little Rock, AR 72201
Phone: (501) 375-7000
Fax: (501) 375-7040
E-mail: arfamcoun@aol.com

Arkansas Policy Foundation
Michael W. Watson, President
900 South Shakelford Road, Suite 300
Little Rock, AR 72211
Phone: (501) 851-0831
Fax: (501) 978-1051
Web site: http://www.GeoCities.com/Heartland/
Creek//2355
E-mail: aggiemw2@aol.com

CEO America
Fritz Steiger, President
P.O. Box 330
Bentonville, AR 72712-0330
Phone: (501) 273-6957
Fax: (501) 273-9362
Web site: http://www.ceoamerica.org
E-mail: ceoamerica@ceoamerica.org

Children First America
901 McClain, Suite 802
Bentonville, AR 72712
Phone: (501) 273-6957
Fax: (501) 273-9362

CSF–Arkansas
Lawrence Gunnells, Executive Director
Libby Davis, Program Administrator
111 Center Street, Suite 1540
Little Rock, AR 72201
Phone: (501) 907-0044
Fax: (501) 907-0047
E-mail: csflr@mail.snider.net;
lgunnells@aristotle.net

Christian Educational Assistance Foundation
P.O. Box 21867
Little Rock, AR 72221
Phone: (501) 219-2323

Endnotes

1   For sources, see "An Explanation of the State Profile Categories."

2   Ronald J. Hy and Gary Wekkin, *Mandate for Public Education Reform*, Murphy Commission, May 1997.

3   See Children's Scholarship Fund Web site at *http://www.scholarshipfund.org*.

4   The Friedman–Blum *Educational Freedom Report*, No. 71, May 21, 1999.

5   See Center for Education Reform Web site at *http://www.edreform.com*.

California

State Profile[1]

School Choice Status

- Public school choice: Limited
- Charter schools: Established 1992
    - Strength of law: Strong
    - Number of charter schools in operation (fall 1999): 234
    - Number of students enrolled in charter schools (fall 1999): 85,000
- Publicly funded private school choice: N/A

K–12 Public and Private Students and Schools

- Public school enrollment (fall 1998) and number of schools (1997–1998): 5,844,111 in 8,178 schools
- Private school enrollment and number of schools (1997–1998): 609,506 in 3,332 schools

K–12 Public and Private School Student Academic Performance

NAEP Test Results—percentage of students at each performance level for both public and private schools, with national percentages in parentheses

Performance Level	Reading 4th grade 1998	Reading 8th grade 1998	Math 4th grade 1996	Math 8th grade 1996	Science 8th grade 1996
Advanced	4% (6%)	1% (2%)	1% (2%)	3% (4%)	1% (3%)
Proficient	16 (23)	21 (28)	10 (18)	14 (19)	19 (24)
Basic	28 (31)	42 (41)	35 (42)	34 (38)	27 (33)
Below Basic	52 (39)	36 (28)	54 (38)	49 (39)	53 (40)

- SAT weighted rank (1999): 10 out of 24 states and the District of Columbia
- ACT weighted rank (1999): N/A

K–12 Public School Expenditures

- Current expenditures (1999–2000): $31,959,025,000
- Amount of revenue from the federal government (1998–1999): 8.9%
- Current per-pupil expenditures (1999–2000): $5,531

K–12 Public School Teachers (1998–1999)

- Number of teachers: 260,539
- Average salary: $45,400
- Students enrolled per teacher: 22.4
- Leading teachers union: NEA

Background

Although Arizona has the greatest number of charter schools in the United States, California has the largest charter school enrollment with over 85,000 students in 234 schools as of fall 1999. There is enormous variety among the state's charter schools. Programs include home-based education, independent learning, programs for the gifted, schools for students expelled from traditional public schools, schools for international studies, multilingual schools, and programs for youth released from detention centers, among others.

In September 1992, former Governor Pete Wilson, a Republican, signed the California Charter School Act, sponsored by then-Senator Gary Hart, a Democrat. The act also included a reform package of amendments (AB 544). The act and its amendments allowed for 250 charter schools during the 1998 academic year and 100 schools each subsequent year.

A charter can be created with petitions signed either by half the teachers in an existing school who wish to convert to charter status or by 50 percent of parents or 50 percent of teachers who indicate a "meaningful intent" to teach at a newly created (start-up) charter school. The California law allows the charter school to operate as a nonprofit public benefit corporation and requires school districts to provide space to charter schools if space is available. It also requires teachers to possess a credential. Charter schools largely are free from state and district oversight and not subject to the district's collective bargaining agreement (although both the schools and their employees are governed by the state's public employee collective bargaining laws, and charter school teachers may organize if they vote to do so).

Funding per student is 100 percent of the average spending per pupil in the school district, with funding "captured" through a charter school block or "categorical" grant. District "oversight" fees are limited to 1 percent of the school's budget or 3 percent if the district provides a school building or site. However, charter schools and sponsor districts may negotiate separate fees for services (such as payroll or special education) for districts to provide charter schools. Charters are granted by school districts for five years, with subsequent five-year renewals. Districts must provide in writing the reasons for denying a charter, specifying how the

charter petition has failed to provide a comprehensive description of the school's curriculum and other items required by charter law or how the petitioners have failed to demonstrate their ability to implement and operate the charter. If a local district denies a charter, the petitioner may appeal to a county or the state board of education.[2]

In addition, another law was enacted that allows charter schools to participate in revolving loans used by new school districts; clarifies that charter schools are subject to the same statewide assessment tests given to public schools; and requires that charter school petitions address dispute resolution matters. The law was backed by the Little Hoover Commission, a state watchdog agency that also has issued a favorable study on charter schools.

Private reports, such as one submitted by the San Diego Chamber of Commerce, have assessed the progress of California's charter schools very favorably. Charter operations also have received validation within the California legal system. "In two separate cases in August 1996, superior court judges upheld the charter schools' exemption from the state's collective bargaining laws, further strengthening legal precedence in favor of charter flexibility and autonomy in the state."[3]

California has three inter-district student transfer laws and one intra-district transfer law. Student transportation varies across these laws. The long-standing inter-district transfer law and the residency status inter-district transfer law make no provision for transfer student transportation. The district-of-choice law and the intra-district transfer law allow parents to request transportation for their transfer student in accordance with standard district transportation practices.

Publicly funded private school choice became a major political issue in 1993. Proposition 174 would have amended the state constitution to provide $2,600 vouchers to families to enroll their school-age children in public, private, or religiously affiliated schools. The initiative, however, attracted only 30 percent of the vote, with the California Teachers Association contributing at least $10 million of the approximately $16 million spent on the campaign to defeat it. Supporters of the measure were able to raise only $2.7 million. Several attempts to pass school choice legislation since then have failed.

In March 1998, Wall Street philanthropist Ted Forstmann pledged to raise funding to provide vouchers of $1,000 for four years to at least 5,000 low-income children in the Los Angeles area. A few months later, the Children's Scholarship Fund (CSF), a $100 million foundation underwritten by Forstmann and John Walton, selected Los Angeles as one of 40 "partner cities" to receive matching donations for private scholarships to help low-income students attend a school of choice. At least 381,000 students—75 percent of Los Angeles Unified District public school students—are eligible for these scholarships. The CSF joined Mike Ovitz (chairman of the Los Angeles effort), Eli Broad, Ron Burkle, and other donors to fund 4,000 new scholarships with $16 million. On September 28, 1998, the San Francisco Bay Area also was named a "partner" by the CSF, which will match funds raised by Bay Area residents to fund approximately 500 private scholarships for low-income students to attend a school of choice. Recipients of these scholarships, awarded for at least four years to children entering kindergarten through 8th grade for the coming year in both cities, were determined by lottery in April 1999.[4]

On June 2, 1998, California voters rejected Proposition 226, the Paycheck Protection initiative, which would have required unions to obtain annual written consent from their members before spending membership dues on political causes. The California Teachers Association alone spent $6.4 million to defeat this measure.

Developments in 1999

Tim Draper, a Silicon Valley venture capitalist and former Republican-appointed member of the California Board of Education, gathered suggestions over the Internet (*www.localchoice.com*) on how to draft a statewide school choice initiative. First drafted and submitted in 1998, the initiative was withdrawn by its backers and resubmitted to the Secretary of State in 1999. In order to qualify for the November 2000 ballot, the measure will need 670,816 signatures. If passed, the National Average School Funding Guarantee and Parental Right to Choose Quality Education Amendment would set funding for support of public schools at a "national average dollar per pupil funding amount" and provide a scholarship of $4,000 to parents who wish to enroll their children in non-public schools. For parents with children already in private schools, the full scholarship amount would be phased in over three years. The initiative also would erect a "regulatory firewall" by requiring a three-fourths vote of each house of the legislature to pass additional statutes pertaining to private schools.[5]

The news for charter school supporters in 1999 was mixed. The good news is that California joined a select group of states in which charter laws have been challenged and subsequently upheld. In October 1999, the California Court of Appeals upheld a lower court decision that rejected a state constitutional challenge to charter school laws. In its decision, the Court of Appeals upheld both the new and old charter school laws, including a provision permitting charter schools to be operated as nonprofit benefit corporations. The plaintiffs had challenged the statutes on numerous constitutional grounds, arguing that the legislature had improperly delegated authority for education to "private" entities, created a second school system, and opened the doors of charter schools to religious institutions. The Court of Appeals disagreed.

The bad news, however, is that the Democrat-controlled legislature, with the cooperation of a newly elected Democrat governor, sought to impose new regulations on charter schools. In April, Assemblywoman Carole Migden (D–San Francisco) introduced AB 842, a bill that would make all California charter school employees subject to the collective bargaining agreement of the sponsor district. This effort was defeated after a vigorous campaign, including a rally on the Capitol steps attended by more than 1,000 charter supporters, and surprisingly strong opposition from Oakland mayor, former California governor, and 1992 presidential candidate Jerry Brown. Nevertheless, by March 2000, charter schools will have to declare whether they or their sponsor district will be the Public School Employer for purposes of California's Education Employee Regulations Act. According to Pamela Riley of the Pacific Research Institute, charter schools across the state have reported an increased amount of union organizing on their campuses.[6]

The legislature also narrowly defeated an effort to restrict charter petitioners from "shopping" for sympathetic sponsor districts. The measure would have required charter schools intending to locate in a site outside of the sponsor district to seek permission from the district in which the school intends to locate. The legislature, however, did seriously restrict the ability of charter schools to operate independent or home-study programs affecting more than 27,000 students or one-third of the total charter school student population.

A Senate bill to create a scholarship program to allow students in poorly performing schools to attend other public schools or certain participating private schools failed to win approval.

In April 1999, the Independent Institute announced the creation of the Independent School Scholarship Fund, a program that will offer need- and merit-based tuition scholarships to enable low-income to moderate-income K–12 students in Alameda and Contra Costa counties in the San Francisco Bay Area to attend schools of choice.[7] The institute awarded 107 scholarships for the 1999–2000 academic year. This initial phase will be followed by a full-scale launch for the 2000–2001 academic year. The program's goal will be to offer 500–1,000 scholarships per year over the next three years.

On April 22, 1999, the Children's Scholarship Fund announced the winners of the largest private scholarship program in the country. The recipients were selected randomly by computer-generated lottery. In the Bay Area, 1,200 recipients were chosen from 6,890 applicants; in Los Angeles, 3,750 recipients were chosen from 54,444 applicants.[8]

Position of the Governor/Composition of State Legislature

Governor Joseph Graham (Gray) Davis, Jr., a Democrat, opposes taxpayer-financed school vouchers.[9] Both houses of the legislature are led by Democrats.

State Contacts

Archdiocese of Los Angeles Education Foundation
Hugh Ralston, Executive Director
3424 Wilshire Boulevard
Los Angeles, CA 90010
Phone: (213) 637-7576
Fax: (213) 637-6111

Assemblyman Steve Baldwin
State Capitol
Sacramento, CA 95814
Phone: (916) 445-3266

Fax: (916) 323-8470
E-mail: Steve.Baldwin@asm.ca.gov

The BASIC Fund
LaVois Hooks, Executive Director
268 Bush Street, #2717
San Francisco, CA 94104
Phone: (415) 986-7221
Fax: (415) 986-5358

California Department of Education
721 Capitol Mall
P.O. Box 944272
Sacramento, CA 94244-2720
Phone: (916) 657-2451
Web site: http://goldmine.cde.ca.gov/

California Public Policy Foundation
John Kurzweil, President
P.O. Box 931
Camarillo, CA 93011
Phone: (805) 445-9183
E-mail: calprev@gte.net

Capitol Resource Institute
Mark Washburn, President
1414 K Street, Suite 200
Sacramento, CA 95814
Phone: (916) 498-1940
Fax: (916) 448-2888
Web site: http://www.capitolresource.org
E-mail: capitolres@aol.com

Center for the Study of Popular Culture
David Horowitz, President
9911 West Pico Boulevard, Suite 1290
Los Angeles, CA 90035
Phone: (800) 752-6562
Fax: (310) 843-3692
Web site: http://www.cspc.org
E-mail: dhorowitz@cspc.org

Children's Scholarship Fund–Los Angeles
Julia MacInnes, Executive Director
1650 Ximeno Street, #245
Long Beach, CA 90804
Phone: (562) 961-9250, ext. 5; (888) 965-9009
Fax: (562) 961-9240

CEO/Oakland
Nancy Berg, CPA, Administrator
P.O. Box 21456
Oakland, CA 94614
Phone: (510) 483-7971
Fax: (510) 339-6770

CEO of Southern California
Jan Harrigan, Administrator
P.O. Box 459
Cerritos, CA 90702-0459
Phone: (562) 926-0900
Fax: (562) 926-1399

Charter Schools Project
Eric Premack
Institute for School Reform
Sacramento State University
600 J Street
Sacramento, CA 95819
Phone: (916) 278-4600

Claremont Institute
Dr. Larry Arnn, President
250 West First Street, Suite 330
Claremont, CA 91711
Phone: (909) 621-6825
Fax: (909) 626-8724
Web site: http://www.claremont.org

Golden State Center for Public Policy Studies
Brian Kennedy, Director
The Golden State Project
1127 11th Street, Suite 206
Sacramento, CA 95814
Phone: (916) 446-7924
Fax: (916) 446-7990
Web site: http://www.claremont.org
E-mail: britrav@aol.com

The Guardsmen Scholarship Fund
Greg Wettersten, Executive Director
120 Montgomery Street, #225
San Francisco, CA 94101

Independent Institute
David J. Theroux, Founder and President
100 Swan Way
Oakland, CA 94621
Phone: (510) 632-1366
Fax: (510) 568-6040
Web site: http://www.independent.org
E-mail: info@independent.org

Independent Scholarship Fund
Michelle Moore, Development Director
Deborah Wright, ISF Director
100 Swan Way
Oakland, CA 94621-1428
Phone: (510) 632-1366
Fax: (510) 568-6040
Web site: http://www.independent.org
E-mail: scholarships@independent.org

Local Choice 2000
Tim Draper
Web site: http://www.localchoice2000.com

Office of Senator Charles Poochigran
State Capitol
Sacramento, CA 95831
Phone: (916) 445-9600

Pacific Research Institute for Public Policy
Pamela Riley, Co-Director, Center for School Reform
755 Sansome Street, Suite 450
San Francisco, CA 94111
Phone: (415) 989-0833
Fax: (415) 989-2411
Web site: http://www.pacificresearch.org

San Francisco Independent Scholars Fund
Liza Watkins
Phone: (415) 561-4607

Reason Public Policy Institute
Richard Seder, Director of Education Studies
3415 South Sepulveda Boulevard, Suite 400
Los Angeles, CA 90034
Phone: (310) 391-2245
Fax: (310) 391-4395
Web site: http://www.reason.org

RPP International
Paul Berman
2200 Powell Street, Suite 250
Emeryville, CA 94710
Phone: (510) 450-2550

Senate Office of Research
Patty Quate
1020 N Street, Suite 200
Sacramento, CA 95814
Phone: (916) 445-1727
Fax: (916) 324-3944

Senate Republican Fiscal Committee
Ann McKinney, Education Consultant
State Capitol
Room 2209
Sacramento, CA 95831
Phone: (916) 323-9221

Endnotes

1   For sources, see "An Explanation of the State Profile Categories."

2   Correspondence from Pamela Riley, Pacific Research Institute, received November 8, 1999.

3 Center for Education Reform, *School Reform in the United States: State by State Summary*, Spring 1997.

4 See Children's Scholarship Fund Web site at *http://www.scholarshipfund.org*.

5 Jon Matthews, "Voucher Plan Would Allot Each Child $4,000," *The Sacramento Bee*, February 3, 1999. See also *http://www.localchoice2000.com*.

6 Correspondence from Pamela Riley, Pacific Research Institute, received November 8, 1999.

7 Correspondence from the Independent Institute, April 1, 1999.

8 See Children's Scholarship Fund Web site at *http://www.scholarshipfund.org*.

9 Dan Smith, "California Gets 1st Democrat Chief in 16 Years," *The Sacramento Bee*, November 4, 1998, p. A16.

Colorado

State Profile[1]

School Choice Status
- Public school choice: Statewide
- Charter schools: Established 1993
    Strength of Law: Strong
    Number of charter schools in operation (fall 1999): 70
    Number of students enrolled in charter schools (1998–1999): 12,572
- Publicly funded private school choice: N/A

K–12 Public and Private Students and Schools
- Public school enrollment (fall 1998) and number of schools (1997–1998): 699,135 in 1,497 schools
- Private school enrollment and number of schools (1997–1998): 52,563 in 353 schools

K–12 Public and Private School Student Academic Performance
NAEP Test Results—percentage of students at each performance level for both public and private schools, with national percentages in parentheses

Performance Level	Reading 4th grade 1998	Reading 8th grade 1998	Math 4th grade 1996	Math 8th grade 1996	Science 8th grade 1996
Advanced	7% (6%)	2% (2%)	2% (2%)	3% (4%)	2% (3%)
Proficient	27 (23)	28 (28)	20 (18)	22 (19)	30 (24)
Basic	35 (31)	46 (41)	45 (42)	42 (38)	36 (33)
Below Basic	31 (39)	24 (28)	33 (38)	33 (39)	32 (40)

- SAT weighted rank (1999): N/A
- ACT weighted rank (1999): 8 out of 26 states

K–12 Public School Expenditures
- Current expenditures (1999–2000): $3,739,880,000
- Amount of revenue from the federal government (1998–1999): 5.4%
- Current per-pupil expenditures (1999–2000): $5,336

K–12 Public School Teachers (1998–1999)
- Number of teachers: 38,089
- Average salary: $38,025
- Students enrolled per teacher: 18.4
- Leading teachers union: NEA

Background

In 1990, the Colorado legislature adopted the Public Schools of Choice Act, which requires all districts to establish policies and procedures for open enrollment in all programs or schools for resident pupils, subject to space restrictions or in cases where open enrollment would produce noncompliance with desegregation plans. In 1994, the law was amended to allow students from other districts to enroll without tuition payments from parents, subject to space and staff limitations. The state's open enrollment policies therefore allow parents to choose a public school for their children either within or outside their district. There are, however, four limitations: There must be space in the school; it must offer appropriate services for the child if needed (as in the case of special needs, either cognitive or physical); the child must meet any eligibility requirements; and admission must not create a need to modify the curriculum.

In November 1992, a full school choice ballot initiative known as Choice School Reform failed by a margin of 62 percent to 37 percent. The initiative would have given parents a voucher, worth 50 percent of the existing per-pupil expenditure, that they could use to send their children to a public, private, or religious school of choice.

In June 1993, the legislature passed the Charter Schools Act. Under this legislation, any group of concerned parents, teachers, or members of the community may submit a charter school application. The bill defines a charter school as a "public" school and includes provisions that allow it to be slightly independent from state and local regulations while remaining within the school district. Enrollment in charter schools is open. Funding for each charter is 95 percent of per-pupil revenues (the per-student amount determined yearly by the state legislature plus capital reserve and liability insurance). According to finance guidelines, state and federal funds flow from the state to the county, then to the district, and finally to the charter school. In addition, local funds flow from the district to the charter school.

Charter schools are not completely free from state and local regulations. Each charter, through the application process, must seek waivers from specific school district policies. Charter schools may petition the state Board of Education for waivers from state law and regulations.

A challenge to the state school board's authority to overrule a local district's rejection of a charter application was upheld by the Colorado Supreme Court. Though the state board can order a district to approve an application, the terms of the contract are to be sorted out at the local level.

In 1995, a commission on charter schools made recommendations to strengthen the state's charter school law. Some of these recommendations were adopted in 1996. A recommendation to increase charter school funding from 80 percent to 95 percent of the average per-pupil expenditure, however, was vetoed in July 1997 by then-Governor Roy Romer, a Democrat.

Although Colorado has yet to implement a publicly funded private school choice program, several programs like Denver's Educational Options for Children (EOC) provide partial scholarship support to low-income students to attend a school of choice for a four-year period. This program is funded entirely by grants from the Adolph Coors Foundation to a special EOC fund established at the Denver Foundation. A total of $200,000 was awarded for the 1999–2000 school year, enabling approximately 110 students to attend a school of their choice.

In May 1997, a group of African–American parents who claimed that Denver was failing to teach basic skills to poor and minority students filed a lawsuit in state court. Since then, over 3,500 parents (including white and Hispanic parents) have joined the class-action suit against the Denver public school system. The suit calls for the district to grant poor families tuition vouchers that could be used at either public or private schools. In early 2000, a Colorado appeals court ruled against the parents; the decision has been appealed to the Colorado Supreme Court.

Colorado voters rejected a refundable tuition tax credit ballot initiative (Initiative 17) in the 1998 general election. The amount of the credit would have been at least 50 percent of the state's per-pupil expenditure, but no more than 80 percent of the actual cost of private school tuition. (For children with special needs, the credits would have been higher.) The initiative was voted down on November 3, 1998, by a margin of 60 percent to 40 percent.

In 1998, according to the Colorado League of Charter Schools, lawmakers passed legislation streamlining the charter school waiver process and providing charter schools with access to financing for tax-exempt facilities. They also changed the state's school finance act to provide additional financial support to rural school districts with charter schools. Additionally, the legislature removed the sunset provision of the Charter Schools Act, making it a permanent law.

Developments in 1999

On March 31, 1999, Governor Bill Owens signed into law a requirement that school districts fully fund charter schools at 95 percent of per-pupil revenue. Districts currently fund only 80 percent of charter school costs. The measure—formerly H.B. 1113, sponsored by Representative Doug Dean (R–18) and Senator Ken Arnold (R–23)—will increase total funding to Colorado's charter schools by about $6 million.[2] The bill also allows a school district to keep 5 percent of district per-pupil revenues to pay for charter school administrative overhead costs and permits charter schools to enter into contracts with the school districts for supportive services other than administrative overhead.

In June 1999, the governor signed S.B. 52, which authorizes charter schools to develop and maintain on-line programs either by themselves or in conjunction with other charter schools, school districts, or boards of cooperative services. S.B. 100, a measure to create state charter school districts with the state school board as their board of education, died in April 1999. Another charter school bill, H.B. 1044, sponsored by Representative Nancy Spence (R–39), would have allowed local school boards to waive nearly all state regulations without approval by local accountability boards, parents, teachers, or administrators, but it faltered in the Senate Committee on Education after being passed by the House.[3]

Two choice bills were introduced in the legislature this session, but neither made it out of committee. S.B. 162, introduced by Senator John Andrews, a Republican and vice-chairman of the Senate Education Committee, would have created a tuition tax credit bill for preschool tuition costs. S.B. 55, introduced by Senator Doug Linkhart, a Democrat, would have allowed taxpayers to take tax credits worth 25 percent of cash donations to a school in the state. Although S.B. 55 was approved by the Senate Finance Committee, it died in the Appropriations Committee.[4]

Colorado NAACP President Willie Breazell was asked to resign after voicing his support for publicly funded private school choice in an August 17 opinion piece in *The Colorado Springs Gazette*.

Developments in 2000

Conservative lawmakers and minority activists will promote at least two initiatives during the 2000–2001 legislative session. The first measure, backed by Senator Andrews, is a statewide voucher program called the School Guarantee Act. Under this plan, parents who were dissatisfied with their child's academic, moral, or physical well-being would receive a voucher to enroll their child in a school of choice. Once parents outlined their specific complaint or complaints, the school would have up to three months to respond. If parents were still dissatisfied, they would receive a voucher of about 80 percent of the money a school receives for each student—around $5,000. This plan was defeated on February 9, 2000. Lawmakers are also promoting legislation to allow parents to apply for a charter school through their state board of education if dissatisfied with their school districts.

Another measure, promoted by a group of conservative activists, is a pilot voucher plan for Denver similar to the one in Milwaukee.

Meanwhile, a group of Colorado business leaders is trying to raise $300,000 to support Republican Governor Bill Owens' education platform, which includes tough sanctions for failing schools.[5]

In early February 2000, a group of voucher advocates launched a private scholarship program that would award $1 million annually to low-income Denver students to attend a school of choice. The group, called the Alliance for Choice in Education, will award 500–700 grants each year.

Position of the Governor/Composition of State Legislature

Governor Bill F. Owens, a Republican, believes that public schools can be improved by closing down the state's worst schools, ending grants of tenure to new teachers, yearly testing, and requiring every high school junior to take the ACT college entrance exam. As a state senator, he sponsored the Charter School Act and wrote the law that legalizes home schooling in Colorado. The governor's education budget contains $3.4 million to establish seven special charter schools designed for disruptive students. Both houses of the legislature are led by Republicans.

State Contacts

Alliance for Choice in Education
511 16th Street, Suite 300
Denver, CO 80202
Phone: (303) 573-1603
Fax: (303) 573-7340
E-mail: www.gotoschool.org

Association of Christian Schools International
Burt Carney
P.O. Box 35097
Colorado Springs, CO 80935-3509
Phone: (719) 528-6906
Fax: (719) 531-0631

Colorado Department of Education
Cindy Howerter, Assistant to the Commissioner
201 East Colfax
Denver, CO 80203-1799
Phone: (303) 866-6806
Fax: (303) 866-6938
Web site: http://www.cde.state.co.us

Colorado League of Charter Schools
Jim Griffin, Director
7700 West Woodard Drive
Lakewood, CO 80227
Phone: (303) 989-5356
Fax: (303) 985-7721
E-mail: clcs@rmi.net

Education Commission of the States
Kathy Christie, Director of Information Clearinghouse
707 17th Street, Suite 2700
Denver, CO 80202-3427
Phone: (303) 299-3613
Fax: (303) 296-8332
Web site: http://www.ecs.org
E-mail: kchristie@ecs.org

Educational Options for Children
Sheryl Glaser, Program Administrator
c/o Adolph Coors Foundation
3773 Cherry Creek North Drive
Denver, CO 80209
Phone: (720) 981-2557
Fax: (303) 948-5923

Greater Educational Opportunities Foundation
Dave Akridge
928 Osage
Manitou Springs, CO 80829
Phone: (303) 296-4311
E-mail: davidageo@aol.com

Independence Institute
Jon Caldara, President
14142 Denver West Parkway, Suite185
Golden, CO 80401
Phone: (303) 279-6536
Fax: (303) 279-4176
Web site: http://www.i2i.org

National Conference of State Legislatures
William Pound, Executive Director
Eric Hirsch, Policy Specialist
1560 Broadway, Suite 700
Denver, CO 80202
Phone: (303) 830-2200
Fax: (303) 863-8003
Web site: http://www.ncsl.org
E-mail: info@ncsl.org

Endnotes

1   For sources, see "An Explanation of the State Profile Categories." Charter count is from Colorado League of Charter Schools.

2   Dan Luzadder, "With the Stroke of a Pen, Owens Puts More into Education," *Denver Rocky Mountain News*, March 31, 1999, p. A10.

3   Michelle Dally Johnston, "House OK's GOP School Bills," *Denver Post*, January 30, 1999.

4   The Friedman–Blum *Educational Freedom Report*, No. 71, May 21, 1999.

5   Michael Cardman, "Colorado Business Leaders Back Governor's Education Plan," *Education Daily*, January 24, 2000.

Connecticut

State Profile[1]

School Choice Status
- Public school choice: Statewide
- Charter schools: Established 1996
  - Strength of Law: Strong
  - Number of charter schools in operation (fall 1999): 17
  - Number of students enrolled in charter schools (1998–1999): 1,938
- Publicly funded private school choice: N/A

K–12 Public and Private Students and Schools
- Public school enrollment (fall 1998) and number of schools (1997–1998): 545,663 in 1,058 schools
- Private school enrollment and number of schools (1997–1998): 69,293 in 339 schools

K–12 Public and Private School Student Academic Performance
NAEP Test Results—percentage of students at each performance level for both public and private schools, with national percentages in parentheses

Performance Level	Reading 4th grade 1998	Reading 8th grade 1998	Math 4th grade 1996	Math 8th grade 1996	Science 8th grade 1996
Advanced	11% (6%)	4% (2%)	3% (2%)	5% (4%)	3% (3%)
Proficient	35 (23)	38 (28)	28 (18)	26 (19)	33 (24)
Basic	32 (31)	40 (41)	44 (42)	39 (38)	32 (33)
Below Basic	22 (39)	18 (28)	25 (38)	30 (39)	32 (40)

- SAT weighted rank (1999): 8 out of 24 states and the District of Columbia
- ACT weighted rank (1999): N/A

K–12 Public School Expenditures
- Current expenditures (1999–2000): $5,225,466,000
- Amount of revenue from the federal government (1998–1999): 4.3%
- Current per-pupil expenditures (1999–2000): $9,476

K–12 Public School Teachers (1998–1999)
- Number of teachers: 39,209
- Average salary: $51,584
- Students enrolled per teacher: 13.9
- Leading teachers union: NEA

Background

School districts in Connecticut offer transportation to private school students and are reimbursed by the state. This currently is the only manner in which public funds are used to support private education in the state.

In 1995, Governor John Rowland, a Republican, authorized the appointment of a school choice commission (the Governor's Commission on School Choice) in response to students' poor performance on the Connecticut Mastery Tests. The commission included among its 16 members public and private school teachers and administrators, public officials, business professionals, and a student from the private school system. The commission recommended four major initiatives.

- **An early childhood educational choice program.** This statewide pilot choice program would give financial assistance to all families to place their children in a broad range of accredited public and private early childhood education programs. The assistance could be achieved through a tax credit against the state income tax for a portion of the tuition and fees paid to accredited early childhood education programs. Families with no tax liability would be eligible for a periodic credit to be applied to tuition and fees.

- **Project Concern.** This public school choice program, operating in Greater Hartford, would expand its options as soon as possible. These options could include accredited private schools and public schools for students in participating suburban districts. Parents of Project Concern students who choose a private school would receive either an income tax credit or a scholarship in an amount not to exceed 50 percent of the district's spending per pupil; the district would be entitled to retain the remaining 50 percent. Existing state funding for transportation of Project Concern students would be increased.

The commission also recommended the implementation of a program that would work in conjunction with the voluntary transfer of urban students to suburban public schools. Financial incentives would be offered to urban public schools to attract out-of-district students. Any urban school that accepted out-of-district students would receive a grant per student equal to 100 percent of the receiving district's revenue per pupil. The commission urged the legislature to explore all financial incentives to encourage other school districts to participate in Project Concern.

- **Charter schools with full autonomy from local boards of education.** These schools would be funded publicly on an equal basis with other public schools and would receive 100 percent of the school district's average spending per pupil. They would not charge tuition, but would subsidize start-up costs by raising private funds. Although the commission failed to approve religious charter schools, it recommended that new charter schools should be free to structure their own curricula and areas of study and should be exempt from teacher tenure and certification laws.

- **A school choice implementation study.** The commission called on the governor and the legislature to study the implementation of school choice programs. The commission would serve as a watchdog for the success or failure of any school choice reform initiatives enacted.

On June 4, 1996, Governor Rowland signed a charter school bill authorizing the creation of 24 charter schools. The law went into effect on October 4, 1996.

During the 1997 legislative session, the General Assembly increased the grant amount for Project Concern students from $468 to $2,000 per student. The program remains voluntary. The legislature also increased the enrollment cap for charter schools from 1,000 to 1,500.

In 1997, the legislature enacted the Enhanced Educational Choice and Opportunities Act, which requires school districts to provide opportunities for students to interact with students and teachers from other racial, ethnic, and economic backgrounds. The law also required that districts report by October 1, 1998, on the programs and activities they had initiated to foster this interaction; phase in and operate a statewide inter-district attendance program beginning in the 1998–1999 school year with Bridgeport, New Haven, and Hartford, and then extend it statewide by 2005; and develop and implement written policies and procedures for encouraging parent–teacher communication.

A private scholarship foundation, CEO Connecticut, serves low-income students in Hartford as well as those already served in Bridgeport. The CEO program offered 301 scholarships for the 1998–1999 school year. Scholarships are for five years for students in kindergarten through 6th grade, and there is a waiting list of 960 students.

Developments in 1999

The CEO Connecticut program doubled in size for the 1999–2000 school year, thanks to a $1 million donation. The donation will provide 250 additional four-year scholarships to low-income students in kindergarten through 5th grade in Hartford.[2]

Position of the Governor/Composition of State Legislature

Governor John Rowland, a Republican, strongly supports public and private school choice. He also supports the final recommendations of the Governor's Commission on School Choice and has vowed to fight for serious education reform. The governor indicated in his state of the state address that he wanted a $500 tax credit for parents of students who attend private or religious schools.[3] Both houses of the legislature are led by Democrats.

State Contacts

Connecticut Answer for Responsible Education
Linda LaRue
442 Steele Road
New Hartford, CT 06057
Phone: (860) 693-6793

CEO Connecticut
Bill Heinrichs, Executive Director
97 Crescent Street
Hartford, CT 06106
Phone: (860) 297-4254
Fax: (860) 987-6218
E-mail: wheinrichs@juno.com

Connecticut Federation of Catholic School Parents
Matthew T. Boyle
238 Jewett Avenue
Bridgeport, CT 06606
Phone: (203) 372-4301
Fax: (203) 371-8698

Family Institute of Connecticut
Kenneth Von Kohorn, Chairman
P.O. Box 5222
Westport, CT 06881
Phone: (203) 454-7283
Fax: (203) 226-1636
Web site: www.ctfamily.org
E-mail: faminst@ibm.net

Yankee Institute for Public Policy Studies
Lewis M. Andrews, Executive Director
97–1999 Crescent Street
Hartford, CT 06106
Phone: (860) 297-4217
Fax: (860) 987-6218
E-mail: 104415.1625@compuserve.com

Endnotes

1 For sources, see "An Explanation of the State Profile Categories."

2 Correspondence from CEO Foundation, March 31, 1999.

3 Jeff Archer, "Rowland Proposing Tuition Tax Credits for Connecticut," *Education Week*, February 16, 2000, p.19.

Delaware

State Profile[1]

School Choice Status
- Public school choice: Statewide
- Charter schools: Established 1995
    - Strength of law: Strong
    - Number of charter schools in operation (fall 1999): 5
    - Number of students enrolled in charter schools (1998–1999): 995
- Publicly funded private school choice: N/A

K–12 Public and Private Students and Schools
- Public school enrollment (fall 1998) and number of schools (1997–1998): 113,082 in 185 schools
- Private school enrollment and number of schools (1997–1998): 24,193 in 103 schools

K–12 Public and Private School Student Academic Performance
NAEP Test Results—percentage of students at each performance level for both public and private schools, with national percentages in parentheses

Performance Level	Reading 4th grade 1998	Reading 8th grade 1998	Math 4th grade 1996	Math 8th grade 1996	Science 8th grade 1996
Advanced	5% (6%)	2% (2%)	1% (2%)	3% (4%)	1% (3%)
Proficient	20 (33)	23 (28)	15 (18)	16 (19)	20 (24)
Basic	32 (31)	41 (41)	38 (42)	36 (38)	30 (33)
Below Basic	43 (39)	34 (28)	46 (38)	45 (39)	49 (40)

- SAT weighted rank (1999): 15 out of 24 states and the District of Columbia
- ACT weighted rank (1999): N/A

K–12 Public School Expenditures
- Current expenditures (1999–2000): $911,261,000
- Amount of revenue from the federal government (1998–1999): 7.3%
- Current per-pupil expenditures (1999–2000): $8,037

K–12 Public School Teachers (1998–1999)
- Number of teachers: 7,073
- Average salary: $43,164
- Students enrolled per teacher (fall 1998): 16.0
- Leading teachers union: NEA

Background

Delaware enacted a bill establishing public school choice in September 1996. The law allows parents to enroll their children in any public school in the state, both between and within districts, if the school's capacity is adequate. The burden of transportation costs for out-of-district students rests on families, but the law does provide a funding mechanism for transportation costs associated with inter-district choice. Parents, however, may not use these funds for private or religious schools.

Governor Thomas Carper, a Democrat, signed the Charter School Act of 1995 into law on July 10, 1995. This act allowed for the establishment of up to 15 public charter schools through 1999; however, it prohibits religious, home-based, or sectarian charter schools. Each charter is awarded for three years but is subject to review and termination by the approving authority at any point. The legislation contains a complex set of rules and regulations on teacher hiring and certification, funding procedures, and transportation financing. It also allows charter schools some freedom from state and local regulations. Overall, the Charter School Act of 1995 may have set the stage for education reform; but because of its limits on the number and types of schools that may be chartered, it still does not qualify as a serious education initiative.

Delaware's first two charter schools opened in September 1996. One of these schools is targeted specifically at the education of at-risk students.

In June 1997, State Representative Deborah H. Capano (R–12) introduced a bill to create a private school choice program. To offset the costs of private school tuition, the program would provide annual scholarships to the parents or guardians of any student attending an accredited non-public school whose public school district chose to participate in the program by a vote of the school board or by referendum. Scholarship amounts would vary based on family income, with a maximum value of $2,700. The bill died in the Education Committee.

Developments in 1999

A bill offering a $500 tax credit for each K–12 student in a non-public school was defeated.[2]

Position of the Governor/Composition of State Legislature

Governor Thomas G. Carper, a Democrat, supports both public school choice and charter schools. During the 1995 legislative session, he signed bills into law that established both. However, he opposes any form of voucher plan involving private or religiously affiliated schools. The House is led by Republicans, and the Senate is led by Democrats.

State Contacts

Delaware Department of Education
Dr. Larry Gabbert
P.O. Box 1402
Dover, DE 19903-1402
Phone: (302) 739-4601
Fax: (302) 739-4654

Delaware Public Policy Institute
Pete Du Pont, Chairman
Suzanne Moore, Executive Director
1201 North Orange Street
Wilmington, DE 19801
Phone: (302) 655-7221
Fax: (302) 654-0691

Focus on the Kids, Inc.
Ms. Martha Manning
100 West 10th Street, Suite 1006
Wilmington, DE 19801
Phone: (302) 778-5999
Fax: (302) 778-5998
E-mail: MarthMLM@aol.com

Endnotes

1 For sources, see "An Explanation of the State Profile Categories."

2 The Friedman–Blum *Educational Freedom Report*, No. 71, May 21, 1999.

District of Columbia

District Profile[1]

School Choice Status
- Public school choice: Citywide
- Charter schools: Established 1996
    Strength of law: Strong
    Number of charter schools in operation (winter 2000): 31
    Number of students enrolled in charter schools (1998–1999): 3,586
- Publicly funded private school choice: N/A

K–12 Public and Private Students and Schools
- Public school enrollment (fall 1998) and number of schools (1997–1998): 79,434 in 146 schools
- Private school enrollment and number of schools (1997–1998): 16,671 in 87 schools

K–12 Public and Private School Student Academic Performance
NAEP Test Results—percentage of students at each performance level for both public and private schools, with national percentages in parentheses

Performance Level	Reading 4th grade 1998	Reading 8th grade 1998	Math 4th grade 1996	Math 8th grade 1996	Science 8th grade 1996
Advanced	3% (6%)	1% (2%)	1% (2%)	1% (4%)	0% (3%)
Proficient	4 (23)	10 (28)	4 (18)	4 (19)	5 (24)
Basic	21 (31)	33 (41)	15 (42)	15 (38)	15 (33)
Below Basic	72 (39)	56 (28)	80 (38)	80 (39)	81 (40)

- SAT weighted rank (1999): 23 out of 24 states and the District of Columbia
- ACT weighted rank (1999): N/A

K–12 Public School Expenditures
- Current expenditures (1999–2000): $563,537,000
- Amount of revenue from the federal government (1998–1999): 15.2%
- Current per-pupil expenditures (1999–2000): $7,105

K–12 Public School Teachers (1998–1999)
- Number of teachers: 5,462
- Average salary: $47,150
- Students enrolled per teacher: 14.5
- Leading teachers union: AFT

Background

In 1995, working with community leaders and the mayor, U.S. Representative Steve Gunderson (R–WI) developed an education plan to increase educational options for the District of Columbia's poorest students. Gunderson's amendment to the FY 1996 D.C. appropriations bill was designed to help fund charter schools, give $3,000 vouchers to students whose family income fell below the poverty level, and give $1,500 vouchers to students whose family incomes are up to 80 percent above the poverty level. The vouchers would have been redeemable at a public, private, or religious school located in the District or the surrounding counties in Northern Virginia and Maryland.

Representative Gunderson's voucher proposal died in the Senate following a filibuster led by Senator Edward Kennedy (D–MA), but his charter school plan was passed. It was amended in 1997. The law, considered to be fairly strong, sets up two chartering authorities: the D.C. Board of Education and a newly formed Public Charter School Board. It allows any entity interested in opening a charter school to submit an application and offers an automatic waiver from most state and district education laws.

The 1997 charter school amendments adjusted the annual payment for facilities' costs to charter schools (previously, the per-pupil allocation for District charter schools made no provision for funding facilities or other capital costs); raised annual charter school funding from $1.235 million to $3.376 million from local funds (rather than funds already made available for D.C. public schools); and created the New Charter School Fund revolving account (with unexpected FY 1997 funds and subsequent unexpected fiscal year funds) to give new charter schools advances for their startup costs. The amendments also expanded the approval period for charter school applications to any time during the calendar year and gave $400,000 to the Public Charter School Board to help board members maintain a meaningful role in the process.[2]

The District's two chartering authorities, the Public Charter School Board and Board of Education, by law can open as many as 20 charter schools each year. Many of the charters granted are provisional, which means that schools must provide additional information or secure a building before receiving a full charter.

Talk of a D.C. school choice plan was revisited when Representative Richard Armey (R–TX) and then-Representative Floyd Flake (D–NY), along with Senator Joseph Lieberman (D–CT) and then-Senator Dan Coats (R–IN), introduced the D.C. Student Opportunity Scholarship Act of 1997. This federal school choice legislation was similar to the Gunderson plan. It would have provided up to $3,200 in scholarships for approximately 1,800 of D.C.'s poorest students in kindergarten through 12th grade to attend a public, private, or religious school of choice in the D.C. metropolitan area.

The Senate approved the choice bill by voice vote on November 9, 1997, and the House passed it by a vote of 214 to 206 on April 30, 1998. However, President Clinton vetoed the measure soon thereafter.

Three days after the President's veto, *The Washington Post* released the results of a May 11–17, 1998, poll of District residents' views on this issue. The poll showed that 65 percent of African–Americans who reside in the District and have incomes under $50,000 favor using federal dollars to send children to private or religious schools. Furthermore, 56 percent of D.C. residents overall support school choice.[3]

Meanwhile, the Children's Scholarship Fund, a $100 million foundation underwritten by Ted Forstmann and John Walton, selected Washington, D.C., as a "partner city" to receive matching donations for private scholarships to help low-income students attend a school of choice. At least 40,000 students—68 percent of the District's public school students in kindergarten through 8th grade—are eligible for these scholarships. The CSF joined Joe Robert, chairman of the Washington Scholarship Fund, and other donors to fund 400 new scholarships with $2 million. This brought the total number of scholarships as of September 1999 to 2,000.[4]

Developments in 1999

The D.C. Public Charter School Board has approved 10 applications for charter school status in the 1999–2000 school year, bringing the total to 29 and the total enrollment to over 7,000 (or 10 percent of D.C. public school students).[5] One of the charter schools that was approved is Paul Junior High School, a community public school since 1926. Superintendent Arlene Ackerman, however, has asked the school to vacate its building even though the

1995 School Reform Act as passed by Congress fully intended that an existing public school converting to a public charter school should retain its existing building—and even though Paul Junior High's conversion to a charter school could not have been effected without the approval of two-thirds of the faculty and two-thirds of the school's parents. The school, which is one of the District's most academically successful, intends to open its doors next September as a charter school with 725 students.

On April 22, 1999, the Children's Scholarship Fund announced the winners of the largest private scholarship program in the country. The recipients were selected randomly by computer-generated lottery. In the District, 500 scholarship recipients were chosen from 10,770 applicants.[6]

An analysis of African–American Catholic and public school children in the District by the Heritage Foundation found that, after holding demographic and socioeconomic factors constant, Catholic school children perform better in math than their public school counterparts. In fact, between the 4th and 8th grades, the performance gap between public and Catholic school students increases considerably; 4th grade Catholic school students score 6.5 percent higher than public school children, and this figure grows to over 8.2 percent by the 8th grade. Thus, the average 8th grade African–American Catholic school student in the District outscored 72 percent of his or her public school peers.[7]

Developments in 2000

The mayor has asked for full control of the city's school system, but the city council has been reluctant to eliminate the elected D.C. Public School Board.

A new study of 810 students who benefit from the Washington Scholarship Fund scholarships finds that, after one year, African–American elementary school students in grades 2 to 5 who transferred to private schools were much happier and performed better in mathematics and reading than their public school counterparts. The students outscored their public school counterparts by six percentage points on math tests and by two points in reading. Results were not as positive for students in grades 6 to 8. In addition, 40 percent of private school parents gave their schools an "A" compared with 15 percent of public school parents.[8]

Position of the Mayor

Mayor Anthony Williams, a Democrat, is in favor of public school choice but does not support vouchers.

District Contacts

AppleTree Institute for Education Innovation
Jack McCarthy and Lex Towle
401 M Street, SW, Room 100
Washington, DC 20024
Phone: (202) 488-3990
Fax: (202) 488-3991

Friends of Choice in Urban Schools (FOCUS)
Malcolm Peabody
1530 16th Street, NW
Washington, DC 20036
Phone: (202) 387-0405
Fax: (202) 667-3798
Web site: http://www.focus-dccharter.org
E-mail: info@focus-dccharter.org

Friends of International Education
Dorothy Goodman
P.O. Box 4800
Washington, DC 20008
Phone: (202) 362-2946
Fax: (202) 363-7499
E-mail: dgoodman@crosslink.net

D.C. Parents for School Choice
Virginia F. Walden, Executive Director
15030 16th Street, NW, Suite 003
Washington, DC 20036
Phone: (202) 518-4140
Fax: (202) 518-4148
E-mail: Gfwalden@aol.com

The Washington Scholarship Fund
Patrick Purtill
1010 16th Street, NW, Suite 500
Washington, DC 20036
Phone: (202) 293-5560
Fax: (202) 293-7893
Web site: www.wsf-dc.org
Application Line: (202) U-CHOOSE (824-6673)

Endnotes

1 For sources, see "An Explanation of the State Profile Categories."

2 From conversations with and information via fax from Lex Towle, Managing Director, AppleTree Institute, January 6, 1997.

3 Sari Horwitz, "Poll Finds Backing for D.C. School Vouchers: Blacks Support Idea More Than Whites," *The Washington Post*, May 24, 1998, pp. F1, F7.

4 See Children's Scholarship Fund Web site at *http://www.scholarshipfund.org*.

5 Susan Ferrechio, "D.C. Board Approves 2 Charters Out of 13," *The Washington Times*, February 18, 1999, p. A1.

6 See Children's Scholarship Fund Web site at *http://www.scholarshipfund.org*.

7 Kirk A. Johnson, "Comparing Math Scores of Black Students in D.C.'s Public and Catholic Schools," *Center for Data Analysis Report* No. CDA99–08, October 7, 1999.

8 Paul Peterson, William Howell, and Patrik Wolfe, "School Choice in Washington, D.C.: An Evaluation After One Year," February 2000; paper prepared for the Conference on Vouchers, Charters, and Public Education, sponsored by the Program on Education Policy and Governance, Harvard University, March 2000.

Florida

State Profile[1]

School Choice Status

- Public school choice: Limited
- Charter schools: Established 1996
  Strength of law: Strong
  Number of charter schools in operation (fall 1999): 112
  Number of students enrolled in charter schools (1998–1999): 9,881
- Publicly funded private school choice: "Opportunity Scholarships"
  Program description: Enacted in 1999, the program allows any child who has attended a failing school for two years out of any four-year period to attend a higher performing public school or a private or religious school of choice. In the first year (1999–2000), 134 families from two elementary schools in Pensacola were offered scholarships; children from 78 of these families attended public schools. Students in as many as 50 schools could qualify in the 2000–2001 school year. The private school choice component of this program was struck down on May 14, 2000. An appeal has been filed.

K–12 Public and Private Students and Schools

- Public school enrollment (fall 1998) and number of schools (1997–1998) 2,333,570 in 2,877 schools
- Private school enrollment and number of schools (1997–1998): 273,628 in 1,481 schools

K–12 Public and Private School Student Academic Performance

NAEP Test Results—percentage of students at each performance level for both public and private schools, with national percentages in parentheses

Performance Level	Reading 4th grade 1998	Reading 8th grade 1998	Math 4th grade 1996	Math 8th grade 1996	Science 8th grade 1996
Advanced	5% (6%)	1% (2%)	1% (2%)	2% (4%)	1% (3%)
Proficient	18 (23)	22 (28)	14 (18)	15 (19)	20 (24)
Basic	31 (31)	42 (41)	40 (42)	37 (38)	30 (33)
Below Basic	46 (39)	35 (28)	45 (38)	46 (39)	49 (40)

- SAT weighted rank (1999): 16 out of 24 states and the District of Columbia
- ACT weighted rank (1999): N/A

K–12 Public School Expenditures

- Current expenditures (1999–2000): $13,014,924,000
- Amount of revenue from the federal government (1998–1999): 7.6%
- Current per-pupil expenditures (1999–2000): $5,436

K–12 Public School Teachers (1998–1999)

- Number of teachers: 129,731
- Average salary: $35,916
- Students enrolled per teacher: 18.0
- Leading teachers union: NEA

Background

As explained below, Florida is now the first state in the nation to offer a "money back guarantee" for students trapped in failing schools. This statewide school choice plan allows students trapped for two out of four years in a failing school an opportunity to attend a better public, private, or religious school of choice. Florida also has a charter school law, enacted on May 17, 1995, that authorizes both the formation of new charter schools and the granting of charter school status to existing public schools. Charter schools may be run by nonprofit private groups under contract with or chartered by the school boards. Most of these schools have programs designed specifically for students with special needs, such as children with attention deficit disorder (ADD), students transferred or expelled from traditional schools, and at-risk students with bad grades or such behavioral problems as truancy. At least one school focuses on discipline and citizenship, and others provide individual learning plans for students.

Florida also has a law, passed in 1997, that allows each school district to develop its own public school choice plan, subject to the approval of the state Department of Education. Five counties (Bay, Dade, Lee, Manatee, and St. Lucie) have received grants from the state and federal governments to implement their school choice proposals.

On September 28, 1998, Miami and Tampa Bay were named two of the 40 "partner cities" for the Children's Scholarship Fund (CSF) challenge grant. The CSF is a $100 million foundation underwritten by entrepreneurs Ted Forstmann and John Walton. It will match funds raised by residents of Miami and Tampa Bay to fund approximately 2,000 private scholarships to enable low-income children entering kindergarten through 8th grade (1,250 in Miami and 750 in Tampa Bay) to attend a school of choice for at least four years.[2]

Developments in 1999

On April 28, leaders in the Florida House and Senate approved Governor Jeb Bush's "A-plus Plan" for education, making Florida the first state to offer state-paid tuition scholarships for children in failing public schools to attend a public, private, or religious school of choice. The legislation will set up a grading system for Florida's public schools. Based on standardized test scores (the Florida Comprehensive Assessment Test), schools will be assigned a grade between A and F. Schools that improve their scores will be rewarded with up to $100 per pupil. Students attending schools receiving a grade of F for two consecutive years will be able to transfer either to a higher-scoring public school or to a private or parochial school by applying the opportunity scholarship, which will be worth up to $4,000 a year. During the first year, the program was limited to two schools in Pensacola and around 1,000 students (already deemed by the state to be failing). Within two years, as many as 78 public schools may be included in the program. The Florida House approved the measure by a vote of 70–48, and the Senate by a vote of 26–14. Governor Bush signed the plan into law on June 21.

The day after the Florida program was signed into law, the National Association for the Advancement of Colored People (NAACP), Florida teachers unions, and others filed a lawsuit against the plan in Leon County Circuit Court claiming that the program violates both Florida's constitution and the U.S. Constitution. Interestingly, the Urban League of Greater Miami, represented by the Washington-based Institute for Justice (IJ), was named as a defendant.[3] On July 29, 1999, the American Federation of Teachers filed a second lawsuit against the Florida plan. A state judge struck down the private school choice provision of the program on March 14, 2000. An appeal has been filed.

The Children's Scholarship Fund announced the winners of the largest private scholarship program in the country on April 22, 1999. The recipients were selected randomly by computer-generated lottery. In Miami, 625 scholarship recipients were chosen from 27,098 applicants; in Tampa and St. Petersburg, 750 recipients were chosen from 12,509 applicants.

Position of the Governor/Composition of State Legislature

Governor Jeb Bush, a Republican, is an avid proponent of parental choice in education. During his first term, he successfully championed a plan allowing students in chronically poor-performing schools to attend private schools with tax-paid vouchers, stating that "We must dismantle the bureaucracy and make our schools parent-oriented and performance-driven."[4] Both houses of the legislature are led by Republicans.

State Contacts

CEO Foundation of Central Florida
Sally Simmons, Executive Director
George Noga, Founder/Chairman Emeritus
Douglas Doudney, Chairman of the Board
1101 North Lake Destiny Road, Suite 225
Maitland, FL 32751
Phone: (407) 629-8787
Fax: (407) 629-1319, (407) 660-9232
Web site: http://www.ceoamerica.org
E-mail: ceocenfla@aol.com

CSF–Tampa Bay
Michele L. Cuteri, Executive Director
601 North Ashley Drive, Suite 500
Tampa, FL 33602
Phone: (813) 222-8009
Fax: (813) 222-8001

CSF–Miami
P.O. Box 01–2497
Miami, FL 33101
Phone: (305) 576-1035

Family First
Mark Merrill, President
101 East Kennedy Boulevard, Suite 1070
Tampa, FL 33602
Phone: (813) 222-8300
Fax: (813) 222-8301
E-mail: info@thefamilyfirst.org

Florida Catholic Conference
Larry Keough, Associate for Education
313 South Calhoun Street
Tallahassee, FL 32301-1807
Phone: (850) 222-3803
Fax: (850) 681-9548

Florida Department of Education
Turlington Building (TUR)
325 West Gaines Street
Tallahassee, FL 32399-0400
Phone: (850) 488-1234
Web site: http://www.firn.edu/doe/doe-home.htm

Mr. Tracey Bailey
Director, Office of Charter Schools
Phone: (850) 414-0780
Fax: (850) 488-9022
E-mail: baileyt@mail.doe.state.fl.us

Florida Federation of Catholic Parents
Joe Magri, President
5510 West Cypress Avenue
Tampa, FL 33607
Phone: (727) 441-2699

Floridians for School Choice
Dr. Patrick Hefferman
1000 Brickell Avenue, Suite 900
Miami, FL 33131
Phone: (305) 702-5576
Fax: (305) 379-7114
Web site: http://www.floridians.org
E-mail: info@floridians.org

The Honorable Tom Gallagher
State Commissioner of Education
Capitol Building, Room PL 08
Tallahassee, FL 32399-0400
Phone: (850) 487-1785
Fax: (850) 413-0378

Independent Voices for Better Education
Kathy Dillenbeck
1408 Viola Drive
Brandon, FL 33511
Phone: (813) 685-3458

James Madison Institute/A Foundation for Florida's Future
Dr. Stanley Marshall, Chairman
Michael G. Strader, Executive Director
Center for Education Entrepreneurs
P.O. Box 37460
Tallahassee, FL 32315
Phone: (850) 386-3131
Fax: (850) 385-8360
Web site: http://www.jamesmadison.org
E-mail: jmi@jamesmadison.org

The Honorable Jerry Melvin
Chairman, Education Innovation Committee
Florida House of Representatives
Suite 1301, The Capitol
Tallahassee, FL 32399-1300

Miami Inner City Angels (MICA)
Michael Carricarte, President
Anne DeLa Pena, Executive Director
P.O. Box 01-2497
Miami, FL 33101
Phone: (305) 576-1035
Fax: (305) 576-1037

Suncoast Baptist Association
Cathy Lloyd, Discipleship Program Associate
6559 126th Avenue North
Largo, FL 33773
Phone: (727) 530-0431
Fax: (727) 530-1225

Urban League of Greater Miami
T. Willard Fair
8500 NW 25th Avenue
Miami, FL 33147
Phone: (305) 696-4450
Fax: (305) 696-4455

Representative Steve Wise
P.O. Box 7914, Suite 4B
5655 Timuquana Road
Jacksonville, FL 32238-0914
Phone: (904) 573-3925
Fax: (904) 573-3928
Tallahassee Office:
221 The Capitol
402 South Monroe Street
Tallahassee, FL 32399-1300
Phone: (850) 488-5102
Fax: (904) 488-4330

Endnotes

1 For sources, see "An Explanation of the State Profile Categories."

2 See Children's Scholarship Fund Web site at *http://www.scholarshipfund.org.*

3 The Friedman–Blum *Educational Freedom Report*, No. 72, June 18, 1999.

4 National Governors' Association, press release, November 4, 1998, at *http://www.nga.org/Releases/PR-4November1998Issues.htm#Education.*

Georgia

State Profile[1]

School Choice Status
- Public school choice: N/A
- Charter schools: Established 1993
    - Strength of law: Strong
    - Number of charter schools in operation (fall 1999): 32
    - Number of students enrolled in charter schools (1998–1999): 18,190
- Publicly funded private school choice: N/A

K–12 Public and Private Students and Schools
- Public school enrollment (fall 1998) and number of schools (1997–1998): 1,401,291 in 1,823 schools
- Private school enrollment and number of schools (1997–1998): 107,065 in 588 schools

K–12 Public and Private School Student Academic Performance
NAEP Test Results—percentage of students at each performance level for both public and private schools, with national percentages in parentheses

Performance Level	Reading 4th grade 1998	Reading 8th grade 1998	Math 4th grade 1996	Math 8th grade 1996	Science 8th grade 1996
Advanced	5% (6%)	1% (2%)	1% (2%)	2% (4%)	1% (3%)
Proficient	19 (23)	24 (28)	12 (18)	14 (19)	20 (24)
Basic	31 (31)	43 (41)	40 (42)	35 (38)	28 (33)
Below Basic	45 (39)	32 (28)	47 (38)	49 (39)	51 (40)

- SAT weighted rank (1999): 24 out of 24 states and the District of Columbia
- ACT weighted rank (1999): N/A

K–12 Public School Expenditures
- Current expenditures (1999–2000): $8,471,318,000
- Amount of revenue from the federal government (1998–1999): 6.6%
- Current per-pupil expenditures (1999–2000): $6,046

K–12 Public School Teachers (1998–1999)
- Number of teachers: 88,654
- Average salary: $39,675
- Students enrolled per teacher: 15.8
- Leading teachers union: N/A (The state has an independent teachers organization, the Professional Association of Georgia Educators.)

Background

In 1992, then-Governor Zell Miller, a Democrat, proposed an education reform package with a charter school initiative. A year later, he signed bills creating a Council for School Performance and charter schools. The Council is tasked with evaluating and publishing reports on the progress of Georgia's schools.

In 1995, Governor Miller signed an amendment to simplify the restrictions on forming and renewing a charter by changing the teacher-support requirement from a two-thirds vote to a simple majority. The charter school law also was amended to extend the charter from three to five years. The governor was able to include $5,000 grants to assist charter schools in their planning process.

Currently, there is no limit on the number of charter schools that may be formed within the state or district. The law allows only existing public schools to convert to charter schools and forbids open enrollment. In addition, the state school board can revoke a charter at any time if it believes the school is failing to fulfill its terms.

During the 1998 legislative session, both houses of the Georgia legislature passed House Bill 353, which improved Georgia's charter law. Introduced by State Representative Kathy Ashe (R–46) and State Senator Clay Land (R–16), and supported by State Superintendent of Schools Linda C. Schrenko, the law would permit local schools, private individuals and organizations, or state or local entities to operate charter schools. The state and local boards of education must approve each charter.[2] Governor Miller signed the bill into law on April 20, 1998.

In 1993, Glenn Delk, president of Georgia Parents for Better Education, rediscovered a 1961 law that provided education grants to help white families avoid desegregated public schools. Later, minority parents and children used the same law to obtain school choice. The 1961 law provided educational grants for students to attend a public or private school of choice. State officials have deemed the law "unusable," but strong public interest encouraged Lieutenant Governor Pierre Howard, a Democrat, to call for special public hearings before the Senate Education Committee. In 1994, the Southeastern Legal Foundation took up the cause on behalf of some of Georgia's poorest families to get the state and its local school districts to enforce the law with tuition vouchers for children in kindergarten through 12th grade. On March 17, 1997, the Georgia Supreme Court handed down its decision. The court did not challenge the constitutionality of this law, but it also did not order the state to enforce it, leaving the matter up to the state legislature.

On September 28, Atlanta and Savannah were named two of 40 "partner cities" for the Children's Scholarship Fund (CSF) challenge grant. The CSF is a $100 million foundation underwritten by entrepreneurs Ted Forstmann and John Walton. It will match funds raised by residents of Atlanta and Savannah to fund approximately 750 private scholarships for low-income students (500 in Atlanta and 250 in Savannah) to attend a school of choice.[3]

Developments in 1999

Senator Land (R–Columbus) introduced his Early HOPE Scholarship bill (S. 68) in the Georgia Senate. The bill was designed to award state-funded scholarships worth around $3,500 to families earning less than two times the federal poverty guidelines whose children were attending poor performing public schools. Senate Democrats blocked consideration of the bill by the Education Committee. As a result, Senator Land introduced the Early HOPE measure as a floor amendment to another education bill, and a two-hour school choice debate ensued. The bill ultimately failed along party lines but likely will receive closer scrutiny in 2000, according to state contact Tim Kelly,[4] for the following reasons:

- The Georgia Council for School Performance has identified 94 public schools that are failing to provide an adequate education to the children of Georgia. Because these schools are often in poor neighborhoods where families spend disproportionate sums on the lottery, many minority parents and leaders are calling for the use of state lottery proceeds to fund K–12 opportunity scholarships. This issue also raises constitutional questions since the state constitution specifies explicitly that the state must provide an "adequate" education to its citizens.

- During 1999, Governor Roy Barnes created an Education Reform Commission to study ways to improve public education in the state. The commission's Accountability

Committee, comprised of elected officials and business and education leaders, recommended mostly "top-down" education reforms such as increased spending on teacher training and recruitment, criterion-referenced testing, and reconstitution of failing schools. But the proposals also included a plan to end teacher tenure, which is the key plan promoted by the governor. Meanwhile, the Republican caucus in the Georgia Senate proposed an accountability package similar to the commission's proposal but included opportunity scholarships for families whose students are attending failing public schools. This plan has been endorsed by Georgia School Superintendent Linda Schrenko.

- Despite vast public appeal, the education establishment in Georgia does not support the independent public charter school movement, which enjoys vast support from the public. This raises public and media concerns about the motives and loyalties of public school officials and fuels interest in opportunity scholarships.

Finally, on April 22, 1999, the Children's Scholarship Fund announced the winners of the largest private scholarship program in the country. The recipients were selected randomly by computer-generated lottery. In Atlanta, 380 scholarship recipients were chosen from 13,798 applicants; in Savannah, 250 recipients were selected from 4,015 applicants. The use of many of the CSF scholarships at schools operated by local churches has caused influential African–American religious leaders, including CSF board member and former U.N. Ambassador Andrew Young, to question why the government feels compelled to deny low-income parents the opportunity to choose the best education alternatives to their children.[5]

Developments in 2000

The House Education Committee defeated several Republican amendments to give parents with children in failing public schools publicly funded private school vouchers to attend a school of choice.

Position of the Governor/Composition of State Legislature

During the work of his Education Reform Commission, Governor Roy Barnes, a Democrat, indicated that all education reform options were on the table for consideration. So far, he has made the elimination of teacher tenure the cornerstone of his education reform plan in 2000; he also has said publicly that he would promote vouchers if the legislature does not end teacher tenure. Both houses of the legislature are led by Democrats.

State Contacts

CSF–Atlanta
(Program handled by Louisiana CSF office)
Faith Sweeney, Executive Director
2120 Dublin Street
New Orleans, LA 70118
Phone: (504) 821-5060, ext. 228
Fax: (504) 821-5271

Georgia Community Foundation, Inc.
James P. Kelly III, Executive Director
P.O. Box 2054
Alpharetta, GA 30023
Phone: (770) 521-0523
Fax: (770) 521-0467
E-mail: jkellyiii@aol.com

Georgia Department of Education
Linda Schrenko, Superintendent of Schools
Suite 2066, Twin Towers East
205 Butler Street
Atlanta, GA 30334
Phone: (404) 656-2800
Fax: (404) 651-8737

Georgia Family Council
Randall Hicks
5380 Peachtree Industrial Boulevard, Suite 100
Norcross, GA 30071-1565
Phone: (770) 242-0001
Fax: (770) 242-0501

Georgia Parents for Better Education
Glenn Delk, President
1355 Peachtree Street, NE, Suite 1150
Atlanta, GA 30309
Phone: (404) 876-3335
Fax: (404) 876-3338

Georgia Public Policy Foundation
Kelly McCutchen, President
4340 Georgetown Square, Suite 608
Atlanta, GA 30338
Phone: (770) 455-7600
Fax: (770) 455-4355
Web site: http://www.gppf.org
E-mail: gppf@gppf.org

Senator Clay Land
P.O. Box 2848
Columbus, GA 31902
Phone: (706) 323-2848
Fax: (706) 323-4242

CFS–Savannah
Maggie Keenan, Administrator
428 Bull Street
Savannah, GA 31401
Phone: (912) 238-3288
Fax: (912) 231-8082

Southeastern Legal Foundation
Matthew J. Glavin
3340 Peachtree Road, NE, Suite 2515
Atlanta, GA 30326
Phone: (404) 365-8500
Fax: (404) 365-0017
E-mail: mglavin@southeasternlegal.org

Endnotes

1   For sources, see "An Explanation of the State Profile Categories."

2   The full text of this bill is available on the Internet at *www.ganet.org/*.

3   See Children's Scholarship Fund Web site at *http://www.scholarshipfund.org*.

4   E-mail correspondence received November 19, 1999, from Tim Kelly, Georgia Community Foundation.

5   *Ibid.*

Hawaii

State Profile[1]

School Choice Status
- Public school choice: N/A
- Charter schools: Established 1994
    Strength of law: Weak
    Number of charter schools in operation (fall 1999): 2
    Number of students enrolled in charter schools (fall 1999): 606
- Publicly funded private school choice: N/A

K–12 Public and Private Students and Schools
- Public school enrollment (fall 1998) and number of schools (1997–1998): 187,395 in 250 schools
- Private school enrollment and number of schools (1997–1998): 33,300 in 126 schools

K–12 Public and Private School Student Academic Performance
NAEP Test Results—percentage of students at each performance level for both public and private schools, with national percentages in parentheses

Performance Level	Reading 4th grade 1998	Reading 8th grade 1998	Math 4th grade 1996	Math 8th grade 1996	Science 8th grade 1996
Advanced	3% (6%)	1% (2%)	2% (2%)	2% (4)%	1% (3%)
Proficient	14 (23)	18 (28)	14 (18)	14 (19)	14 (24)
Basic	28 (31)	41 (41)	37 (42)	35 (38)	27 (33)
Below Basic	55 (39)	40 (28)	47 (38)	49 (39)	58 (40)

- SAT weighted rank (1999): 18 out of 24 states and the District of Columbia
- ACT weighted rank (1999): N/A

K–12 Public School Expenditures
- Current expenditures (1999–2000): $1,149,798,000
- Amount of revenue from the federal government (1998–1999): 8.5%
- Current per-pupil expenditures (1999–2000): $6,075

K–12 Public School Teachers (1998–1999)
- Number of teachers: 11,019
- Average salary: $40,377
- Students enrolled per teacher: 17.0
- Leading teachers union: NEA

Background

In 1994, the Hawaii legislature passed a charter school bill that grants four-year charters to public schools. The bill limits the number of charters to 25 for the entire state. In 1997 and 1998, the state had two charter schools (termed "student-centered" schools) in operation that were serving 565 students.

Developments in 1999

An income tax credit bill for private school students was introduced in the Senate Education Committee but was later defeated.[2] The legislature replaced its "student-centered" charter school law with a bill that creates up to a total of 25 New Century charter schools and designates the two existing student-centered schools as the first such schools. Over 15 programs or schools have applied to become New Century charters. To qualify, each charter applicant must develop a detailed implementation plan.

Position of the Governor/Composition of State Legislature

Governor Benjamin J. Cayetano, a Democrat, supports public school choice but opposes any voucher program that would shift the cost of private education to the taxpayers. The governor also supports the current charter school system. Both houses of the legislature are led by Democrats.

State Contacts

Hawaii Department of Education
Dr. Paul LeMahieu, Superintendent
P.O. Box 2360
Honolulu, HI 96804
Phone: (808) 586-3310
Fax: (808) 586-3320
Web site: http://www.k12.hi.us
Yvonne Hashizume, Administrator for Planning
Phone: (808) 586-3285
Fax: (808) 586-3440
E-mail: yvonne.hashizume@notes.k12.hi.us

Representative David Pendleton
Minority Floor Leader
State Capitol
415 South Beretania Street
Honolulu, HI 96813
Phone: (808) 586-9490
Fax: (808) 586-9496

Endnotes

1 For sources, see "An Explanation of the State Profile Categories."

2 The Friedman–Blum *Educational Freedom Report*, No. 71, May 21, 1999.

Idaho

State Profile[1]

School Choice Status
- Public school choice: Statewide
- Charter schools: Established 1998
    Strength of law: Strong
    Number of charter schools in operation (fall 1999): 8
    Number of students enrolled in charter schools (1998–1999): N/A
- Publicly funded private school choice: N/A

K–12 Public and Private Students and Schools
- Public school enrollment (fall 1998) and number of schools (1997–1998): 244,623 in 636 schools
- Private school enrollment and number of schools (1997–1998): 9,635 in 82 schools

K–12 Public and Private School Student Academic Performance
NAEP Test Results—percentage of students at each performance level for both public and private schools, with national percentages in parentheses

Performance Level	Reading 4th grade 1998	Reading 8th grade 1998	Math 4th grade 1996	Math 8th grade 1996	Science 8th grade 1996
Advanced	n/a	n/a	n/a	n/a	n/a
Proficient	n/a	n/a	n/a	n/a	n/a
Basic	n/a	n/a	n/a	n/a	n/a
Below Basic	n/a	n/a	n/a	n/a	n/a

- SAT weighted rank (1999): N/A
- ACT weighted rank (1999): 14 out of 26 states

K–12 Public School Expenditures
- Current expenditures (1999–2000): $1,296,873,000
- Amount of revenue from the federal government (1998–1999): 6.9%
- Current per-pupil expenditures (1999–2000): $5,275

K–12 Public School Teachers (1998–1999)
- Number of teachers: 13,399
- Average salary: $34,063
- Students enrolled per teacher: 18.3
- Leading teachers union: NEA

Background

Idaho makes a variety of educational options available to students and their parents. Within certain limitations, such as enrollment capacity, students may choose the public school they wish to attend in a district. State funds follow the child to the school of choice. During the 1997–1998 school year, 3,090 children participated in Idaho's inter-district school choice program.

In February 1998, the House Revenue and Taxation Committee defeated a $1,500 private school tuition tax credit proposal; but on March 11, 1998, Idaho became the 30th state to enact a charter school law. The measure authorizes the formation of up to 12 new schools per year for the first five years, with no limitation thereafter. It prohibits permanently hiring non-certified teachers, contracting operations out to a for-profit company, and converting secular private schools. Eight charter schools were approved to open in the fall of 1999.

After a five-year phase-in period, the new law will allow the granting of an unlimited number of charters for fully autonomous schools. Existing public schools may convert to charter schools with the approval of the local school board, 60 percent of the parents, and 60 percent of the teachers. The schools are funded directly by the Idaho Department of Education, and charter applicants have the right to appeal a denial to the State Superintendent of Public Instruction.[2]

Developments in 1999

A bill proposing a school choice tax credit pilot program was introduced in the Idaho legislature but did not pass. The tax credit is modeled after the Universal Tax Credit plan created by the Michigan-based Mackinac Center for Public Policy. Under this plan, which would be phased in over a six-year period:

- Any individual or corporation would be allowed to take a dollar-for-dollar tax credit for amounts donated to any child not enrolled in the public school system.

- The donation would go directly to the child's parents, who could use the funds to pay the cost of tuition.

- For individuals making donations, the following caps would apply: $250 in 2000 and 2001; $500 in 2002 and 2003; $750 in 2004; and $1,000 in 2005 and each year thereafter. For corporations making donations, the following caps would apply: $1,000 in 2000 and 2001; $2,500 in 2002 and 2003; $5,000 in 2004; and $10,000 in 2005 and each year thereafter.

- The amount of the tax credit would be restricted to a maximum of 40 percent of the donor's overall income tax liability.

- A child could receive donations from an unlimited number of donors, provided that total donations did not exceed the per-child cap of 50 percent of the cost of educating a child in the public school system (65 percent for special needs students).

- School districts would be allowed to provide up to 50 percent of the cost of educating a child in the public school system (65 percent for special needs children) for a child to transfer out of the public school system.[3]

Position of the Governor/Composition of State Legislature

Governor Dirk Kempthorne, a Republican, has expressed interest in school choice. Both houses of the legislature are led by Republicans.

State Contacts

Idaho Department of Education
Marilyn Howard, Superintendent
P.O. Box 83720
Boise, ID 83720-0027
Phone: (208) 336-2372
Web site: http://www.sde.state.id.us/Dept/

Idahoans for Tax Reform
Laird Maxwell, Chairman
1608 Bedford Drive
Boise, ID 83705
Phone: (208) 331-1996
Fax: (208) 384-1998
E-mail: lmaxwell@rmci.net

Endnotes

1 For sources, see "An Explanation of the State Profile Categories."

2 Correspondence from Jim Spady, Co-Director, Education Excellence Coalition, Seattle, Washington, March 19, 1998.

3 Draft of Idaho school choice tax credit pilot program (RSMLI054), provided by Idahoans for Tax Reform.

Illinois

State Profile[1]

School Choice Status
- Public school choice: N/A
- Charter schools: Established 1996
    Strength of law: Strong
    Number of charter schools in operation (fall 1999): 18
    Number of students enrolled in charter schools (1999–2000): 5,600
- Publicly funded private school choice: Educational expense tax credits
    Program description: Enacted in 1999, this plan allows parents to claim a non-refundable tax credit of up to $500 for tuition, books, and lab fees at any public, private, or religious school of choice. The credit is equal to 25 percent of educational expenditures after the first $250, for a maximum of $500 per family. A parent would need to spend $2,250 to qualify for the maximum credit.

K–12 Public and Private Students and Schools
- Public school enrollment (fall 1998) and number of schools (1997–1998): 2,011,530 in 4,228 schools
- Private school enrollment and number of schools (1997–1998): 298,620 in 1,408 schools

K–12 Public and Private School Student Academic Performance
NAEP Test Results—percentage of students at each performance level for both public and private schools, with national percentages in parentheses

Performance Level	Reading 4th grade 1998	Reading 8th grade 1998	Math 4th grade 1996	Math 8th grade 1996	Science 8th grade 1996
Advanced	n/a	n/a	n/a	n/a	n/a
Proficient	n/a	n/a	n/a	n/a	n/a
Basic	n/a	n/a	n/a	n/a	n/a
Below Basic	n/a	n/a	n/a	n/a	n/a

- SAT weighted rank (1999): N/A
- ACT weighted rank (1999): 12 out of 26 states

K–12 Public School Expenditures
- Current expenditures (1999–2000): $11,807,233,000
- Amount of revenue from the federal government (1998–1999): 6.6%
- Current per-pupil expenditures (1999–2000): $5,856

K–12 Public School Teachers (1998–1999)

- Number of teachers: 122,122
- Average salary: $45,569
- Students enrolled per teacher: 16.5
- Leading teachers union: NEA

Background

A 1988 state law led to the decentralization of the Chicago public schools and authorized city-wide public school choice beginning with the 1991–1992 school year. Its implementation, however, was delayed indefinitely.

In 1995, following a failed attempt to devolve power over education and funding to local school councils, the legislature placed Chicago Mayor Richard M. Daley in control of the city's 413,000-student system. Daley appointed his budget director, Paul Vallas, as CEO to oversee efforts to reform the school system. Vallas brought the city's education finances under control, eliminated a $1.3 billion deficit, and privatized the school maintenance division.[2]

In 1997, Vallas established a new curriculum and gained nationwide fame for putting in place a policy of "no social promotions." He also made principals more accountable, put schools on probation, and laid off a number of administrative staff employees. In July 1997, he identified seven persistently failing high schools as targets for "reconstitution," which entails requiring employees of the school to reapply for their positions.[3]

Meanwhile, the legislature passed a bill in 1996 to allow for the creation of up to 45 charter schools—15 in Chicago, 15 in the Chicago suburbs, and 15 in the rest of the state. Any not-for-profit organization, including a school district, may sponsor a charter school if the charter is approved by the local or state board of education.

Illinois opened its first charter school in 1996. Sponsored by the Peoria Board of Education, the Peoria Alternative Charter School serves students with behavioral difficulties.

Apart from Chicago and Peoria, however, local school boards in 1996 and 1997 uniformly rejected charter school applications. In December 1997, state legislators strengthened the charter school law to allow charters rejected at the local level to be submitted to the state board of education for approval.

In 1997, State Representatives Peter Roskam (R) and Roger McAuliffe (R) introduced a bill to provide means-tested vouchers for children in a selected area of Chicago. The bill died in the House Rules Committee. Another bill, sponsored by Representative Kevin McCarthy (D) and Senator Dan Cronin (R), would have allowed parents with at least $250 in school expenses for children in kindergarten through 12th grade to claim one-fourth of those expenses as a tax credit, with a maximum credit of $500 per family. Items covered by the credit would have included tuition, books, and lab fees for K–12 classes at public, private, or parochial schools. This bill was approved by the legislature but then was vetoed by then-Governor Jim Edgar on January 2, 1998. (Edgar's successor, George Ryan, eventually signed it into law on June 3, 1999.)

Illinois is cracking down on low-income parents who "fraudulently" register their children in public schools in affluent neighboring school districts. A law passed in January 1997 would send these parents to jail for 30 days and fine them $500.

A random poll in 1998 of 3,000 Chicago residents conducted by the Metro Chicago Information Center indicated support by 81 percent of Chicago residents and 75 percent of Cook County residents for charter schools. Of all Chicago residents, 62 percent supported using tax money to send low-income students to private schools and 55 percent supported using vouchers for religious private schools. When asked about non–means-tested vouchers, 49 percent of Chicago residents supported the idea.[4]

A two-year study released in 1998 by the Special Task Force on Catholic Schools revealed that the Archdiocese of Chicago risks having to close or downsize some of its 270 elementary schools in Cook and Lake Counties unless it finds substantial additional funding within the next year. In addition to other needs, the Archdiocese is calling for between $25 million and $30 million to increase teacher salaries to 75 percent of market value. (Catholic school teachers currently make about one-half of what their public school counterparts make.) The Archdiocese called on Governor George Ryan to approve a voucher or tax credit program which would help offset the costs of educating children, many of whom are from poor urban neighborhoods and 80 percent to 90 percent of whom, though not Catholic, attend Chicago Catholic schools.[5]

On September 28, 1998, Chicago was named one of 40 "partner cities" for the Children's Scholarship Fund (CSF) challenge grant. The CSF is a $100 million foundation underwritten by entrepreneurs Ted Forstmann and John Walton. The program matches funds raised by residents of Chicago to fund approximately 2,500 private scholarships for low-income students to attend a school of choice. The scholarships were awarded for at least four years to children entering kindergarten through 8th grade in the spring of 1999.[6]

Developments in 1999

The Illinois House and Senate approved the Illinois Educational Expenses Tax Credit plan (Senate Bill 1075) that would provide a tax credit of up to 25 percent of education-related expenses (tuition, book fees, lab fees) exceeding $250. The credit can be up to $500 per family. The primary House sponsor of this legislation was Representative Kevin McCarthy (D). As a freshman legislator in 1997, McCarthy had introduced a similar tax credit bill that was passed by both chambers only to be summarily vetoed by then-Governor Jim Edgar (R). A key difference between the earlier bill and the one signed by Edgar's successor, George Ryan, is that a refundability provision—making the credit available as a tax refund to low-income families who pay no state taxes—was removed from the later measure. If parents could claim the tax credit for every child in Illinois private schools, their annual tax savings would be $160 million; but with the credit limited to a maximum of $500 for each taxpaying family, actual savings are estimated to be, at most, between $50 million and $60 million.

Governor Ryan signed the bill into law on June 3, 1999, at St. Stanislaus Kosta Catholic School in Chicago. The tax credit takes effect in the 2000 tax year. Illinois has over 321,000 private school students in grades K–12 who could benefit from this legislation, including approximately 250,000 students in Catholic schools.

In July 1999, the local chapter of the American Federation of Teachers filed a lawsuit against the tax credit plan, alleging that it violates the state prohibition against any establishment of religion, in the circuit court of rural Franklin County, Illinois. On December 7, 1999, the Franklin County Circuit Court dismissed the lawsuit. An appeal has been filed.

A second lawsuit, filed by a coalition of nine groups led by the Illinois Education Association in Sangamon County Circuit Court, challenging the program on religious establishment and other state constitutional grounds is pending in Springfield, Illinois. The tax credit legislation is also in jeopardy because of bureaucratic maneuvers by opponents. A concerted effort is underway to make the credit inoperable by manipulating the process by which rules and regulations are written.

The Illinois legislature also considered a voucher plan. The bill (SB 329) was voted down in the Senate Education Committee. Introduced by Senate Education Committee Chairman Dan Cronin, the bill would have provided Educational Opportunity Grants for students in Chicago, East St. Louis, Joliet, Peoria, and Rockford to use at a school of choice, including religious schools. The grants would have provided $2,000 to elementary students and $3,000 to high school students.

Meanwhile, an October 1999 survey by the Chicago-based Coalition for Consumer Rights showed that concern about education in public schools was the top concern in all three regions of Illinois: Chicago, the suburbs, and downstate. The education issue beat out other issues such as food safety, retirement income, and illegal drugs in the community.

A telephone survey of over 1,000 Illinois residents, taken shortly before the Illinois General Assembly voted to provide education expense tax relief for parents, showed that three out of four respondents (77 percent) support the idea of parents and students being able to choose the child's school. More than half (56 percent) agreed that per-student tax dollars for education should follow the student to whichever school the parent and student choose, with only 31 percent saying that tax money should go only to public schools authorized by the school board. The poll was commissioned by the Glen Ellyn-based Illinois Family Institute.

In another survey, conducted in 1999 by the Metro Chicago Information Center, 62 percent of respondents in the Chicago metropolitan six-county area supported vouchers for low-income children to attend private schools, and 55 percent supported vouchers for use at religious schools.[7]

On April 22, 1999, the Children's Scholarship Fund announced the winners of the largest private scholarship program in the country. The recipients were selected randomly by computer-generated lottery. In Chicago, 2,500 scholarship recipients were chosen from 59,186 applicants.[8]

Developments in 2000

Several charter school bills have been introduced in the legislature. H 2975 would expand the number of Chicago area charters from 15 to 20 but reduce the charters for downstate Illinois by five. H 2852 would eliminate the Illinois State Board of Education's power to reverse local charter school denial upon appeal. And SB 508 would establish a state charter school chartering board, removing the Illinois State Board of Education's power to approve charter schools.[9]

Position of the Governor/Composition of State Legislature

Governor George H. Ryan, a Republican, supports tax credits for educational expenses. He also seems receptive to school choice. The Illinois House is led by Democrats; the Senate is led by Republicans.

State Contacts

Big Shoulders Fund
Judith Silekis, Executive Director
One First National Plaza, Suite 2500
Chicago, IL 60603
Phone: (312) 751-8337
Fax: (312) 751-5235
E-mail: bgshlder@interaccess.com

Catholic Conference of Illinois
Doug Delaney, Executive Director
65 East Wacker Place
Chicago, IL 60610
Phone: (312) 368-1066
Fax: (312) 368-1090
E-mail: Delaney@aol.com
Springfield Office
Joan McKinney, Education Expert
108 East Cook Street

Springfield, IL 62704
Phone: (217) 528-9200
Fax: (217) 528-7214

Charter Consultants
The Illinois Charter School Facs
Paul Seibert, Director
219 West Main Street
Belleville, IL 62220
Phone: (618) 233-0428
Fax: (618) 233-0541
Web site: http://www.gfacademy.com
E-mail: chrsch@gfacademy.com

Chicago Public Schools
Paul Vallas, CEO
125 South Clark Street
Chicago, IL 60603
Phone: (773) 553-1535
Fax: (773) 553-1500
E-mail: pvallas@csc.cps.k12.il.us
Greg Richmond, Director of Charter School Office
Phone: (773) 553-1535
Fax: (773) 553-1559
E-mail: grichmond@csc.cps.k12.il.us

Children's Scholarship Fund–Chicago
Bo Kemper, Executive Director
68 East Wacker Place, Suite 1600
Chicago, IL 60601
Phone: (312) 960-0205, ext. 11;
(800) 260-2022
Fax: (312) 849-3400

Daniel Murphy Scholarship Foundation
Joe Walsh, Executive Director
3030 South Wells Street, Suite 910
Chicago, IL 60606
Phone: (312) 341-4080
Fax: (312) 341-4081
Web site: http://www.dmsf.org
E-mail: dmsf@mcs.com

Family Taxpayers Foundation
Jack Roeser, Chairman
8 East Main Street
Carpentersville, IL 60110
Phone: (847) 428-0212
Fax: (847) 428-9206

The FOCUS Fund
Patrick J. Keleher, President
Joan M. Ferdinand, Vice President, Operations
Georgetown Square
522 Fourth Street
Wilmette, IL 60091-2829
Phone: (847) 256-8476

Fax: (847) 256-8482
Web site: http://homepage.interaccess.com/
~duck/teach.htm
E-mail: TEACH522@aol.com

Heartland Institute
Joseph L. Bast, President
19 South LaSalle, Suite 903
Chicago, IL 60603-1405
Phone: (312) 377-4000
Fax: (312) 377-5000
Web site: http://www.heartland.org
E-mail: think@heartland.org

George Clowes
Managing Editor, School Reform News
E-mail: clowesga@aol.com

Illinois Family Institute
Dr. John Koehler, President
799 West Roosevelt Road
Building 3, Suite 218
Glen Ellyn, IL 60137
Phone: (630) 790-8370
Fax: (630) 790-8390
Web site: http://www.ilfaminst.com
E-mail: ilfaminst@aol.com

Illinois State Board of Education
100 North First Street
Springfield, IL 62777
Phone: (217) 782-4321
Chicago: (312) 814-2220
Mount Vernon: (618) 244-8383
Web site: http://www.isbe.state.il.us/

Leadership for Quality Education
One First National Plaza
21 South Clark Street, Suite 3120
Chicago, IL 60603
Phone: (312) 853-1214

Link Unlimited
Robert Anderson, Executive Director
7759 South Everhart
Chicago, IL 60619
Phone: (773) 487-5465
Fax: (773) 487-8626

TEACH America
Patrick J. Keleher, President
Joan M. Ferdinand, Vice President, Operations
Georgetown Square
522 Fourth Street
Wilmette, IL 60091
Phone: (847) 256-8476
Fax: (847) 256-8482
Web site: http://homepage.interaccess.com/
~duck/teach.htm
E-mail: TEACH522@aol.com

Endnotes

1 For sources, see "An Explanation of the State Profile Categories."

2 Correspondence with Charter School Office of the Chicago Public Schools, November 1998.

3 *Ibid.*

4 Dr. Garth Taylor, "Charter Schools, Educational Vouchers, and the Fairness of Public School Funding," Metro Chicago Information Center, March 1998, available at *www.mcic.org.*

5 Steve Kloehn and Rick Pearson, "Catholic School Alarm," *The Chicago Tribune*, December 16, 1998.

6 See Children's Scholarship Fund Web site at *http://www.scholarshipfund.org.*

7 E-mail correspondence from state contact George Clowes, Heartland Institute, December 7, 1999.

8 See Children's Scholarship Fund Web site at *http://www.scholarshipfund.org.*

9 *The Illinois Charter School Facs*, Paul Seibert, ed., January 31, 2000; facsimile available from the author upon request.

Indiana

State Profile[1]

School Choice Status
- Public school choice: Limited
- Charter schools: N/A
- Publicly funded private school choice: N/A

K–12 Public and Private Students and Schools
- Public school enrollment (fall 1998) and number of schools (1997–1998): 988,094 in 1,859 schools
- Private school enrollment and number of schools (1997–1998): 105,358 in 768 schools

K–12 Public and Private School Student Academic Performance
NAEP Test Results—percentage of students at each performance level for both public and private schools, with national percentages in parentheses

Performance Level	Reading 4th grade 1998	Reading 8th grade 1998	Math 4th grade 1996	Math 8th grade 1996	Science 8th grade 1996
Advanced	n/a	n/a	2% (2%)	3% (4%)	2% (3%)
Proficient	n/a	n/a	22 (18)	21 (19)	28 (24)
Basic	n/a	n/a	48 (42)	44 (38)	35 (33)
Below Basic	n/a	n/a	28 (38)	32 (39)	35 (40)

- SAT weighted rank (1999): 19 out of 24 states and the District of Columbia
- ACT weighted rank (1999): N/A

K–12 Public School Expenditures
- Current expenditures (1999–2000): $6,594,280,000
- Amount of revenue from the federal government (1998–1999): 4.5%
- Current per-pupil expenditures (1999–2000): $6,658

K–12 Public School Teachers (1998–1999)
- Number of teachers: 57,840
- Average salary: $41,163
- Students enrolled per teacher: 17.1
- Leading teachers union: NEA

Background

Indiana currently provides transportation to children attending private schools if their schools are on the public school bus routes. Low-income children attending private and parochial schools are entitled to state financial support for textbooks.

State Senator Teresa Lubbers (R) has tried to pass a charter school bill six years in a row but has failed each time.

The state has no publicly sponsored private school choice program, but since 1991, the Educational CHOICE Charitable Trust has helped low-income Indianapolis children attend private school by awarding scholarships for up to half of the cost of tuition. Despite vigorous attacks by the education establishment on Golden Rule CEO J. Patrick Rooney, who designed the scholarship program, parental response has been overwhelmingly positive. The Educational CHOICE Charitable Trust is helping 2,600 low-income Indianapolis children attend area private or parochial schools during the 1999–2000 school year.

On September 28, Indianapolis was named one of 40 "partner cities" for the Children's Scholarship Fund (CSF) challenge grant. The CSF is a $100 million foundation underwritten by entrepreneurs Ted Forstmann and John Walton. It will match funds raised by residents of Indianapolis to fund approximately 500 private scholarships for low-income students to attend a school of choice. The scholarships are awarded for at least four years to children entering kindergarten through 8th grade the following year.[2]

Developments in 1999

On April 22, 1999, the Children's Scholarship Fund announced the winners of the largest private scholarship program in the country. The recipients were selected randomly by computer-generated lottery. In Indianapolis, 500 scholarship recipients were chosen from 4,637 applicants. The Educational CHOICE Charitable Trust will administer the scholarships in Indianapolis.[3]

Developments in 2000

The chairman of the House Education Committee, Representative Greg Porter (R–Indianapolis), said he will not hold hearings on charters or vouchers this year. The Senate has approved a public school choice bill and a charter school bill, although its chances of survival are slim because of House inaction.[4] Meanwhile, the Indianapolis-based Greater Educational Opportunities Foundation is working to educate the grassroots about the benefits of school choice.

Position of the Governor/Composition of State Legislature

Governor Frank O'Bannon, a Democrat, supports public charter schools and public school choice. The Indiana House is led by Democrats; the Senate is led by Republicans.

State Contacts

Educational CHOICE Charitable Trust
Tim Ehrgott, Executive Director
7440 Woodland Drive
Indianapolis, IN 46278-1719
Phone: (317) 293-7600, ext. 7378
Fax: (317) 297-0908
E-mail: timothyp16@aol.com

Greater Educational Opportunities Foundation
Kevin Teasley
1800 North Meridian Street, Suite 506
Indianapolis, IN 46202
Phone: (317) 283-4711
Fax: (317) 283-4712
Web site: http://www.GEOFoundation.org

Hudson Institute
Michael Garber
Director, Education Policy
Herman Kahn Center
P.O. Box 26-919
Indianapolis, IN 46226
Phone: (317) 545-1000
Fax: (317) 545-9639
E-mail: mgarber@aol.com

Indiana Chamber of Commerce
David Holt, Director of Education Policy
115 West Washington, Suite 850 South
Indianapolis, IN 46204-3407
Phone: (317) 264-6883
Fax: (317) 264-6855
E-mail: dholt@indianachamber.com

Indiana Department of Education
Room 229, State House
Indianapolis, IN 46204-2798
Phone: (317) 232-6610
Fax: (317) 233-6326
Web site: http://doe.state.in.us/

Indiana Family Institute
Micah Clark, Associate Director
70 East 91st Street, Suite 210
Indianapolis, IN 46240
Phone: (317) 582-0300
Fax: (317) 582-1438
E-mail: ifi@hoosier.org

Indiana Non-Public Education Association
Glen Tebbe, Executive Director
1400 North Meridian Street
Indianapolis, IN 46202-2367
Phone: (317) 236-7329
Fax: (317) 236-7328
E-mail: impea@iquest.net

Indiana Policy Review Foundation
Tom Hession, President
P.O. Box 12306
Fort Wayne, IN 46863-2306
Phone: (317) 236-7360; (219) 424-7104
Fax: (317) 236-7370

Endnotes

1 For sources, see "An Explanation of the State Profile Categories."

2 See Children's Scholarship Fund Web site at *http://www.scholarshipfund.org.*

3 *Ibid.*

4 E-mail correspondence from Kevin Teasley, Greater Educational Opportunities Foundation, January 27, 2000, and February 22, 2000.

Iowa

State Profile[1]

School Choice Status
- Public school choice: Statewide
- Charter schools: N/A
- Publicly funded private school choice: Education tax credits
  Program description: The plan offers a $250 credit for any education-related expenses at a public, private, or religious school of choice.

K–12 Public and Private Students and Schools
- Public school enrollment (fall 1998) and number of schools (1997–1998): 502,570 in 1,548 schools
- Private school enrollment and number of schools (1997–1998): 50,138 in 277 schools

K–12 Public and Private School Student Academic Performance
NAEP Test Results—percentage of students at each performance level for both public and private schools, with national percentages in parentheses

Performance Level	Reading 4th grade 1998	Reading 8th grade 1998	Math 4th grade 1996	Math 8th grade 1996	Science 8th grade 1996
Advanced	7% (6%)	n/a	1% (2%)	4% (4%)	3% (3%)
Proficient	28 (23)	n/a	21 (18)	27 (19)	33 (24)
Basic	35 (31)	n/a	52 (42)	47 (38)	35 (33)
Below Basic	30 (39)	n/a	26 (38)	22 (39)	29 (40)

- SAT weighted rank (1999): N/A
- ACT weighted rank (1999): 3 out of 26 states

K–12 Public School Expenditures
- Current expenditures (1999–2000): $2,947,320,000
- Amount of revenue from the federal government (1998–1999): 4.0%
- Current per-pupil expenditures (1999–2000): $5,919

K–12 Public School Teachers (1998–1999)
- Number of teachers: 33,415
- Average salary: $34,927
- Students enrolled per teacher: 15.0
- Leading teachers union: NEA

Background

Iowa offers a statewide inter-district open enrollment program. During the 1998–1999 school year, 16,269 students participated in this program.[2] Transportation is provided for students attending non-public schools if both their homes and their non-public schools are located on regular public school bus routes; if not, parents can be reimbursed for transportation costs.

Iowa's voucher payment for school transportation costs has survived several legal challenges. School districts may deny students an inter-district transfer if the transfer interferes with racial desegregation efforts. The limits of this restriction were tested in Des Moines in December 1992 when the school board refused to grant transfers for 122 white students for the following school year while granting requests from six minority students. The reason: During the first two years of choice, 402 of the 413 students who chose to transfer from Des Moines to surrounding suburban districts were white; only 11 were members of minority groups. Of the 32,000 students in the Des Moines school district, only 20 percent were members of minority groups. Parents appealed the court's decision, which subsequently was overturned because the school board had no written policy on which to base the denial of student transfers. After this decision, the school board imposed explicit restrictions on student transfers, including a policy establishing strict racial ratios for school districts. The board has used the new restrictions to deny more requests for transfers.

The state also permits post-secondary enrollment in college courses for high school juniors and seniors.

In 1997, then-Governor Terry E. Branstad, a Republican, included a provision in his budget proposal that would have more than doubled the state's tax credit for private school tuition costs from $100 to $250. The provision was approved by the Senate Education Committee and passed by the Senate Ways and Means Committee in April 1997. In the final days of the legislative session, a group of senators attached an amendment to allow tax credits for fees at public and non-public schools, thereby increasing the cost of the legislation by over $3 million.[3]

On May 6, 1998, Governor Branstad signed into law House File 2513, which increases Iowa's tuition tax credit from $100 to $250 on the first $1,000 of tuition expenses. The bill also expands the definition of allowable tuition and textbook expenses to include "expenses which relate to extracurricular activities (i.e., sporting events, speech activities, etc.)" at a school of choice.

Developments in 1999

On January 11, 1999, the first day of the legislative session, House Speaker Ron Corbett (R–52) introduced House File 12, which would have increased the state's education tax credit from 29 percent to a maximum of 50 percent of the first $1,000 of expenses. The tax credit had been raised from $100 to $250 in 1998. The increase to 50 percent eventually would have cost $8 million more to fund.[4] The bill was later defeated.

Position of the Governor/Composition of State Legislature

Governor Tom Vilsack, a Democrat, does not support school choice. Both houses of the legislature are led by Republicans.

State Contacts

Iowa Department of Education
Grimes State Office Building
Des Moines, IA 50319-0146
Phone: (515) 281-5294
Fax: (515) 242-5988

Public Interest Institute
Dr. Don Racheter, President
600 North Jackson Street
Mount Pleasant, IA 52641
Phone: (319) 385-3462
Fax: (319) 385-3799
Web site: www.limitedgovernment.org
E-mail: piiatiwc@se-iowa.net

Endnotes

1   For sources, see "An Explanation of the State Profile Categories."

2   Update from Jim Tyson, Iowa Department of Education.

3   The Blum Center's *Educational Freedom Report*, No. 54, December 19, 1997.

4   The Friedman–Blum *Educational Freedom Report*, No. 71, May 21, 1999.

Kansas

State Profile[1]

School Choice Status
- Public school choice: N/A
- Charter schools: Established 1995
    - Strength of law: Weak
    - Number of charter schools in operation (fall 1999): 15
    - Number of students enrolled in charter schools (1998–1999): 1,594
- Publicly funded private school choice: N/A

K–12 Public and Private Students and Schools
- Public school enrollment (fall 1998) and number of schools (1997–1998): 469,758 in 1,453 schools
- Private school enrollment and number of schools (1997–1998): 40,573 in 241 schools

K–12 Public and Private School Student Academic Performance
NAEP Test Results—percentage of students at each performance level for both public and private schools, with national percentages in parentheses

Performance Level	Reading 4th grade 1998	Reading 8th grade 1998	Math 4th grade 1996	Math 8th grade 1996	Science 8th grade 1996
Advanced	6% (6%)	2% (2%)	n/a	n/a	n/a
Proficient	28 (23)	33 (28)	n/a	n/a	n/a
Basic	37 (31)	46 (41)	n/a	n/a	n/a
Below Basic	29 (39)	19 (28)	n/a	n/a	n/a

- SAT weighted rank (1999): N/A
- ACT weighted rank (1999): 7 out of 26 states

K–12 Public School Expenditures
- Current expenditures (1999–2000): $2,875,217,000
- Amount of revenue from the federal government (1998–1999): 5.9%
- Current per-pupil expenditures (1999–2000): $6,112

K–12 Public School Teachers (1998–1999)
- Number of teachers: 31,899
- Average salary: $37,405
- Students enrolled per teacher: 14.7
- Leading teachers union: NEA

Background

In April 1994, Kansas enacted a restrictive charter school law that allowed for the creation of 15 charters statewide, with each district allowed no more than two charters at a given time. Under current law, any group not affiliated with a religious organization may apply for a charter. To apply, the group must submit a petition to the local school board. Once the local board approves the charter, the application is sent to the state Board of Education for review and approval. The charter school then may apply to the local school board for a waiver from local district rules and regulations. If these waivers are approved, the charter school may apply to the state board for additional waivers from state regulations. Because a charter school remains a legal entity of the local school district, the charter school movement is essentially controlled by the public school system. As of the fall 1999 school year, the number of charter schools in Kansas had grown to the allowable maximum of 15. Efforts to strengthen the law have been unsuccessful.

In February 1995, State Representative Kay O'Connor (R–14), the state's leading choice proponent, and 10 co-sponsors introduced a voucher program known as the Kansas G.I. Bill for Kids. A companion bill was introduced in the Senate by Senators Phil Martin (D–13) and Michael Harris (R–27). These bills would have established school choice by phasing in, over five years, both the number of families eligible to participate in the voucher program and the amount of the vouchers. Opponents were able to deny debate on the bill in the House; consequently, the Senate did not act on its version.

On February 14, 1997, Representative O'Connor introduced the Parent Control of Education Act to establish a statewide choice program, to be phased in over six years. This voucher program would have allowed students in kindergarten through 12th grade to attend a school of choice. The value of the voucher would have been phased in, with students in 9th through 12th grades eligible for a full per-pupil state allocation by the end of the sixth year. No further action was taken on this bill.[2]

On September 28, 1998, Kansas City was named one of the 40 "partner cities" for the Children's Scholarship Fund (CSF) challenge grant. The CSF is a $100 million foundation underwritten by entrepreneurs Ted Forstmann and John Walton. It will match funds raised by Kansas City residents to fund approximately 1,250 private scholarships for low-income students to attend a school of choice. The scholarships were awarded for at least four years to children entering kindergarten through 8th grade in the spring of 1999.[3]

Developments in 1999

Representative Kay O'Connor re-submitted her Parental Control of Education Act (HB 2462). In addition, the Kansas Educational Opportunities Certificate Pilot Program Act (HB 2504 and SB 295) was introduced to provide vouchers worth 80 percent of the base state aid per pupil for tuition costs at non-public schools.[4] Both bills were defeated. Representative O'Connor plans to re-introduce school choice during the 2000 legislative session.

On April 22, 1999, the Children's Scholarship Fund announced the winners of the largest private scholarship program in the country. The recipients were selected randomly by computer-generated lottery. In Kansas City, 1,250 scholarship recipients were chosen from 11,531 applicants.[5]

Position of the Governor/Composition of State Legislature

Governor Bill Graves, a Republican, has not publicly endorsed school choice. He has indicated that he believes the merits and details of a choice program require further study. Both houses of the legislature are led by Republicans.

State Contacts

Cindy Duckett
President, Project Educate
Associate Editor, *Crises in Education*
410 South Kessler
Wichita, KS 67217
Phone: (316) 942-4545
Web site: http://www2southwind.net/~educate
E-mail: YSZW26A@prodigy.com

Kansas Department of Education
John A. Tompkins, Commissioner
120 Southeast 10th Avenue
Topeka, KS 66612
Phone: (785) 296-3201
Fax: (785) 296-7933

Kansas Public Policy Institute
Bob Corkins, Executive Director
P.O. Box 1946
Topeka, KS 66601-1946
Phone: (785) 357-7709
Fax: (785) 357-7524
Web site: http://www.kppi.org
E-mail: bcorkins@kppi.org

Parents in Control
Kay O'Connor, Executive Director
P.O. Box 2232
Olathe, KS 66051
Phone: (913) 393-1991; 1 (877) IAM4PIC
Fax: (913) 393-3903
E-mail: kayoisok@msn.com

Senator Barbara Lawrence
State Capitol
Topeka, KS 66612-1504
Phone: (785) 296-7386

Representative Kay O'Connor
State Capitol
Topeka, KS 66612-1504
Phone: (785) 276-7649;
(800) 277-6368, ext. 3092

Endnotes

1 For sources, see "An Explanation of the State Profile Categories."

2 The Blum Center's *Educational Freedom Report*, No. 54, December 19, 1997.

3 See Children's Scholarship Fund Web site at *http://www.scholarshipfund.org.*

4 The Friedman–Blum *Educational Freedom Report*, No. 71, May 21, 1999.

5 Children's Scholarship Fund Web site at *http://www.scholarshipfund.org.*

Kentucky

State Profile[1]

School Choice Status
- Public school choice: N/A
- Charter schools: N/A
- Publicly funded private school choice: N/A

K–12 Public and Private Students and Schools
- Public school enrollment (fall 1998) and number of schools (1997–1998): 638,830 in 1,352 schools
- Private school enrollment and number of schools (1997–1998): 70,731 in 370 schools

K–12 Public and Private School Student Academic Performance
NAEP Test Results—percentage of students at each performance level for both public and private schools, with national percentages in parentheses

Performance Level	Reading 4th grade 1998	Reading 8th grade 1998	Math 4th grade 1996	Math 8th grade 1996	Science 8th grade 1996
Advanced	6% (6%)	2% (2%)	1% (2%)	1% (4%)	2% (3%)
Proficient	23 (23)	27 (28)	15 (18)	15 (19)	21 (24)
Basic	34 (31)	45 (41)	44 (42)	40 (38)	35 (33)
Below Basic	37 (39)	26 (28)	40 (38)	44 (39)	42 (40)

- SAT weighted rank (1999): N/A
- ACT weighted rank (1999): 22 out of 26

K–12 Public School Expenditures
- Current expenditures (1999–2000): $3,791,098,000
- Amount of revenue from the federal government (1998–1999): 8.9%
- Current per-pupil expenditures (1999–2000): $5,876

K–12 Public School Teachers (1998–1999)
- Number of teachers: 39,000
- Average salary: $35,526
- Students enrolled per teacher: 16.4
- Leading teachers union: NEA

Background

Kentucky has neither a school choice program nor charter schools, although a 1990 law gives parents limited authority to remove their children from a public school. The law was enacted after the Kentucky Supreme Court ruled in June 1989 that the state's entire system of public education was unconstitutional because resources were not allocated equally among schools. The 1990 law, concerned mainly with school organization and accountability guidelines in dealing with this decision, permits students to withdraw from an assigned public school if state authorities deem the school a failure. Students are not allowed to choose the public school to which they will be transferred.

In response to the court's decision, the General Assembly passed a series of reform initiatives in the Kentucky Education Reform Act of 1990 (KERA). KERA was signed by then-Governor Wallace G. Wilkinson on April 11, 1990, and went into effect on July 13, 1990. It establishes high educational goals and an assessment process and accountability system, determined by the people of Kentucky, that will (1) reward schools that are improving their students' level of academic success; (2) intervene when schools are struggling to make progress; (3) overhaul early childhood education programs for at-risk children; (4) increase funding for longer school days, weeks, and years (with new funding mechanisms to alleviate the financial discrepancies between wealthier and poorer school districts); and (5) change the governing structure of Kentucky's schools to eliminate bureaucracy.

So far, the evidence with respect to KERA's effectiveness is inconclusive.

The Jefferson County (greater Louisville area) school system has a limited choice program that includes traditional and magnet schools. Traditional schools (kindergarten through 12th grade) emphasize the basics of reading, writing, math, and science; are strong in discipline; have specific dress and behavior codes; and require active parental involvement and support. Parents put their names on a list for the traditional school serving their district. Selection is made by a "draw" system that is guided by desegregation laws and the school district. The Jefferson County magnet program (for 1st through 12th grades) requires an application for a specific curriculum area such as science, math, computer science, performing arts, and visual arts.

References, grades, school records, and a personal interview determine a child's ability and talent in the requested area.

In 1998, a new $1 million privately funded scholarship program, School CHOICE Scholarships, Inc., awarded over 300 scholarships to children from low-income families to attend a private school of choice in Jefferson County. The scholarships cover 50 percent of tuition (up to $1,000) for three years.

Developments in 1999

School CHOICE Scholarships, Inc., in Louisville has increased by 200 the number of grants to be awarded in its second scholarship lottery.

Position of the Governor/Composition of State Legislature

Governor Paul Patton, a Democrat, has no stated position on school choice. The House is led by Democrats; the Senate is led by Republicans.

State Contacts

Kentucky Department of Education
Jim Parks
Capitol Plaza Tower, 19th Floor
Frankfort, KY 40601
Phone: (502) 564-4770
Web site: http://www.kde.state.ky.us/

Kentucky League for Educational Alternatives
Harry Borders, Program Director
1042 Burlington Lane
Frankfort, KY 40601
Phone: (502) 875-8010
Fax: (502) 875-2841

School CHOICE Scholarships, Inc.
Pamela Thorpe, Executive Director
P.O. Box 221546
Louisville, KY 40252-1546
Phone: (502) 254-7274
Fax: (502) 245-4792
E-mail: scsiky@aol.com

Endnote

1 For sources, see "An Explanation of the State Profile Categories."

Louisiana

State Profile[1]

School Choice Status
- Public school choice: Limited
- Charter schools: Established 1995
    Strength of law: Strong
    Number of charter schools in operation (fall 1999): 17
    Number of students enrolled in charter schools (1998–1999): 1,431
- Publicly funded private school choice: N/A

K–12 Public and Private Students and Schools
- Public school enrollment (fall 1998) and number of schools (1997–1998): 764,939 in 1,476 schools
- Private school enrollment and number of schools (1997–1998): 141,633 in 452 schools

K–12 Public and Private School Student Academic Performance
NAEP Test Results—percentage of students at each performance level for both public and private schools, with national percentages in parentheses

Performance Level	Reading 4th grade 1998	Reading 8th grade 1998	Math 4th grade 1996	Math 8th grade 1996	Science 8th grade 1996
Advanced	3% (6%)	1% (2%)	0% (2%)	0% (4%)	1% (3%)
Proficient	16 (23)	17 (28)	8 (18)	7 (19)	12 (24)
Basic	29 (31)	46 (41)	36 (42)	31 (38)	27 (33)
Below Basic	52 (39)	36 (28)	56 (38)	62 (39)	60 (40)

- SAT weighted rank (1999): N/A
- ACT weighted rank (1999): 25 out of 26 states

K–12 Public School Expenditures
- Current expenditures (1999–2000): $4,178,023,000
- Amount of revenue from the federal government (1998–1999): 11.4%
- Current per-pupil expenditures (1999–2000): $5,441

K–12 Public School Teachers (1998–1999)
- Number of teachers: 48,721
- Average salary: $32,510
- Students enrolled per teacher: 15.7
- Leading teachers union: AFT (also known as Louisiana Federation of Teachers)

Background

In 1995, then-Governor Edwin Edwards signed a charter school bill, sponsored by State Senator Cecil Picard (D–25), authorizing a charter school demonstration program to give parents, teachers, and concerned citizens an opportunity to create independent public schools. Up to eight school boards can volunteer to participate in the pilot program. These school boards, in turn, may authorize the groups eligible to operate the schools. The groups would be allowed to establish at least one charter school in the district and up to one for every 20,000 pupils enrolled in the public and non-public schools within the charter school's jurisdiction.

Under this law, only the following may apply for the five-year charters:

- A group of three or more teachers holding Louisiana teaching certificates;

- A group of 10 or more citizens;

- A public service organization;

- A business or corporate entity;

- A Louisiana college or university; or

- An existing public school, which may convert to a charter school if two-thirds of the full-time faculty and instructional staff and two-thirds of the parents sign a petition in favor of the charter.

At least 75 percent of the teachers employed by the charter school must be state certified; the remaining 25 percent must meet other requirements. Charter schools are not bound by any district-wide collective bargaining agreement if this stipulation is written into their charters.

One of the strengths of the new law is its funding provision. All charter schools approved by the local school board would receive a per-pupil amount equal to the amount the district currently spends on average per pupil. In addition, charter schools would be eligible for federal, state, or local operating funds for which the student qualifies. New charter schools may not be operated by religious or home study groups, or for the purpose of becoming religiously affiliated schools in the future.

On May 1, 1997, the Louisiana Senate Education Committee defeated a $300 million voucher bill introduced by Senator Tom Greene (R–17). This legislation would have made vouchers available through an Educational Voucher Program based on state per-pupil expenditure and would have phased in the use of vouchers over a 12-year period, beginning with kindergarten and 1st grade. The bill was opposed by the Louisiana School Board Association, the American Civil Liberties Union, and local teachers unions. Ed Steimel, former president of the Louisiana Association of Business and Industry and the Public Affairs Research Council, has been a leading supporter.[2]

On September 28, 1998, New Orleans and Baton Rouge were named two of the 40 "partner cities" for the Children's Scholarship Fund (CSF) challenge grant. The CSF is a $100 million foundation underwritten by entrepreneurs Ted Forstmann and John Walton. It will match funds raised by New Orleans and Baton Rouge residents to fund approximately 1,500 private scholarships for low-income students (1,250 in New Orleans and 250 in Baton Rouge) to attend a school of choice. Scholarships are awarded for at least four years to children entering kindergarten through 8th grade the following year.[3]

Developments in 1999

On April 22, 1999, the Children's Scholarship Fund announced the winners of the largest private scholarship program in the country. The recipients were selected randomly by computer-generated lottery. In New Orleans, 1,500 scholarship recipients were chosen from 29,152 applications; in Baton Rouge, 250 recipients were chosen from 5,568 applicants.[4]

According to the Public Affairs Research Council of Louisiana, several voucher bills were introduced in the state legislature in 1999.[5]

- HB 725 would have created the Right to Learn Program, a pre-K program limited to low-income students that would later expand to the 3rd grade and include all children. This program would issue vouchers for $1,500 or the amount charged by the non-public school, whichever is less, to be used at an approved school of choice.

- HB 1652, SB 299, and SB 964 would have enacted a voucher program that would start from kindergarten and slowly be phased in until all K–12 public and private students and schools, including students attending nonpublic schools, are eligible.

- HB 1770 would have enacted the School Choice Awards Program to expand the TOPS college scholarship program to include certain elementary and secondary school students. Under this plan, the governor initially would designate, with local school board approval, three to 10 low-performing schools that are in the bottom 20 percent in a district. Students in these schools would then receive an award (or voucher) of $1,000 or 50 percent of the nonpublic school tuition, whichever is less, to attend a school of choice. The governor could expand the program in subsequent years. All potential cost savings from this program would be re-allocated to the local school district.

- HB 1953 would have enacted the Louisiana Alternative Education Grant Program. This program would have been limited to students in parishes with a minimum population of 240,000 based on the latest decennial census. It would be limited at first to students in kindergarten but gradually would expand to include all grades. The voucher amount would not exceed the average per-pupil cost of education of the other students.

- SB 1029 would have enacted a five-year pilot choice program targeted at low-income students in pre-K through first grade to attend a school of choice.

None of these proposals was enacted.

Position of the Governor/Composition of State Legislature

Governor M. J. "Mike" Foster, Jr., a Republican, has no stated position on school choice. He has proposed expanding the state's pilot charter school program.[6] Both houses of the legislature are led by Democrats.

State Contacts

CSF–Baton Rouge
Boys and Girls Club
Pat Van Burkleo, Executive Director
263 Third Street, Suite 308
Baton Rouge, LA 70801
Phone: (225) 387-6840
Fax: (225) 344-2582

CSF–New Orleans
Faith Sweeney, Executive Director
3110 Canal Street
New Orleans, LA 70119
Phone: (504) 821-5060
Fax: (888) 239-9350

Jacklyn Ducote & Associates–
Empowerment Resources
Jackie Ducote
P.O. Box 14588
Baton Rouge, LA 70898
Phone: (225) 343-7020
Fax: (225) 383-1967
E-mail: Jhducote@aol.com

Louisiana Association of Business and Industry
Mona Davis, Director of Education Council
3113 Valley Creek Drive
P.O. Box 80258
Baton Rouge, LA 70898-0258
Phone: (504) 928-5388
Fax: (504) 929-6054

Public Affairs Research Council
Richard Omdal
4664 Jamestown Avenue, Suite 300
P.O. Box 14776
Baton Rouge, LA 70898-4776
Phone: (504) 926-8414
Fax: (504) 926-8417
Web site: www.la-par.org

Endnotes

1 For sources, see "An Explanation of the State Profile Categories."

2 The Blum Center's *Educational Freedom Report*, No. 54, December 19, 1997.

3 See Children's Scholarship Fund Web site at *http://www.scholarshipfund.org*.

4 *Ibid.*

5 *PAR Legislative Bulletin*, Vol. 45, No. 3 (April 27, 1999).

6 Center for Education Reform, *School Reform in the United States: State by State Summary*, Spring 1997, p. 22.

Maine

State Profile[1]

School Choice Status
- Public school choice: Limited
- Charter schools: N/A
- Publicly funded private school choice: Tuitioning law since 1954
    Program description: Maine reimburses parents who live in districts without a public school for the cost of sending their children to a non-religious private school, either within or outside the state, or to a public school in a neighboring district of choice. During the 1998–1999 school year, 14,541 students participated in the program. Of those, 5,295 attended 39 private schools.

K–12 Public and Private School Students and Schools
- Public school enrollment (fall 1998) and number of schools (1997–1998): 210,927 in 697 schools
- Private school enrollment and number of schools (1997–1998): 17,187 in 135 schools

K–12 Public and Private School Student Academic Performance
NAEP Test Results—percentage of students at each performance level for both public and private schools, with national percentages in parentheses

Performance Level	Reading 4th grade 1998	Reading 8th grade 1998	Math 4th grade 1996	Math 8th grade 1996	Science 8th grade 1996
Advanced	8% (6%)	4% (2%)	3% (2%)	6% (4%)	4% (3%)
Proficient	28 (23)	38 (28)	24 (18)	25 (19)	37 (24)
Basic	37 (31)	42 (41)	48 (42)	46 (38)	37 (33)
Below Basic	27 (39)	16 (28)	25 (38)	23 (39)	22 (40)

- SAT weighted rank (1999): 11 out of 24 states and the District of Columbia
- ACT weighted rank (1999): N/A

K–12 Public School Expenditures
- Current expenditures (1999–2000): $1,540,000,000
- Amount of revenue from the federal government (1998–1999): 6.3%
- Current per-pupil expenditures (1999–2000): $7,365

K–12 Public School Teachers (1998–1999)
- Number of teachers: 15,086
- Average salary: $34,906
- Students enrolled per teacher: 14.0
- Largest teachers union: NEA

Background

Since 1954, school districts in Maine that lack public schools have provided aid for students to attend non-religious private schools (although religious schools were included at one time) or other districts' public schools. Bills concerning both charter schools and vouchers for religious schools have been introduced several times but have not been passed.

On July 31, 1997, the Washington, D.C.-based Institute for Justice filed a lawsuit in the case of *Bagley* v. *Town of Raymond* on behalf of parents living in "tuitioning towns" in Maine who wished to send their children to a religious school. Under current law, parents can place their children in non-religious private schools if the district in which they reside does not have a public school. The lawsuit argued that excluding religious schools violates the constitutions of the United States and Maine, both of which guarantee the free exercise of religion and equal protection under the law. Cumberland County Superior Court in Portland ruled against the parents on April 24, 1998.[2] On April 26, 1999, the Maine Supreme Court upheld the Cumberland County Superior Court's decision; and in October 1999, the U.S. Supreme Court refused to review the Maine Supreme Court's decision, thus letting stand the exclusion of religious schools from Maine's tuitioning program.

During the 1998 legislative session, with support from the Maine School Choice Coalition, State Representative Adam Mack (R– Standish) attempted to attach an amendment to the state supplemental budget to establish 3,000 scholarships of $5,000 each to enable children to attend a school of choice. Scholarships would have gone to children whose families earn less than $30,000 per year and who live in school "administrative units" with test scores in the lowest 25 percent. The amendment failed.

Developments in 1999

On April 23, 1999, the Maine Judicial Supreme Court upheld the Cumberland County Superior Court's 1998 decision in *Bagley* v. *Town of Raymond*, ruling against the parents who want to include religious schools in the choices available to students in "tuitioning towns."[3] A similar lawsuit by the American Center for Law and Justice was rejected by the First Circuit Court of Appeals in May 1999. In October, the U.S. Supreme Court refused to review these decisions. The refusal lets stand the 1980 Maine law that excludes religious schools from Maine's tuitioning program.

Several school choice and charter school bills were introduced, but none was enacted. Two charter school bills were held over for consideration during the 2000 legislative session. Representative Judy Powers (D–Rockport) is the sponsor of one of the charter school bills, which would allow five new charters with a total enrollment of 200 in the first year. Representative Carol Weston (R–Montville) is the sponsor of a bill that would create a charter school authority (similar to the Maine "Finance Authority").

Position of the Governor/Composition of State Legislature

Governor Angus S. King, Jr., an Independent, supports limited school choice, especially public school choice. Both houses of the legislature are led by Democrats.

State Contacts

Maine Association for Charter Schools
Judith Jones
199 Hatchet Mountain Road
Hope, ME 04847
Phone: (207) 763-3576
Fax: (207) 763-4552

Maine Department of Education
Phone: (207) 287-5800

Maine Education Choice Coalition
Frank Heller, State Coordinator
12 Belmont Street
Brunswick, ME 04011
Phone: (207) 729-6090
Fax: (207) 729-1590
Web site: http://www.netschoolofmaine.com
E-mail: global@gwi.net

Representative Adam Mack (candidate for U.S. Congress)
476 Pond Road
Standish, ME 04084
Phone: (207) 892-4024
Fax: (207) 892-4019
Toll Free: 1-877-BIG-MACK
Web Site: http://www.bigmack.net

Endnotes

1 For sources, see "An Explanation of the State Profile Categories."

2 Correspondence from Maureen Blum, Institute for Justice, December 16, 1998.

3 Correspondence from the Institute for Justice, April 26, 1999.

Maryland

State Profile[1]

School Choice Status
- Public school choice: N/A
- Charter schools: N/A
- Publicly funded private school choice: N/A

K–12 Public and Private School Students and Schools
- Public school enrollment (fall 1998) and number of schools (1997–1998): 841,671 in 1,298 schools
- Private school enrollment and number of schools (1997–1998): 129,898 in 655 schools

K–12 Public and Private School Student Academic Performance
NAEP Test Results—percentage of students at each performance level for both public and private schools, with national percentages in parentheses

Performance Level	Reading 4th grade 1998	Reading 8th grade 1998	Math 4th grade 1996	Math 8th grade 1996	Science 8th grade 1996
Advanced	7% (6%)	4% (2%)	3% (2%)	5% (4%)	2% (3%)
Proficient	22 (23)	27 (28)	19 (18)	19 (19)	23 (24)
Basic	32 (31)	41 (41)	37 (42)	33 (38)	30 (33)
Below Basic	39 (39)	28 (28)	41 (38)	43 (39)	45 (40)

- SAT weighted rank (1999): 9 out of 24 states and the District of Columbia
- ACT weighted rank (1999): N/A

K–12 Public School Expenditures
- Current expenditures (1999–2000): $5,935,581,000
- Amount of revenue from the federal government (1998–1999): 5.1%
- Current per-pupil expenditures (1999–2000): $6,991

K–12 Public School Teachers (1998–1999)
- Number of teachers: 49,249
- Average salary: $42,526
- Students enrolled per teacher: 17.1
- Largest teachers union: NEA

Background

Former Baltimore Mayor Kurt Schmoke's task force held public forums in 1996 to discuss education options ranging from vouchers to charter schools and later issued a report recommending charter schools, open enrollment, and post-secondary enrollment options, as well as an expansion of magnet school programs. The state assumed partial control of the Baltimore City school system in 1997, with the mayor and the governor charged jointly with selecting new board members for the city. The new policy included a mild provision for charter schools that, operating under contract to the school district, would be somewhat free from district management.[2]

In 1998, TEACH Maryland started to garner support for an education tax credit bill modeled after a recently enacted Arizona plan. A modified version of the TEACH Maryland plan was introduced as H.B. 1075 by State Delegate James F. Ports, Jr. (R–Baltimore County). The bill, which would have capped the credit at $50 per year, was defeated in the Ways and Means Committee.

On September 28, 1998, Baltimore was named one of the 40 "partner cities" for the Children's Scholarship Fund (CSF) challenge grant. The CSF is a $100 million foundation underwritten by entrepreneurs Ted Forstmann and John Walton. Baltimore residents have raised $1 million, which the CSF will match to fund 500 private scholarships for low-income students to attend a school of choice. A lottery in April 1999 determined who would receive the scholarships, which were awarded for at least four years to children entering kindergarten through 8th grade in the spring of 1999. Baltimore recipients were able to choose from about 2,600 openings at 60 private or parochial schools with average yearly tuition costs of $2,900.[3]

Developments in 1999

In March, a charter school bill (S.B. 761) was approved by both chambers of the legislature, but the Senate later refused to concur with amendments attached to it in the House. S.B. 761 would establish a pilot program to allow certain low-income children to attend public charter schools. Key differences between the Senate and House versions of the bill were as follows:

- The Senate version allowed teachers to be unionized but did not require it as the House version did.

- The Senate bill restricted participation in the pilot program to low-income students, while the House version had a wider eligibility.

- The Senate version did not make provision for a charter appeals process as did the House version.

- Neither the Senate nor the House version of the bill allowed current private schools to convert to charter status.[4]

By the end of the legislative session, Maryland had not enacted a charter school law. A tuition tax-credit and deduction bill was reported unfavorably in the House Committee on Ways and Means. H.B. 564 would have allowed reimbursements to parents or taxpayers for any "education related expenses." It would have allowed Maryland families a tax deduction for up to $1,500 per dependent child in kindergarten through 6th grade and up to $2,500 per dependent child in 7th through 12th grades. For low-income parents (with combined incomes below $33,500), a tax credit for $2,000 would have been available.[5]

On April 22, 1999, the Children's Scholarship Fund announced the winners of the largest private scholarship program in the country. The recipients were selected randomly by computer-generated lottery. In Baltimore, 500 scholarship recipients were chosen from 20,145 applicants. Among Baltimore's eligible parents, 44 percent applied for CSF scholarships. This was the highest percentage in the country; the national average was 24 percent.[6]

On October 21, 1999, the Maryland State Department of Education requested that private entities apply for contracts to manage "reconstitution eligible" (RE) public schools in Baltimore City. "RE" schools are poor-performing schools that, three or four years previously, were given an ultimatum to improve. Those that have not improved are to be turned over to the private sector. However the stipulations in the contracts are very vague. The Maryland State Department of Education has said that it is working to clarify the contracts. Those that receive final approval will begin managing public school(s) in the fall of 2000.

Developments in 2000

Representative Nancy Stocksdale (R–Carroll County) has introduced legislation in the Maryland House to give tax credits to parents for educational expenses for all Children from grades K–12.[7] Three bills to allow students in "RE" schools to attend a private school of choice have also been introduced.[8]

Position of the Governor/Composition of State Legislature

Governor Parris N. Glendening, a Democrat, supports public school choice but not private school choice. Both houses of the legislature are led by Democrats.

State Contacts

Calvert Institute for Policy Research
Douglas P. Munro, Ph.D., President
2604 Sisson Street, 3rd Floor
Baltimore, MD 21211
Phone: (410) 662-7252
Fax: (410) 662-7254
Web site: http://www.calvertinstitute.org

Charles J. O'Malley & Associates
Charles O'Malley, President
442 Cranes Roost Court
Annapolis, MD 21401
Phone: (410) 349-0139
Fax: (410) 349-0140

CSF–Baltimore
Suzanna Duvall
2604 Sisson Street, 3rd Floor
Baltimore, MD 21211
Phone: (410) 243-2510
Fax: (410) 243-8149

Doyle and Associates
Denis Doyle
110 Summerfield Road
Chevy Chase, MD 20815
Phone: (301) 986-9350
Fax: (301) 907-4959
E-mail: dpdoyle@bellatlantic.net

Maryland State Department of Education
Nancy S. Grasmick, Ph.D.
State Superintendent of Schools
200 West Baltimore Street
Baltimore, MD 21201
Phone: (410) 767-0100
Fax: (410) 333-6033
Web site: http://www.state.md.us/msde/

Representative Nancy R. Stocksdale
39 Ridge Road
Westminister, MD 21157
Phone: (410) 840-8088
Fax: (410) 840-8088

TEACH Maryland
John Schiavone
P.O. Box 43573
Baltimore, MD 21234
Phone: (410) 592-3390
Fax: (410) 592-5265
E-mail: JDSchiavo@aol.com

Endnotes

1 For sources, see "An Explanation of the State Profile Categories."

2 Correspondence with Douglas P. Munro, Calvert Institute, December 14, 1998.

3 See Children's Scholarship Fund Web site at *http://www.scholarshipfund.org.*

4 Correspondence from Douglas P. Munro, Calvert Institute, March 3, 1999.

5 Correspondence from John Schiavone, TEACH Maryland, March 11, 1999.

6 See Children's Scholarship Fund Web site at *http://www.scholarshipfund.org.*

7 Correspondence from Nancy Stocksdale, received February 1, 2000. The bill can be found at *http://mlis.state.md.us.*

8 See Education Commission of the States Web site at *http://www.ecs.org.*

Massachusetts

State Profile[1]

School Choice Status
- Public school choice: Limited
- Charter schools: Established 1993
    Strength of law: Strong
    Number of charter schools in operation (fall 1999): 39
    Number of students enrolled in charter schools (fall 1999): 12,424
- Publicly funded private school choice: N/A

K–12 Public and Private School Students and Schools
- Public school enrollment (fall 1998) and number of schools (1997–1998): 948,313 in 1,858 schools
- Private school enrollment and number of schools (1997–1998): 127,165 in 657 schools

K–12 Public and Private School Student Academic Performance
NAEP Test Results—percentage of students at each performance level for both public and private schools, with national percentages in parentheses

Performance Level	Reading 4th grade 1998	Reading 8th grade 1998	Math 4th grade 1996	Math 8th grade 1996	Science 8th grade 1996
Advanced	8% (6%)	3% (2%)	2% (2%)	5% (4%)	4% (3%)
Proficient	29 (23)	33 (28)	22 (28)	23 (19)	33 (24)
Basic	36 (31)	44 (41)	47 (42)	40 (38)	32 (33)
Below Basic	27 (39)	20 (28)	29 (38)	32 (39)	31 (40)

- SAT weighted rank (1999): 6 out of 24 states and the District of Columbia
- ACT weighted rank (1999): N/A

K–12 Public School Expenditures
- Current expenditures (1999–2000): $7,058,413,000
- Amount of revenue from the federal government (1998–1999): 5.1%
- Current per-pupil expenditures (1999–2000): $7,387

K–12 Public School Teachers (1998–1999)
- Number of teachers: 64,985
- Average salary: $45,075
- Students enrolled per teacher: 14.6
- Largest teachers union: NEA

Background

A 1991 public school choice law permits students in Massachusetts to attend a public school out of district only if the recipient district participates in the program. The law was amended in 1993. Under the amended law, a school district that chooses not to accept incoming students from another district must opt out annually by a vote of the local school committee. Districts that participate may determine, without state review, the number of seats available for out-of-district students. Schools accepting students can receive tuition from the state equivalent to 75 percent of actual spending per pupil in the district, up to $5,000. The state Board of Education has established an information system to help parents choose among participating districts. (Special education is paid at a rate of 100 percent.) Transportation assistance is provided for low-income children who cross district lines to attend schools of choice. As of December 1999, 7,172 students were taking advantage of this choice program.

Massachusetts also has several intra-district choice programs. The two most prominent are in Boston and Cambridge. Boston introduced intra-district choice in 1989 at the prodding of its frustrated business community. The Boston school district is divided into three school zones for kindergarten through 8th grade, and students in those grades are allowed to choose a school from among all the city schools as long as their choice does not undermine the state's guidelines for racial integration. In 1981, Cambridge launched a public school choice program for students in kindergarten through 8th grade, but eliminated the system of zones that governed the school a child attended. Schools may accept any child and are constrained only by available space and state desegregation requirements.

A 1997 study of the state's inter-district public school choice program by the Massachusetts-based Pioneer Institute shows that the districts that lost large numbers of students at the outset of the program responded by improving their policies and programs to encourage former students to return and to attract transfer students from other districts. Consequently, these districts lost fewer students in subsequent years. Conversely, districts that lost only a small number of students initially made few changes and lost more students in subsequent years—further evidence that a competitive market can have positive effects on the quality of public education.[2]

Although the state choice program does not give parents the option of private schools, there are private scholarships that make it possible for low-income students to attend parochial schools. Direct private assistance is available for Catholic schools. The Catholic Schools Foundation has given aid to Catholic schools in the Boston area since 1983 and has offered scholarships to low-income children to attend Catholic schools in Boston since 1991. Additionally, on September 28, 1998, Boston was named one of 40 "partner cities" for the Children's Scholarship Fund (CSF) challenge grant. The CSF is a $100 million foundation underwritten by entrepreneurs Ted Forstmann and John Walton. It will match funds raised by Boston residents to fund approximately 500 private scholarships for low-income students to attend a school of choice. A lottery in April 1999 determined who would receive the scholarships, which were awarded for at least four years to children entering kindergarten through 8th grade during the 1999–2000 academic year.[3]

On the charter school front, in 1993, Governor William Weld signed the Education Reform Act. Among other things, the law eliminated tenure, required that teachers be re-certified every five years, and authorized the establishment of up to 25 charter schools beginning with the 1995–1996 school year. Charter schools must be open to all students and may not charge tuition. Under this law, up to 6 percent of district net school spending may be transferred to charter schools in the district. No more than 2 percent of the total public school student population (approximately 19,000 children during the 1998–1999 school year) may be enrolled in charter schools.

Any individual, group, business, corporate entity, two or more certified teachers, or 10 or more parents may apply for a charter; private and parochial schools may not. There are no statutory funding provisions to help charter schools defray their high start-up costs. Federal grants have been awarded, and private funds are available to charter schools in need. An approved charter school is entitled to per-pupil payments equal to the average cost in the student's home district, and charter schools are independent of outside control over their daily operations.

The Boston-based Pioneer Institute has conducted several studies since 1996 on charter schools in the state[4] and has found that they serve traditionally under-served student populations, including a higher percentage of low-income, bilingual, and minority children, than the regular public school system. The studies also found that most of the students in charter schools had been ranked average or below average academically in their previous schools. The charters did not necessarily attract more academically involved parents, but parents of charter school students expressed greater satisfaction with their children's new schools.

A Pioneer Institute 1998 poll found that 60 percent of charter school parents gave their schools an "A," compared with 37 percent of district school parents. Of the charter school parents, almost 90 percent preferred their charter school over the child's previous school; 58 percent said the charter school exceeded their expectations. Nearly two-thirds of parents said their child is performing better academically as a result of moving to a charter school.[5]

Compared with parents of children in district schools, charter school parents are more likely to want to continue sending their children to their current schools. If given the option to send their children to any public, private, or parochial school, 78 percent of charter school parents said they would remain at the current charter school; only 50 percent of district school parents would keep their children in the same district school. More than twice as many district school parents as charter school parents (12 percent and 5 percent, respectively) said that they were looking for a new school for next year.

Charter school parents also reported more frequent communication from their child's school. They reported twice as many in-person meetings with their child's teacher as did district school parents (three meetings per year for charter school parents versus one-and-a half for district school parents). Charter school parents received an annual average of four phone calls from their child's school, whereas district school parents received fewer than three. Charter school parents averaged 3.3 forms of written communication from the school, compared with 1.7 for district school parents. Charter school parents were more confident that their child could easily obtain extra help (90 percent) than were district school parents (71 percent).

A 1998 Pioneer study revealed that the state's charter school teachers found it easier to participate in decision-making at their charter schools than at other schools in which they had worked. The most common reason teachers gave for seeking a position at a charter school was the school's mission and educational philosophy (51 percent); 47 percent selected control over curriculum and instruction, 42.5 percent selected the quality of academic program, and 41 percent cited the collaborative working environment. Nearly half the teachers in charter schools hold a master's or higher degree, and 67 percent hold a Massachusetts teaching certificate. Also, "Charter school teachers are active stakeholders in their schools."[6]

And a 1997 study by the Massachusetts Department of Education shows that students in charter schools were advancing faster than their peers in their former districts.

In 1998, one of Boston's charter schools, the Academy of the Pacific Rim, became the first public school in the nation to grant a "learning guarantee." The school promised that if a student does not pass the 10th grade state assessment test, his or her parents have the right to send that student to another school of their choice. The Academy will transfer the $7,400 per-pupil state expenditure to the recipient school. However, parents must sign weekly progress reports on their child, and if the school feels a student is lagging behind, the student must consent to work with a tutor.

Developments in 1999

On April 22, 1999, the Children's Scholarship Fund announced the winners of the largest private scholarship program in the country. The recipients were selected randomly by computer-generated lottery. In Boston, 325 scholarship recipients were chosen from 11,795 applicants.[7]

Meanwhile, the demand for charter schools continues to rise. In 1995, when the first charter schools opened, there was an average of two applications for each available space. Four years later in 1999, the average had risen to nearly five applications for each space. Current state law caps the number of Commonwealth charter schools at 37—a number that already has been met—and 8,500 students were on a waiting list to attend a charter school of choice as of fall 1999. Legislation is in the works to lift the cap on charter schools.

On April 27, 1999, Republican legislative leaders introduced a bill that would double, to $24 million, the funding for the Metropolitan Council for Educational Opportunity (METCO), and support the addition of more charter schools.

In mid-December, thanks to the work of the Washington-based Becket Fund, state officials certified more than 78,000 signatures on petitions involving school choice.

Position of the Governor/Composition of State Legislature

Governor A. Paul Cellucci, a Republican, supports charter schools. He also favors lifting the cap on the number of charter schools that can be opened statewide and supports publicly funded private school choice. Both houses of the legislature are led by Democrats.

State Contacts

Beacon Hill Institute for Public Policy Research
David Tuerck, Executive Director
Suffolk University
8 Ashburton Place
Boston, MA 02108-2770
Phone: (617) 573-8750
Fax: (617) 720-4272
Web site: http://www.bhi.sclaf.suffolk.edu

CSF–Boston
Cornelius (Con) Chapman
Judy Burnette
Eliot Church of Roxbury
56 Dale Street
Boston, MA 02119
Phone: (617) 357-8700, ext. 103
Fax: (617) 442-8299

Catholic Schools Foundation, Inc.
Archdiocese of Boston
2121 Commonwealth Avenue
Brighton, MA 02135
Phone: (617) 254-0100
Fax: (617) 783-6366

Massachusetts Department of Education
Jose Afonso, Charter School Office
One Ashburton Place, Room 1403
Boston, MA 02108
Phone: (617) 727-0075
Fax: (617) 727-0049

Phylis Rogers, School Finance Office
Phone: (781) 338-6534
Fax: (781) 338-6565
E-mail: progers@doe.mass.edu

Parents' Alliance for Catholic Education (PACE)
Steve Perla, Executive Director
124 Summer Street
Fitchburg, MA 01420
Phone: (978) 665-9890
Fax: (978) 665-9885
E-mail: paceinc@impresso.com

Pioneer Institute for Public Policy Research
Linda Brown, Director, Charter School Resource Center
85 Devonshire Street, 8th Floor
Boston, MA 02109-3504
Phone: (617) 723-2277
Fax: (617) 723-1880
Web site: http://www.pioneerinstitute.org
E-mail: pioneer@pioneerinstitute.org

Worcester Municipal Research Bureau
Dr. Roberta R. Shaefer, Executive Director
500 Salisbury Street
Worcester, MA 01609-1296
Phone: (508) 799-7169
Fax: (508) 756-1780

Endnotes

1 For sources, see "An Explanation of the State Profile Categories."

2 David J. Armor and Brett Peiser, *Competition in Education: A Case Study of Interdistrict Choice* (Boston: Pioneer Institute for Public Policy Research, 1997).

3 See Children's Scholarship Fund Web site at *http://www.scholarshipfund.org*.

4 Pioneer Institute for Public Policy Research, *Massachusetts Charter School Profiles, 1995–96 School Year*, July 1996, and *Massachusetts Charter School Profiles, Interim 1996–1997*, 1997.

5 "Poll Finds Higher Satisfaction Rate Among Charter School Parents," Pioneer Institute for Public Policy Research *Policy Directions*, No. 3, June 1998.

6 Massachusetts Charter School Resource Center, "Study Finds Charter School Teachers Are Stakeholders," Pioneer Institute for Public Policy Research *Policy Directions*, No. 4, July 1998.

7 See Children's Scholarship Fund Web site at *http://www.scholarshipfund.org*.

Michigan

State Profile[1]

School Choice Status
- Public school choice: Statewide
- Charter schools: Established 1993
    - Strength of law: Strong
    - Number of charter schools in operation (fall 1999): 175
    - Number of students enrolled in charter schools (1998–1999): 33,372
- Publicly funded private school choice: N/A

K–12 Public and Private School Students and Schools
- Public school enrollment (fall 1998) and number of schools (1997–1998): 1,696,475 in 3,625 schools
- Private school enrollment and number of schools (1997–1998): 187,740 in 1,096 schools

K–12 Public and Private School Student Academic Performance
NAEP Test Results—percentage of students at each performance level for both public and private schools, with national percentages in parentheses

Performance Level	Reading 4th grade 1998	Reading 8th grade 1998	Math 4th grade 1996	Math 8th grade 1996	Science 8th grade 1996
Advanced	5% (6%)	n/a	2% (2%)	4% (4%)	3% (3%)
Proficient	23 (23)	n/a	21 (18)	24 (19)	29 (24)
Basic	35 (31)	n/a	45 (42)	39 (38)	33 (33)
Below Basic	37 (39)	n/a	32 (38)	33 (39)	35 (40)

- SAT weighted rank (1999): N/A
- ACT weighted rank (1999): 16 out of 26 states

K–12 Public School Expenditures
- Current expenditures (1999–2000): $12,672,855,000
- Amount of revenue from the federal government (1998–1999): 6.6%
- Current per-pupil expenditures (1999–2000): $7,483

K–12 Public School Teachers (1998–1999)
- Number of teachers: 91,233
- Average salary: $48,207
- Students enrolled per teacher: 18.6
- Largest teachers union: NEA

Background

Frustrated by the failure of voters to approve ballot measures for education finance reform, Michigan's legislature in 1993 took the extraordinary step of repealing property taxes as a source of school operating revenue. Governor John Engler, a Republican, and his legislative allies then crafted measures for quality improvement and cost containment, such as school choice, abolition of teacher tenure, alternative certification, mandatory competitive bidding for teacher health insurance, and school employee pension reform. Opponents led by the Michigan Education Association (MEA) succeeded in blocking nearly all these reforms. The MEA also backed legislation to increase school spending and centralize school administration at the state level.

On December 24, 1993, acting under a self-imposed deadline, the legislature passed a series of bills to replace most of the repealed property tax revenue. It then gave voters the option of raising either the state sales tax or, by default, income and business taxes. In addition, legislators overhauled state school aid, folding many categorical programs (such as school transportation and some special education) and separate obligations (such as employer FICA and retirement funds) into a basic per-pupil grant that could not be transferred between districts.

Also in 1993, according to an internal Michigan Education Association document, the MEA vowed to oppose any effort by school districts to privatize school support services, such as cafeteria, custodial, and transportation services, and any revision in state law that would make local privatization easier to implement. However, information made available to the media by the Mackinac Center, a Michigan-based state think tank that has issued studies recommending privatization as a factor in cutting costs and improving quality, indicates that the MEA contracted with private firms for cafeteria, custodial, mailing, and security services at its own headquarters in East Lansing—and that these firms usually were non-union. Since then, there has been an explosion in the number of districts that are contracting out for various services.

The state passed a charter school law in 1993. Shortly after its passage, however, the teachers unions and the American Civil Liberties Union filed a lawsuit claiming that charter schools were unconstitutional because they would use state funds but would not be regulated by the state Board of Education. On November 1, 1994, Ingham County Circuit Judge William Collette ruled that charter schools could not receive public funds. The governor and the legislature responded by drawing up new legislation with stricter state regulations.

Michigan Public Act No. 416 of 1994 was passed on December 14, 1994, to "govern the establishment and operation of a Public School Academy," or charter school. It allows state public universities, community colleges, and local school districts to create public school academies. Universities have the greatest flexibility and are free to enroll students from across the state. Although there is a limit on the number of charter schools the universities may create, there is no cap on the total for the state as a whole. Teachers in charter schools are retained according to performance and do not enjoy tenure rights or guaranteed employment after four years.

Michigan law does not permit the waiver of statutory requirements. However, the state Board of Education may waive the application of an administrative rule if the applicant can meet its intent in a more effective, efficient, or economical manner, or if the waiver can stimulate student performance. For constitutional and school aid purposes, charter schools are defined as "school districts" and therefore may be subject to the same bureaucratic regulations binding school districts in admissions, curriculum, assessment, accreditation, teacher certification, special education, and (in the case of district-authorized charter schools) employee contract provisions.

The high level of parental demand for charter schools has made them diverse. For example, charter schools cater to pregnant teenagers, Hispanic students at risk of dropping out, young people with learning disabilities, Native American children on reservations, and students with an aptitude for creative arts. Charters also are available for technical trade academies, schools with a focus on the environment, and high-level math and science centers.

In November 1997, the Mackinac Center for Public Policy proposed a creative Universal Tuition Tax Credit plan. The measure would allow businesses or individuals paying private or public school tuition to take up to 80 percent of the cost of that tuition off their taxes. The tax credit would be capped at $2,800, half of what Michigan provides per pupil to its public schools. The plan has been endorsed by several groups, including the state's largest religious organization, the Wolverine State Missionary Baptist Convention, and the *Detroit News*.

Also in 1997, TEACH (Toward Educational Accountability and Choice) Michigan, a state-wide grassroots organization that has been seeking to repeal the state's constitutional prohibition against full educational choice, took 20 of Detroit's African–American leaders to Milwaukee to learn more about school choice opportunities. Subsequently, in April 1997, the influential Council of Baptist Pastors of Detroit and Vicinity publicly stated its interest in school choice as an educational reform option. In 1998, the Council released a report, *Empowering Parents to Drive Education Reform*, published by TEACH Michigan, which outlines the group's dedication to the principles of educational choice.

On July 7, 1998, Dr. E. Edward Jones, president of the four million-member National Baptist Convention of America, agreed to join the school choice movement in (1) establishing a new African–American-led scholarship fund for low-income students in kindergarten through 12th grades and (2) campaigning nationally for enactment of tuition tax credits that encourage individuals and businesses to donate to such funds. Jones's stance came in response to a $10 million commitment in matching funds to a new scholarship fund, the United Fund for Educational Opportunity, by philanthropist John Walton.

Meanwhile, private efforts to help low-income students escape failing public schools abound in Michigan. Since1991, CEO (Children's Educational Opportunities) Michigan has been awarding scholarships to low-income students throughout the state.

In Detroit, Cornerstone Schools (schools established by a coalition of church groups, businesses, labor, and community organizations) offer low-income children educational alternatives. Because over half the children in the Cornerstone Schools cannot afford full tuition, the schools set up a Partner Program, which matches each low-income student with a benefactor who gives the student partial scholarship assistance and plays an active role in the student's life.

On September 28, 1998, the entire state of Michigan was named one of 40 "partner" communities for the Children's Scholarship Fund (CSF) challenge grant. The CSF is a $100 million foundation underwritten by entrepreneurs Ted Forstmann and John Walton. In partnership with CEO Michigan, the CSF raised $15 million from Michigan residents to fund approximately 3,750 private scholarships for low-income students to attend a school of choice. A lottery in April 1999 determined who received the scholarships, which were awarded for at least four years to children entering kindergarten through 8th grade the following year.[2]

Developments in 1999

On April 22, 1999, the Children's Scholarship Fund announced the winners of the largest private scholarship program in the country. The recipients were selected randomly by computer-generated lottery. In Michigan, 3,750 scholarship recipients were chosen from 63,000 applicants.[3]

Under the leadership of Amway President and former Michigan Board of Education member Richard DeVos, school choice activists (including TEACH Michigan and Detroit's black pastors) and business leaders have formed Kids First! Yes! to rally around an effort to amend the Michigan constitution to give parents whose children attend "at risk" school districts a publicly funded voucher to attend a school of choice; 38 would qualify at this point.

Kids First! Yes! has gathered 302,000 signatures from registered voters to put the amendment to a statewide vote in November 2000. The amendment would repeal a 1970 amendment passed by voters that outlaws public aid to religious schools, including indirect aid such as tax credits and deductions. Michigan's constitution is regarded by many as the most restrictive in the United States with regard to school choice.

There is strong opposition to the efforts of Kids First! Yes! A coalition of 30 anti-parental choice groups has been organized under the name All Kids First! and is campaigning against the voucher proposal. However, a poll by the *Detroit News* shows that 53 percent of voters favor the Kids First! Yes! proposal; only 23 percent oppose the plan, and 24 percent are undecided.[4]

Meanwhile, the Mackinac Center for Public Policy began a new quarterly journal dedicated to K–12 news and analysis in Michigan. The journal is distributed free of charge to Michigan's 100,000 teachers and is the only source of non-union education information for most teachers. The Center will launch a series of statewide workshops to educate citizens about the benefits of school choice and encourage grassroots support. It also will conduct over 140 two-hour workshops between December 1999 and November 2000.

A 1999 University of Michigan study found that charter schools are beneficial to the state's education system. The study also found, however, that most charter programs are servicing only elementary age students, who are far less expensive to service than high school students, who require more money for such things as athletic equipment, laboratories, and larger libraries. Furthermore, because only 75 percent of Michigan's charter schools offer special education services, the bulk of these expenses are left to the public school districts, which often contract the instruction of harder-to-teach students to private schools.

Position of the Governor/Composition of State Legislature

Governor John Engler is one of the strongest advocates of public school choice and charter schools. However, he does not support the current voucher system proposed by Kids First! Yes! Both houses of the legislature are led by Republicans.

State Contacts

Cornerstone Schools
Ms. Ernestine Sanders, President and CEO
6861 East Nevada
Detroit, MI 48234
Phone: (313) 892-1860
Fax: (313) 892-1861

Crossroads Charter Academy
Dr. Ormand Hook, Principal
215 North State Street
Big Rapids, MI 49307
Phone: (616) 796-9041
Fax: (616) 796-9790

Education Freedom Fund
Linda Ploeg, Executive Director
Pamela Pettibone, Program Administrator
126 Ottawa, NW, Suite 401
Grand Rapids, MI 49503
Phone: (616) 459-2222; (800) 866-8141
Fax: (616) 459-1211
Web site: http://www.educationfreedom-fund.org
E-mail: ceomich@iserv.net

Educational Choice Project
Kimberley Holley, Administrator
34 West Jackson
One River Walk Center
Battle Creek, MI 49017
Phone: (616) 962-2181
Fax: (616) 962-2182

Kids First! Yes!
Jeff Timmer
P.O. Box 16008
Lansing, MI 48901
Phone: (800) 330-KIDS
Web site: http://www.KidsFirstYes.org

Mackinac Center for Public Policy
Lawrence Reed, President
Joe Overton, Senior Vice President
Matthew J. Brouillette, Associate Director of Education Policy
140 West Main Street
P.O. Box 568
Midland, MI 48640
Phone: (517) 631-0900
Fax: (517) 631-0964
Web site: http://www.mackinac.org
E-mail: mcpp@mackinac.org

Michigan Association for Public School Academies (MAPSA)
Daniel L. Quisenberry, President
124 West Allegan, Suite 750
Lansing, MI 48933
Phone: (517) 374-9167
Fax: (517) 374-9197
Web site: http://www.charterschools.org

Michigan Department of Education
608 West Allegan Street
Hannah Building
Lansing, MI 48933
Phone: (517) 373-3324
Web site: http://www.mde.state.mi.us/

Michigan Education Report
Matthew J. Brouillette, Managing Editor
P.O. Box 568
Midland, MI 48640
Phone: (517) 631-0900
Web site: http://www.educationreport.org

Michigan Family Forum
Dan Jarvis, Research and Policy Director
611 South Walnut
Lansing, MI 48933
Phone: (517) 374-1171
Fax: (517) 374-6112
Web site: http://www.mfforum.com

Michigan School Board Leaders Association
Lori Yaklin, Executive Director
3122 Rivershyre Parkway
P.O. Box 608
Davison, MI 48423
Phone: (810) 658-7667
Fax: (810) 658-7557
Web site: http://www.msbla.org

National Heritage Academies
Peter Ruppert, Chairman
989 Spaulding Avenue, SE
Grand Rapids, MI 49546
Phone: (616) 222-1700; (800) 699-9235
Fax: (616) 222-1701
E-mail: jc@superschools.com

TEACH (Toward Educational Accountability and Choice) Michigan
Paul DeWeese, Chairman
Brian Taylor, Executive Director
321 North Pine Street
Lansing, MI 48933
Phone: (517)374-4083; (800) TEACH-MI
Fax: (517) 374-4092
Web site: http://teach-mi.org
E-mail: research@teach-mi.org

Endnotes

1 For sources, see "An Explanation of the State Profile Categories."

2 See Children's Scholarship Fund Web site at *http://www.scholarshipfund.org*.

3 *Ibid.*

4 Michael Cardman, "Michigan: School Vouchers Popular in Newspaper Poll," *Education Daily*, January 21, 2000, p. 2.

Minnesota

State Profile[1]

School Choice Status
- Public school choice: Statewide
- Charter schools: Established 1991
    - Strength of law: Strong
    - Number of charter schools in operation (fall 1999): 57
    - Number of students enrolled in charter schools (1998–1999): 4,899
- Publicly funded private school choice: Income tax credits and deductions
    - Program description: Minnesota offers an education tax deduction of $1,625 per child in grades K–6 and $2,500 per child in grades 7–12 for any education-related expense at a school of choice. For families with annual incomes of $37,500 or less, it provides a refundable tax credit for any education-related expense (except non-public school tuition) of up to $1,000 per child, with a maximum of $2,000 per family. According to the Department of Revenue, 150,000 families claimed the deduction and 38,500 benefited from the credit in 1998.

K–12 Public and Private School Students and Schools
- Public school enrollment (fall 1998) and number of schools (1997–1998): 856,421 in 2,012 schools
- Private school enrollment and number of schools (1997–1998): 90,400 in 580 schools

K–12 Public and Private School Student Academic Performance
NAEP Test Results—percentage of students at each performance level for both public and private schools, with national percentages in parentheses

Performance Level	Reading 4th grade 1998	Reading 8th grade 1998	Math 4th grade 1996	Math 8th grade 1996	Science 8th grade 1996
Advanced	8% (6%)	2% (2%)	3% (2%)	6% (4%)	3% (3%)
Proficient	28 (23)	35 (28)	26 (18)	28 (19)	34 (24)
Basic	33 (31)	44 (41)	47 (42)	41 (38)	35 (33)
Below Basic	31 (39)	19 (28)	24 (38)	25 (39)	28 (40)

- SAT weighted rank (1999): N/A
- ACT weighted rank (1999): 2 out of 26 states

K–12 Public School Expenditures
- Current expenditures (1999–2000): $6,311,575,000
- Amount of revenue from the federal government (1998–1999): 4.5%
- Current per-pupil expenditures (1999–2000): $7,326

K–12 Public School Teachers (1998–1999)

- Number of teachers: 54,035
- Average salary: $39,458
- Students enrolled per teacher: 15.8
- Largest teachers union: Education Minnesota (merged teachers union affiliated with both the NEA and AFT)

Background

Minnesota has led the United States in school choice activity.

Since the 1950s, it has permitted families with children to take a tax deduction for school expenses, even if the children attend a private, parochial, or home school. Deductible expenses include the cost of tuition, transportation, textbooks, and other supplies. The maximum annual deduction for students in the 7th through 12th grades was $1,000 until 1998. In late June 1997, due to the efforts of then-Governor Arne Carlson, a Republican, the legislature approved a school funding bill that increased the current education tax deduction from $650 to $1,625 per child in kindergarten through 6th grade and from $1,000 to $2,500 for children in the 7th through 12th grades. The legislation expands the list of deductible expenses to include academic summer school and camps, tutoring, personal computer hardware, and educational software. It also gives families with annual incomes of $33,500 (this cap was lifted to $37,500 in 1999) or less a refundable education tax credit of $1,000 per child, with a maximum of $2,000 per family. The tax credit applies to all items that qualify for the deduction except tuition. The legislation also expanded the Working Family Tax Credit, which provides an average tax credit increase of $200 to $350 for families making $29,000 or less.

Minnesota also was the first state to permit high school students to enroll in college for dual credit. This program, which began in 1985, allows high school juniors and seniors to take courses at local colleges for both high school and higher education credit. A share of the money allocated for their high school course work follows them to college. To meet the stiff competition posed by the college-run courses, local high schools have doubled their advanced placement (AP) course offerings.

In 1988, Minnesota was the first state to enact statewide open enrollment for all students. All districts are open to any student in the state as long as space is available. The state also offers a "second-chance" program to children who are deficient in basic skills or who have a history of personal or disciplinary problems. A High School Graduation Incentives Program allows these students to attend either a public school or one of several private schools operating under contract with the school districts. Because state revenues follow students, families can select schools designed to deal with their children's specific problems.

In 1991, Minnesota broke new ground by passing the nation's first charter school law, the Charter Schools Act, which permits teachers to create and operate new public schools. Supporters of school choice in Minnesota see this type of institution as one that bridges the gap between public and private schools. The original legislation provided for only eight charter schools; in 1997, however, the legislature lifted the cap on charter schools, allocated a $50,000 start-up fund and lease aids, and authorized private colleges to sponsor charter schools.

Charter schools also now may lease classroom space from religious organizations.

Over half of Minnesota's charter schools target low-income, at-risk, or physically and mentally handicapped students. City Academy in St. Paul—the country's first charter school—was established to meet the growing need for academic programming designed to return alienated young adults to productive and responsible roles within the community. Students typically are between the ages of 16 and 21 and have experienced combinations of academic failure, poverty, chemical dependency, violent or delinquent behavior, and physical or sexual abuse. After five years, City Academy had graduated about 90 percent of its seniors.

A survey of parents of children enrolled in charter schools conducted by the Minnesota House Research Department in 1994 indicated a high degree of satisfaction with charter schools. Most of the parents surveyed listed curriculum and school features as reasons for choosing charter schools. They also liked the smaller classrooms and the school environment. The survey also showed that parents generally were satisfied with the teachers in charter schools and with the positive academic effects on their children.

From 1993 until 1997, the Minneapolis School Board contracted out management of its school system to Public Strategies Group, Inc., a St. Paul-based private consulting firm, to increase the academic achievement of students. The firm managed the district's 80 schools and 14 contracted school programs with a $400 million budget, and was to be paid only if it met specific goals negotiated each year with the city school board. When the contract came to a close at the end of the 1996–1997 school year, PSG had achieved 70 percent of its targeted goals. Since then, achievement has continued to improve.

In January 1998, benefactors Ron and Laurie Eibensteiner pledged $1 million over 10 years to establish the KidsFirst Scholarship Fund of Minnesota, a scholarship fund to enable low-income students in Minneapolis and St. Paul to attend a school of choice. Recipients entering the 1st through 4th grades in the fall of 1998 received 75 percent of their tuition expenses, up to $1,200 per child for three years. For the 1999–2000 school year, the eligibility requirements were expanded to include children living in the entire seven-county metropolitan area. The income ceiling for eligible families was raised to a maximum of $41,125 for a family of four, and scholarships were made available for children in kindergarten through 6th grade. Up to 25 percent of the total scholarships awarded in the 1999–2000 school year were available to children already in private school.

On September 28, 1998, Minneapolis and St. Paul were named two of 40 "partner cities" for the Children's Scholarship Fund (CSF) challenge grant. The CSF is a $100 million foundation underwritten by entrepreneurs Ted Forstmann and John Walton. In partnership with KidsFirst Scholarship Fund of Minnesota, the CSF matches funds raised by residents of Minneapolis and St. Paul to support approximately 1,500 private scholarships for low-income students to attend a school of choice. A lottery in April 1999 determined who would receive the scholarships, which were awarded for four years to children entering kindergarten through 6th grade.[2]

In 1998, Governor Carlson signed into law a bill to create residential academies for disadvantaged children in the 4th through 12th grades. Grants are made to public and public–private cooperating organizations to cover start-up and capital costs. The program is available by choice and can serve up to 900 children.[3]

Developments in 1999

The legislature expanded the state's current education tax credit by raising the household income limit for eligibility from $33,500 to $37,500, thus adding over 30,000 middle-class families to the program. This expansion included a gradual "phase-out" of the tax credit so that families would no longer be penalized for modest increases in their earnings. The 1999 legislation also ensured that all custodial parents are eligible for the tax credit and/or deduction. The state Department of Revenue reported that 38,500 low-income families claimed an education tax credit in 1998 (the first year it was available) and estimated that an additional 150,000 families benefited from the tax deduction.

On May 17, the legislature passed a bill to improve Minnesota's already strong charter law. According to the Washington-based Center for Education Reform, the new law adds $3 million in start-up funds and $6 million in funds to help with leases and other building expenses, and allows cooperatives to sponsor charter schools for the first time.

On April 22, the Children's Scholarship Fund announced the winners of the largest private scholarship program in the country. The recipients were selected randomly by computer-generated lottery. In Minneapolis and St. Paul, 1,000 scholarship recipients were chosen from 4,541 applicants.[4]

Position of the Governor/Composition of State Legislature

Governor Jesse Ventura, a member of the Reform Party, is a strong advocate of public schools. He does not support vouchers[5] but his administration has promoted the current education tax credit and deduction program initiated by former Governor Carlson. The Minnesota House is led by Republicans; the Senate is led by Democrats.

State Contacts

Center for School Change
Hubert Humphrey Institute of Public Affairs
University of Minnesota
Joe Nathan, Director
301 19th Avenue South
Minneapolis, MN 55455
Phone: (612) 625-3506
Fax: (612) 625-6351

Center of the American Experiment
Mitchell B. Pearlstein, President
12 South 6th Street, Suite 1024
Minneapolis, MN 55402
Phone: (612) 338-3605
Fax: (612) 338-3621
Web site: http://www.amexp.org

KidsFirst Scholarship Fund of Minnesota
Ron Eibensteiner, Founder
Margie Lauer, Administrator
1025 Plymouth Building
12 South 6th Street
Minneapolis, MN 55402
Phone: (612) 573-2020
Fax: (612) 573-2021
Web site: http://www.kidsfirstmn.org
E-mail: kids1st@kidsfirstmn.org;
mlauer@visi.com

Minnesota Association of Charter Schools
Steve Dess, Executive Director
1745 University Avenue, Suite 110
St. Paul, MN 55104
Phone: (651) 649-5470
Fax: (651) 649-5472
Web site: http://www.mncharterschools.org
E-mail: stevedess@mncharterschools.org

Minnesota Department of Children, Families, and Learning
1500 Highway 36 West
Roseville, MN 55113
Phone: (651) 582-8700
Fax: (651) 582-8727
Mary S. Pfeifer, Learner Options
E-mail: mary.pfeifer@state.mn.us

Minnesota Family Council
Tom Prichard, Executive Director
2855 Anthony Lane South, Suite 150
Minneapolis, MN 55418-3265
Phone: (618) 789-8811
Fax: (618) 789-8858
Web site: http://www.mfc.org
E-mail: mail@mfc.org

Partnership for Choice in Education
Morgan Brown, Executive Director
46 East 4th Street, Suite 900
St. Paul, MN 55101
Phone: (651) 293-9196
Fax: (651) 293-9285
Web site: http://www.pcemn.org
E-mail: pcemail@pcemn.org

Public Strategies Group, Inc.
Peter Hutchinson, President
275 East 4th Street, Suite 710
St. Paul, MN 55101
Phone: (651) 227-9774
Fax: (651) 292-1482
Web site: http://www.psgrp.com

Republican School Choice Task Force
Ms. Laurie Steinfeldt
480 Cedar Street, Suite 560
St. Paul, MN 55101
Phone: (602) 222-0022

Endnotes

1 For sources, see "An Explanation of the State Profile Categories."

2 See Children's Scholarship Fund Web site at *http://www.scholarshipfund.org.*

3 Jeanne Allen, "Reform News: A Week in Review," Center for Education Reform *Fax Alert*, April 24, 1998.

4 See Children's Scholarship Fund Web site at *http://www.scholarshipfund.org.*

5 Rochelle Olson, "Candidates Push Public Education Proposal," Associated Press, October 11, 1998.

Mississippi

State Profile[1]

School Choice Status
- Public school choice: Limited
- Charter schools: Established 1997
  - Strength of law: Weak
  - Number of charter schools in operation (fall 1999): 1
  - Number of students enrolled in charter schools (1998–1999): 334
- Publicly funded private school choice: N/A

K–12 Public and Private School Students and Schools
- Public school enrollment (fall 1998) and number of schools (1997–1998): 502,379 in 874 schools
- Private school enrollment and number of schools (1997–1998): 54,529 in 212 schools

K–12 Public and Private School Student Academic Performance
NAEP Test Results—percentage of students at each performance level for both public and private schools, with national percentages in parentheses

Performance Level	Reading 4th grade 1998	Reading 8th grade 1998	Math 4th grade 1996	Math 8th grade 1996	Science 8th grade 1996
Advanced	3% (6%)	1% (2%)	0% (2%)	0% (4%)	1% (3%)
Proficient	15 (23)	18 (28)	8 (18)	7 (19)	11 (24)
Basic	30 (31)	42 (41)	34 (42)	29 (38)	27 (33)
Below Basic	52 (39)	39 (28)	58 (38)	64 (39)	61 (40)

- SAT weighted rank (1999): N/A
- ACT weighted rank (1999): 26 out of 26 states

K–12 Public School Expenditures
- Current expenditures (1999–2000): $2,220,349,000
- Amount of revenue from the federal government (1998–1999): 13.8%
- Current per-pupil expenditures (1999–2000): $4,410

K–12 Public School Teachers (1998–1999)
- Number of teachers: 29,939
- Average salary: $29,530
- Students enrolled per teacher: 16.8
- Largest teachers union: NEA

Background

Because school choice was a major issue in the successful 1991 campaign of then-Governor Kirk Fordice, a Republican, he appointed a task force in 1992 to look into options for school reform. Based on the task force report, he proposed a ballot initiative—the People's Right to Initiate Model Education (PRIME) Act—to give the citizens of Mississippi the right to propose changes in school management policies to their local school board. If the board rejects their recommendations, the issue can be submitted (with the requisite number of proper signatures) directly to the voters. The local school board could propose and implement recommendations at the local level. The governor's initiative promoted direct grassroots reform and would have allowed local communities to try different approaches to education; however, the measure was never approved.

The 1997 legislature authorized a pilot charter school program to set up one charter school in each of the five districts and a school in the Delta region. To date, only one charter school has opened.

Since 1995, CEO Metro Jackson has provided private scholarships to disadvantaged students to attend a school of choice.

On September 28, 1998, Jackson was named one of 40 "partner cities" for the Children's Scholarship Fund (CSF) challenge grant. The CSF is a $100 million foundation underwritten by entrepreneurs Ted Forstmann and John Walton. The program matches funds raised by Jackson residents, in conjunction with CEO Metro Jackson, to fund approximately 400 private scholarships for low-income students to attend a school of choice. A lottery in April 1999 determined who would receive the scholarships, which were awarded for at least four years to children entering kindergarten through 8th grade the following year.[2]

Developments in 1999

On April 22, 1999, the Children's Scholarship Fund announced the winners of the largest private scholarship program in the country. The recipients were selected randomly by computer-generated lottery. In Jackson, 325 scholarship recipients were chosen from 4,698 applicants.[3]

Developments in 2000

Two measures to establish a voucher program have been introduced in the state legislature.[4]

Position of the Governor/Composition of State Legislature

Governor Ronnie Musgrove, a Democrat, does not support school vouchers. Both houses of the legislature are led by Democrats.

State Contacts

Children's Scholarship Fund–Jackson
Charles L. Irby, President
Cindy J. Dittus, Executive Director
817 South State Street
P.O. Box 1819
Jackson, MS 39215-1819
Phone: (601) 960-7248
Fax: (601) 960-7231
E-mail: csf@irby.com

Mississippi Family Council
Forest Thigpen, Executive Director
P.O. Box 13514
Jackson, MS 39236
Phone: (601) 969-1200
Fax: (601) 969-1600
E-mail: msfamily@aol.com

Endnotes

1 For sources, see "An Explanation of the State Profile Categories."

2 See Children's Scholarship Fund Web site at *http://www.scholarshipfund.org*.

3 *Ibid.*

4 See Education Commission of the States Web site at *http://www.ecs.org*.

Missouri

State Profile[1]

School Choice Status
- Public school choice: Limited
- Charter schools: Established 1998
  Strength of law: Strong
  Number of charter schools in operation (fall 1999): 15
  Number of students enrolled in charter schools: N/A
- Publicly funded private school choice: N/A

K–12 Public and Private School Students and Schools
- Public school enrollment (fall 1998) and number of schools (1997–1998): 895,304 in 2,194 schools
- Private school enrollment and number of schools (1997–1998): 119,534 in 602 schools

K–12 Public and Private School Student Academic Performance

NAEP Test Results—percentage of students at each performance level for both public and private schools, with national percentages in parentheses

Performance Level	Reading 4th grade 1998	Reading 8th grade 1998	Math 4th grade 1996	Math 8th grade 1996	Science 8th grade 1996
Advanced	5% (6%)	1% (2%)	1% (2%)	2% (4%)	2% (3%)
Proficient	24 (23)	28 (28)	19 (18)	20 (19)	26 (24)
Basic	34 (31)	47 (41)	46 (42)	42 (38)	36 (33)
Below Basic	37 (39)	24 (28)	34 (38)	36 (39)	36 (40)

- SAT weighted rank (1999): N/A
- ACT weighted rank (1999): 6 out of 26 states

K–12 Public School Expenditures
- Current expenditures (1999–2000): $4,761,505 ,000
- Amount of revenue from the federal government (1998–1999): 6.1%
- Current per-pupil expenditures (1999–2000): $5,298

K–12 Public School Teachers (1998–1999)
- Number of teachers: 62,281
- Average salary: $34,746
- Students enrolled per teacher: 14.4
- Largest teachers union: Missouri State Teachers Association (independent teachers organization)

Background

On September 26, 1994, the U.S. Supreme Court agreed, following a decision by U.S. District Court Judge Russell A. Clark, to review for a third time the massive desegregation plan implemented in Kansas City. The Court accepted an appeal brought by the state, which had been forced to bear much of the cost of this plan. The issue was whether a desegregating school district must provide equal educational opportunity and, at the same time, improve student performance and test scores before judicial supervision can be concluded.

In June 1995, in a 5 to 4 decision, the U.S. Supreme Court ruled that equal outcomes are an inappropriate standard. This was a partial victory for the state. The Court did not determine the point at which Judge Clark's supervision of the district should be terminated, only that it should end. Chief Justice William Rehnquist, writing for the majority, "held that, among other things, Judge Clark had exceeded his authority in ordering some kinds of spending."[2] The district court agreed to a settlement proposal that would end state funding for the desegregation effort by 1999 but stopped short of issuing a unitary state declaration. Judge Clark subsequently stepped down from supervision of the case, asking that it be reassigned. The case has been assigned to Judge Dean Whipple.

Subsequently, the Missouri State Board of Education voted to strip the Kansas City school district of its accreditation following the 1999–2000 school year. The school district sought an order from U.S. District Court Judge Dean Whipple preventing the state board from taking the action, but Judge Whipple, in a surprise ruling, rejected the request and dismissed the entire school desegregation case after more than 23 years of court intervention. The school district and the plaintiffs are appealing the district court's ruling to the 8th Circuit Court of Appeals, which overturned Judge Whipple's decision and placed U.S. District Judge Fernando Gaitan in charge of the case.

In January 1998, State Representative Rich Chrismer (R–16) introduced H.B. 1472, the Challenge Scholarships bill, to fund scholarships of $2,500 to $3,000 for children of low-income families whose incomes are up to 200 percent of the poverty line. The scholarships could have been redeemed at a school of choice or for tutoring expenses in kindergarten through 12th grade and applied only to the two areas under desegregation orders, Kansas City and St. Louis. H.B. 1472 failed to pass.

On September 28, 1998, Kansas City and St. Louis were named two of 40 "partner cities" for the Children's Scholarship Fund (CSF) challenge grant. The CSF is a $100 million foundation underwritten by entrepreneurs Ted Forstmann and John Walton. It matches funds raised by residents of Kansas City and St. Louis to fund approximately 1,750 private scholarships for low-income students (1,250 in Kansas City and 500 in St. Louis) to attend a school of choice. A lottery in April 1999 determined who would receive the scholarships, which were awarded for at least four years to children entering kindergarten through 8th grade the following year.[3]

During the 1998 session, the legislature passed a bill that included provisions permitting the establishment of charter schools in the St. Louis and Kansas City school districts. The charters may be operated only by the local school board or a local college or university with an approved teacher education program that meets regional or national standards of accreditation.[4]

Developments in 1999

On April 22, 1999, the Children's Scholarship Fund announced the winners of the largest private scholarship program in the country. The recipients were selected randomly by computer-generated lottery. In Kansas City, 1,250 scholarship recipients were chosen from 11,531 applicants; in St. Louis, 500 recipients were chosen from 9,686 applicants.[5]

Meanwhile, the momentum to give parents choices in their child's education continues to grow. The most exciting developments in Missouri are in the Kansas City area, where 15 charter schools have attracted about 10 percent of the Kansas City School district's enrollment from last year. In addition, many more charter schools are being proposed. In St. Louis, attempts by opponents of charter schools to have Missouri's charter school law invalidated met with an unsuccessful conclusion late in 1999, clearing the way for more charter schools in St. Louis as well as Kansas City.[6]

Developments in 2000

State lawmakers are considering several school choice measures as they seek to respond to the educational problems facing Missouri's two urban school districts, St. Louis and Kansas City. Their efforts are focused on tax relief and incentive initiatives. One popular idea is to offer tax credits to individuals and businesses that make contributions to scholarship charities. Three bills advancing this idea have been pre-filed.[7]

- SB 531, introduced by Senator Harry Wiggins (D–Kansas City), authorizes a state tax credit for contributions to authorized scholarship charities. To qualify as a scholarship charity, the organization must be a 501(c)(3) charitable organization and must allocate at least 90 percent of its annual revenue for educational scholarships to children attending qualified schools. The credit may be claimed, for all taxable years beginning on or after January 1, 2001, in an amount equal to 50 percent of the taxpayer's contribution to the scholarship charity, but cannot exceed $50,000 per taxable year for any taxpayer. The credit is not refundable but may be carried over for up to four succeeding taxable years. The cumulative amount of all scholarship charity tax credits is limited to $5 million per fiscal year. The director of revenue is authorized to allocate the tax credits as necessary to ensure their maximum use.

- SB 592, introduced by Senator Anita Yeckel (R–St. Louis), authorizes, for taxable years beginning on or after January 1, 2000, a state income tax credit for cash contributions, not to exceed $500 per year, to a school tuition organization, defined as a charitable organization that is exempt from federal income tax and that allocates at least 90 percent of its annual revenue for educational scholarships or tuition grants to children. The credit may be carried forward for up to five years but is not allowed if the contribution is part of the taxpayer's itemized deductions on the state income tax return for that taxable year.

- SB 656, introduced by Senator Steve Ehlmann (R–St. Charles), authorizes a state income tax credit for donations to scholarship charities, as determined by the act. A scholarship charity is a tax-exempt charitable organization that allocates at least 90 percent of its annual revenue for scholarships to children to allow them to attend a public or non-discriminatory private elementary or secondary school. The credit is not refundable but may be carried forward and applied to future tax liabilities for up to four years. The total annual amount of credits is limited to $20 million. The Director of the Department of Economic Development shall determine which organizations qualify as scholarship charities. Credits shall be allocated equally at the beginning of each year to all scholarship charities, and those not used by a date determined under rules of the director may be reallocated by the director to ensure that the maximum amount of credits is used each year.

- A tuition deduction plan, introduced by Senator John Schneider (D–Florisant), offers a $2,500 state income tax deduction for high school tuition and other high school expenses. The legislature is also considering H.B. 1373, a pilot voucher program.[8]

A lawsuit by the Missouri School Boards Association challenging the state's charter law was dismissed by a judge in early January 2000.

On February 15, 2000, as many as 750 St. Louis students were given scholarships to escape poorly performing schools. The scholarships, which totaled $3.6 million, were made possible largely by retired St. Louis businessman Eugene Williams and his wife, and by David Farrell, a former chief executive of the May Company Department stores.

Position of the Governor/Composition of State Legislature

Governor Mel Carnahan, a Democrat, opposes school choice. Both houses of the legislature are led by Democrats.

State Contacts

CSF–Kansas City
Carl Herbster, President
4500 Selsa Road
Blue Springs, MO 64015
Phone: (816) 795-8643
Fax: (816) 795-8096

Educational Freedom Foundation
12545 Olive Boulevard, Suite 123
St. Louis, MO 63141
Phone: (314) 434-4171
Fax: (314) 434-4171
Web site: http://www.educational-freedom.org

Gateway Educational Trust
Irene Allen, Executive Director
7716 Forsyth Boulevard
St. Louis, MO 63105
Phone: (314) 721-1375
Fax: (314) 721-1857
E-mail: afer2@aol.com

Elizabeth Lay Midlam Foundation
Christina Holmes, Executive Director
4140 Lindell Boulevard
St. Louis, MO 63108
Phone: (314) 371-0207
Fax: (314) 371-0267
E-mail: stlsupt@impresso.com;
stlsuptsec@impresso.com

Missouri Department of Elementary
and Secondary Education
P.O. Box 480
Jefferson City, MO 65102-0480
Phone: (573) 751-3469
Web site: http://www.dese.state.mo.us

Citizens for Educational Freedom
Mae Duggan, President
9333 Clayton Road
St. Louis, MO 63124
Phone: (314) 997-6361
Fax: (314) 997-6321
Web site: http://www.educational-freedom.org
E-mail: martinmaeduggan@juno.com

Missouri Research Institute
P.O. Box 480018
Kansas City, MO 64148

Parents for School Choice
John Lewis, Chairman
810 South Warson Road
St. Louis, MO 63124-1259
Phone: (314) 993-1255

Endnotes

1   For sources, see "An Explanation of the State Profile Categories."

2   Fax correspondence from Missouri Department of Elementary and Secondary Education, December 22, 1998.

3   See Children's Scholarship Fund Web site at *http://www.scholarshipfund.org.*

4   Angela Dale and David DeSchryver, eds., *The Charter School Workbook: Your Roadmap to the Charter School Movement* (Washington, DC: Center for Education Reform, 1997). Updates available at *http://www.edreform.com/pubs/chglance.htm.*

5   See Children's Scholarship Fund Web site at *http://www.scholarshipfund.org.*

6   Correspondence from Pete Hutchison, Landmark Legal Foundation, January 19, 2000.

7   *Ibid.*

8   See Education Commission of the States Web site at *http://www.ecs.org.*

Montana

State Profile[1]

School Choice Status
- Public school choice: N/A
- Charter schools: N/A
- Publicly funded private school choice: N/A

K–12 Public and Private School Students and Schools
- Public school enrollment (fall 1998) and number of schools (1997–1998): 159,988 in 889 schools
- Private school enrollment and number of schools (1997–1998): 8,341 in 94 schools

K–12 Public and Private School Student Academic Performance

NAEP Test Results—percentage of students at each performance level for both public and private schools, with national percentages in parentheses

Performance Level	Reading 4th grade 1998	Reading 8th grade 1998	Math 4th grade 1996	Math 8th grade 1996	Science 8th grade 1996
Advanced	8% (6%)	2% (2%)	1% (2%)	5% (4%)	3% (3%)
Proficient	29 (23)	36 (28)	21 (18)	27 (19)	38 (24)
Basic	36 (31)	45 (41)	49 (42)	43 (38)	36 (33)
Below Basic	27 (39)	17 (28)	29 (38)	25 (39)	23 (40)

- SAT weighted rank (1999): N/A
- ACT weighted rank (1999): 4 out of 26 states

K–12 Public School Expenditures
- Current expenditures (1999–2000): $978,286,000
- Amount of revenue from the federal government (1998–1999): 10.2%
- Current per-pupil expenditures (1999–2000): $6,213

K–12 Public School Teachers (1998–1999)
- Number of teachers: 10,221
- Average salary: $31,356
- Students enrolled per teacher: 15.7
- Largest teachers union: NEA

Background

A charter school bill, SB 370, was introduced during the 1995 legislative session to authorize the establishment of charter schools through an application to the trustees of a school district. Charters would have been limited to 10 during a fiscal year, restricted to three-year terms, and limited to non-sectarian schools. The bill was passed by the Senate in February 1995 but died in the House Education and Cultural Resources Committee the following month. In 1997, a proposed tuition tax credit bill died on the floor of the legislature. A proposed charter school bill did not make it out of committee.

Developments in 1999

A charter school bill, SB 204, which was introduced by State Senator Tom Keatings (R–5), was tabled in February. The bill would have allowed any person, corporation, or group, including churches, to start a charter school. Charter school employees would have been exempt from the school district's collective bargaining agreements. The bill met with strong opposition in the Senate Education Committee and ultimately died.[2]

Position of the Governor/Composition of State Legislature

Governor Marc F. Racicot, a Republican, believes that school choice is not practical for Montana because of the sparse population in some regions. He has not stated a position on charter schools. Both houses of the legislature are led by Republicans.

State Contact

Montana Conservatives
Robert Natelson, President
1113 Lincolnwood
Missoula, MT 59802
Phone: (406) 721-2266
Fax: (406) 728-2803
E-mail: natelson@montana.com

Endnotes

1   For sources, see "An Explanation of the State Profile Categories."

2   Kathleen McLaughlin, "Foes Say Charter Schools Legislation Dangerous," *The Missoulan*, February 2, 1999, p. A5.

Nebraska

State Profile[1]

School Choice Status
- Public school choice: Statewide
- Charter schools: N/A
- Publicly funded private school choice: N/A

K–12 Public and Private School Students and Schools
- Public school enrollment (fall 1998) and number of schools (1997–1998): 289,981 in 1,353 schools
- Private school enrollment and number of schools (1997–1998): 40,943 in 236 schools

K–12 Public and Private School Student Academic Performance
NAEP Test Results—percentage of students at each performance level for both public and private schools, with national percentages in parentheses

Performance Level	Reading 4th grade 1998	Reading 8th grade 1998	Math 4th grade 1996	Math 8th grade 1996	Science 8th grade 1996
Advanced	n/a	n/a	2% (2%)	5% (4%)	3% (3%)
Proficient	n/a	n/a	22 (18)	26 (19)	32 (24)
Basic	n/a	n/a	46 (42)	45 (38)	36 (33)
Below Basic	n/a	n/a	30 (38)	24 (39)	29 (40)

- SAT weighted rank (1999): N/A
- ACT weighted rank (1999): 5 out of 26 states

K–12 Public School Expenditures
- Current expenditures (1999–2000): $1,711,982,000
- Amount of revenue from the federal government (1998–1999): 4.9%
- Current per-pupil expenditures (1999–2000): $5,870

K–12 Public School Teachers (1998–1999)
- Number of teachers: 20,100
- Average salary: $32,880
- Students enrolled per teacher: 14.4
- Largest teachers union: NEA

Background

In 1989, Nebraska became the fourth state to adopt an open enrollment law permitting parents to choose a school outside their district, subject to space and legal requirements for racial balance. Students are allowed to exercise this transfer option only once in their academic career (unless their family moves). The open enrollment law does not address choice of schools within district boundaries; each district is free to set its own policy. During the 1995 legislative session, a bill was introduced to amend the 1989 open enrollment law and place tougher admission requirements on students with disciplinary problems. It did not pass.

State funds for the transportation of students across district lines are available for all low-income children who qualify for free lunches under the National School Lunch Program. Parents of children who do not qualify must arrange for transportation to the receiving district line, and the receiving district will provide transportation from the district line to the school.

On September 28, 1998, Omaha was named one of 40 "partner cities" for the Children's Scholarship Fund (CSF) challenge grant. The CSF is a $100 million foundation underwritten by entrepreneurs Ted Forstmann and John Walton. It matches funds raised by Omaha residents to fund approximately 500 private scholarships for low-income students to attend a school of choice. A lottery in April 1999 determined who would receive the scholarships, which were awarded for at least four years to children entering kindergarten through 8th grade the following year.[2]

Developments in 1999

State Senator Ardyce Bohlke, who chairs the Education Committee, introduced a voucher bill that would offset education-related expenses for low-income parents. The vouchers, which would be awarded to parents with children in private or parochial school, could be applied to tuition or textbook expenses. The value of the voucher would be based on the child's grade level and family income. Families that earn up to twice the federal poverty level would receive up to $3,000 for a student in grades K–6; up to $4,000 for a student in grades 7–8; and up to $5,000 for a student in grades 9–12. Families earning between two and four times the federal poverty level would receive vouchers for half

these amounts. The program would be capped to those families at or below four times the federal poverty level.[3]

On April 22, 1999, the Children's Scholarship Fund announced the winners of the largest private scholarship program in the country. The recipients were selected randomly by computer-generated lottery. In Omaha, 500 scholarship recipients were chosen from 3,584 applicants.[4]

Position of the Governor/Composition of State Legislature

Governor Mike Johanns, a Republican, supports school choice. He sees vouchers both as an experiment that could help to boost performance and as an intervention strategy for schools that fail to improve their performance.[5] Nebraska has a unicameral nonpartisan legislature.

State Contacts

CSF–Omaha
Patricia Mulcahey, Director
3212 North 60th Street
Omaha, NE 68104-0130
Phone: (402) 554-8493 x219
Fax: (402) 554-8402

Constitutional Heritage Foundation
Richard Thayer
P.O. Box 540787
Omaha, NE 68154-0787
Phone: (402) 334-1214
Fax: (402) 334-1224

Nebraska Department of Education
Phone: (402) 471-2295
Web site: http://nde4.nde.state.ne.us

Endnotes

1 For sources, see "An Explanation of the State Profile Categories."

2 See Children's Scholarship Fund Web site at *http://www.scholarshipfund.org.*

3 The Friedman–Blum *Educational Freedom Report*, No. 70, April 23, 1999.

4 See Children's Scholarship Fund Web site at *http://www.scholarshipfund.org.*

5 See National Governors' Association Web site at *http://www.nga.org.*

Nevada

State Profile[1]

School Choice Status
- Public school choice: Limited
- Charter schools: Established 1997
    - Strength of law: Weak
    - Number of charter schools in operation (fall 1999): 5
    - Number of students enrolled in charter schools (1998–1999): 180
- Publicly funded private school choice: N/A

K–12 Public and Private School Students and Schools
- Public school enrollment (fall 1998) and number of schools (1997–1998): 311,063 in 448 schools
- Private school enrollment and number of schools (1997–1998): 12,847 in 71 schools

K–12 Public and Private School Student Academic Performance
NAEP Test Results—percentage of students at each performance level for both public and private schools, with national percentages in parentheses

Performance Level	Reading 4th grade 1998	Reading 8th grade 1998	Math 4th grade 1996	Math 8th grade 1996	Science 8th grade 1996
Advanced	4% (6%)	1% (2%)	1% (2%)	n/a	n/a
Proficient	17 (23)	23 (28)	13 (18)	n/a	n/a
Basic	32 (31)	45 (41)	43 (42)	n/a	n/a
Below Basic	47 (39)	31 (28)	43 (38)	n/a	n/a

- SAT rank scores rank (1999): N/A
- ACT rank scores rank (1999): 9 out of 26 states

K–12 Public School Expenditures
- Current expenditures (1999–2000): $1,684,435,000
- Amount of revenue from the federal government (1998–1999): 4.4%
- Current per-pupil expenditures (1999–2000): $5,406

K–12 Public School Teachers (1998–1999)
- Number of teachers: 16,653
- Average salary: $38,883
- Students enrolled per teacher: 18.7
- Largest teachers union: NEA

Background

In 1997, the Nevada Senate passed Senate Bill 220, a weak charter school bill to create up to 21 charters statewide, with a cap of no more than 12 per county. SB 220's primary goal is the establishment of charter schools for at-risk students. It authorizes the formation of new charter schools only; existing private schools and certain public schools may not convert to charter schools. The bill would allow two charter schools for every 75,000 students in counties with a population of 400,000 or more; two charter schools in counties with populations of between 100,000 and 400,000; and one charter school in counties with fewer than 100,000 residents. It allows only county school boards to sponsor charter schools and requires that 75 percent of the teachers in a charter school be licensed; the remaining 25 percent may teach if they possess certain skills and must work under the direction of a licensed teacher. Then-Governor Bob Miller, a Democrat, signed this legislation on July 16, 1997.

Developments in 1999

No developments were reported.

Position of the Governor/Composition of State Legislature

Governor Kenny Guinn, a Republican, supports local and parental control of education. He believes that a wider range of options for parents to educate their children will lead to more competitive schools to satisfy their demands. He also supports the establishment of charter schools.[2] The House is led by Democrats; the Senate is led by Republicans.

State Contacts

State of Nevada
Legislative Council Bureau (LCB)
401 South Carson Street
Carson City, NV 89701
Phone: (775) 684-6825

Senator Maurice Washington
P.O. Box 1166
Sparks, NV 89432-1166
Phone: (775) 331-3826

Nevada Policy Research Institute
Judy Cresanta, President
P.O. Box 20312
Reno, NV 89515-0312
Phone: (775) 786-9600
Fax: (775) 786-9604
Web site: http://www.npri.org
E-mail: info@npri.org

Endnotes

1   For sources, see "An Explanation of the State Profile Categories."

2   See National Governors' Association Web site at *http://www.nga.org*.

New Hampshire

State Profile[1]

School Choice Status
- Public school choice: Limited
- Charter schools: Established 1995
    Strength of law: Strong
    Number of charter schools in operation (fall 1999): 0
    Number of students enrolled in charter schools (1998–1999): 0
- Publicly funded private school choice: N/A

K–12 Public and Private School Students and Schools
- Public school enrollment (fall 1998) and number of schools (1997–1998): 203,127 in 513 schools
- Private school enrollment and number of schools (1997–1998): 21,143 in 148 schools

K–12 Public and Private School Student Academic Performance
NAEP Test Results—percentage of students at each performance level for both public and private schools, with national percentages in parentheses

Performance Level	Reading 4th grade 1998	Reading 8th grade 1998	Math 4th grade 1996	Math 8th grade 1996	Science 8th grade 1996
Advanced	7% (6%)	n/a	n/a	n/a	n/a
Proficient	31 (23)	n/a	n/a	n/a	n/a
Basic	37 (31)	n/a	n/a	n/a	n/a
Below Basic	25 (39)	n/a	n/a	n/a	n/a

- SAT weighted rank (1999): 4 out of 24 states and the District of Columbia
- ACT weighted rank (1999): N/A

K–12 Public School Expenditures
- Current expenditures (1999–2000): $1,282,467,000
- Amount of revenue from the federal government (1998–1999): 3.7%
- Current per-pupil expenditures (1999–2000): $6,306

K–12 Public School Teachers (1998–1999)
- Number of teachers: 13,290
- Average salary: $37,405
- Students enrolled per teacher: 15.3
- Largest teachers union: NEA

Background

In 1997, the New Hampshire Supreme Court ruled that varying local property tax rates to fund education is unconstitutional and that the state has a duty to determine educational adequacy and to fund adequacy with a state tax. The court gave the legislature until April 1999 to craft a new school finance system that would be more equitable for all the state's districts. The plan that the legislature produced (after missing the deadline) was rejected by the court in October 1999. A modified property tax plan was agreed upon a month later, but it appears that the issue of school finance is far from settled.

Then-Senator Jim Rubens (R–5) campaigned heavily to allow school districts to control their education choices. Through his efforts on the Senate Education Committee, on May 23, 1995, both houses of the New Hampshire legislature passed the Act Relative to Charter Schools and Open Enrollment. Under the charter school part, two state-certified teachers, 10 parents, or a nonprofit organization may propose a charter school addressing such elements as specialized curriculum needs, academic goals, annual budget, location of facilities, methods of assessment, and other details of operation. Charter schools would be exempt from oversight by both state and local education authorities and would have full authority to oversee their own operations. Provisions that relate to state funding are comparatively weak, however. Each charter school would receive two-thirds of the district's average expenditure per pupil; the remaining one-third would stay in the local public school system.

New Hampshire's charter school law went into effect on July 1, 1995. There is a cap of 35 charter schools for the first five years, and a limit of two charter schools per district. After 2000, the cap on the number of charter schools is eliminated.

The open enrollment provisions of the Rubens bill allow districts to adopt public school choice at their annual school district meetings. The state, which has a tradition of local control, allows each district to decide for itself whether to participate in an open enrollment program.

On June 23, 1997, Governor Jeanne Shaheen, a Democrat, signed a compromise bill, SB 154, amending the state's charter school law. Under this law, the state board may grant no more than 10 charter schools per year until July 2000, when the cap is to be repealed. The location of a new charter school would not need to be determined until the town's ratification vote, and the board of trustees may acquire the property for a charter school before the school is established. The bill also clarified the calculation for providing funding to charter schools; extended by two to three months the submission dates for applications and contracts, school board review, and state board review; and allowed two or more school districts to consolidate their eligible resident pupils into one applicant pool for attendance at a designated charter or open enrollment school, with students to be chosen from this pool by an admissions lottery.

In 1997, a group of legislators drafted HB 2056, which would have enabled school districts to vote on reimbursing parents for public, private, or home schooling tuition costs. A companion bill introduced by Senator Rubens—SB 456, which would have allowed five school districts to authorize school choice—was passed by a vote of 16 to 8 in the Senate but was defeated in the House.

On September 28, 1998, the entire state of New Hampshire was named one of 40 "partner" communities for the Children's Scholarship Fund (CSF) challenge grant. The CSF is a $100 million foundation underwritten by entrepreneurs Ted Forstmann and John Walton. It matches funds raised by New Hampshire residents to fund between 300 and 400 private scholarships for low-income students to attend a school of choice. A lottery in April 1999 determined who would receive the scholarships, which were awarded for at least four years to children entering kindergarten through 8th grade the following year.[2]

Developments in 1999

The state streamlined the approval process for charter schools by cutting the number of steps required for approval from four to two.

The legislature also approved a new state property tax plan to finance schools, but the New Hampshire Supreme Court rejected the plan in October. A modified property tax plan was agreed upon a month later, but it is unclear whether the new plan will meet with the court's approval.

The 1999 School Choice Scholarship Act (HB 633), a school choice bill introduced by Representative Marie Rabideau (R–16), was considered by the House Education Committee. The proposal would provide state-funded scholarships to low- and middle-income families to reimburse them for educational expenditures. Scholarships would be limited to students whose parents make 300 percent of the poverty line or less and who live in districts with schools that score in the bottom one-third on the state assessment tests, or who attend schools that do not meet the state's minimum standards.[3] The bill was approved in the House by a vote of 172–171 on May 20, 1999, but was later defeated by the Senate.

On April 22, 1999, the Children's Scholarship Fund announced the winners of the largest private scholarship program in the country. The recipients were selected randomly by computer-generated lottery. In New Hampshire, 250 scholarship recipients were chosen from 3,086 applicants.[4]

Position of the Governor/Composition of State Legislature

Governor Jeanne Shaheen, a Democrat, opposes vouchers. The House is led by Republicans; the Senate is led by Democrats.

State Contacts

Representative John R. M. Alger
Member, House Education Committee
945 East Rumney Road
Rumney, NH 03266
Phone: (603) 786-9562
Fax: (603) 786-9463
E-mail: john.alger@connriver.net

Josiah Bartlett Center for Public Policy
Daphne A. Kenyon, President
7 South State Street
P.O. Box 897
Concord, NH 03301
Phone: (603) 224-4450
Fax: (603) 224-4329
Web site: http://www.jbartlett.org
E-mail: jbcpp@sprynet.com

Center for Market-Based Education, Inc.
Judy Alger, President
P.O. Box 373
Rumney, NH 03266-0373
Phone: (603) 786-9562
Fax: (603) 786-9463

Children's Scholarship Fund–NH
Karen E. Cabral, Executive Director
P.O. Box 112
Pelham, NH 03076-0112
Phone: (603) 893-0222
Fax: (603) 893-0222
E-mail: csf1nh@aol.com

Citizens' Education Association
Terry Gorham, President
P.O. Box 176
Monroe, NH 03771-0176
Phone: (603) 638-4701
Fax: (603) 638-9336
E-mail: GORHAT@Newnet.com

Ovide M. Lamontagne
Devine, Millimet, & Branch
Victory Park
111 Amhurst Street, Box 719
Manchester, NH 03105
Phone: (603) 695-8516
Fax: (603) 669-8547
E-mail: omlamontagne@dmb.com

Think–NH
11 Laramie Road
Etna, NH 03750
Phone: (603) 643-6059
Fax: (603) 643-0144
E-mail: JimRubens@aol.com

Endnotes

1 For sources, see "An Explanation of the State Profile Categories."

2 See Children's Scholarship Fund Web site at *http://www.scholarshipfund.org*.

3 Correspondence from Jim Rubens, Think New Hampshire, March 9, 1999.

4 See Children's Scholarship Fund Web site at *http://www.scholarshipfund.org*.

New Jersey

State Profile[1]

School Choice Status
- Public school choice: Limited
- Charter schools: Established 1996
    - Strength of law: Strong
    - Number of charter schools: 52
    - Number of students enrolled in charter schools (1998–1999): 4,621
- Publicly funded private school choice: N/A

K–12 Public and Private School Students and Schools
- Public school enrollment (fall 1998) and number of schools (1997–1998): 1,240,874 in 2,313 schools
- Private school enrollment and number of schools (1997–1998): 205,126 in 901 schools

K–12 Public and Private School Student Academic Performance
NAEP Test Results—percentage of students at each performance level for both public and private schools, with national percentages in parentheses

Performance Level	Reading 4th grade 1998	Reading 8th grade 1998	Math 4th grade 1996	Math 8th grade 1996	Science 8th grade 1996
Advanced	n/a	n/a	3% (2%)	n/a	n/a
Proficient	n/a	n/a	22 (18)	n/a	n/a
Basic	n/a	n/a	43 (42)	n/a	n/a
Below Basic	n/a	n/a	32 (38)	n/a	n/a

- SAT weighted rank (1999): 12 out of 24 states and the District of Columbia
- ACT weighted rank (1999): N/A

K–12 Public School Expenditures
- Current expenditures (1999–2000): $12,217,147,000
- Amount of revenue from the federal government (1998–1999): 3.2%
- Current per-pupil expenditures (1999–2000): $9,775

K–12 Public School Teachers (1998–1999)
- Number of teachers: 93,090
- Average salary: $51,193
- Students enrolled per teacher: 13.3
- Largest teachers union: NEA

Background

Some school districts in New Jersey offer inter-district public school choice. Parents are permitted to choose from among the state's schools; if a school is oversubscribed, students are accepted by lottery.

On January 11, 1996, Governor Christine Todd Whitman, a Republican, signed the country's 20th charter school law. Certified teachers, parents, or a combination of teachers and parents may establish a charter school. A charter also may be established by an institution of higher learning or by a private corporation located within New Jersey. Private or religious schools are not eligible to become charter schools. For a public school to be converted to a charter school, 51 percent of the teaching staff at the school and 51 percent of the parents of children attending the school must support the conversion. Charters are granted for an initial four-year period and may be renewed for five-year periods. Charter schools that originally were not public schools are required by law to enroll the lesser of up to 500 pupils or 25 percent of the district's student body. Funding for the charter school equals 90 percent to 100 percent of per-pupil expenditure for the district in which the school is located. Transportation may be provided for students who reside in the district.

Among some of the law's weaker features are provisions relevant to the ability of religious schools to get a charter and the ability of a charter school to adopt its own teacher hiring practices. To gain the support of the New Jersey Education Association, legislators amended the bill to require public schools that become charter schools to hire only government-certified teachers and to guarantee them the same salaries and benefits as other public school teachers. The law took effect immediately after it was signed.

Governor Whitman also issued Executive Order No. 30 to create an Advisory Panel on School Vouchers. The panel, chaired by former Governor Thomas H. Kean, released its report on proposed school voucher legislation on January 3, 1996. The Kean panel found that:

- School tuition vouchers may serve as an appropriate vehicle for education reform because they give parents the ability to select schools and programs that best suit their children's individual educational needs.

- A limited pilot program should be established to allow children residing in an eligible district to attend a participating non-public or public school and pay tuition in full or in part with a tuition voucher.

- The amount of the tuition voucher should be no more than $2,500 for kindergarten through 8th grade and $3,500 for pupils in grades 9 through 12.

- Transportation should be provided for all students accepting a voucher, regardless of whether the charter school lies within or outside the student's residing district.

- A non-public school should be designated by the U.S. Department of Education as currently eligible to receive publicly funded services.

In mid-February 1997, the Lincoln Park School District board approved a plan to permit access by its high school students to other public or private schools. The decision was spurred by parents who, because Lincoln Park had no high school, must send their children to Boonton High School in a neighboring district. The program was challenged by the teachers union and others who alleged violations of the state constitution and statutes (but did not raise federal constitutional issues). Shortly after the State Commissioner of Education decided that the school board lacked the authority to create its school choice plan, there was a school board election in which a slate backed by the teachers union captured three seats formerly held by supporters of the plan. These new members joined two incumbents in voting down the plan 5–4, effectively ending the program and the controversy surrounding it.

On September 28, 1998, Newark was named one of 40 "partner cities" for the Children's Scholarship Fund (CSF) challenge grant. The CSF is a $100 million foundation underwritten by entrepreneurs Ted Forstmann and John Walton. It matches funds raised by Newark residents to fund approximately 1,000 private scholarships for low-income students to attend a school of choice. A lottery in April 1999 determined who would receive the scholarships, which were awarded for at least four years to children entering kindergarten through 8th grade the following year.[2]

The CSF also selected Jersey City as a "partner city" to receive matching donations for private scholarships to help 400 low-income students to attend a school of choice. At least 21,000 students (84 percent of Jersey City's public school students in kindergarten through 8th grade) are eligible for these scholarships. The CSF will join efforts by Jersey City Mayor Bret Schundler and other donors to fund the 200 four-year scholarships.

Developments in 1999

A bill creating a pilot voucher program (A–2320) was introduced in the New Jersey Assembly.[3] It would create a five-year pilot program that would permit one public school in each county to become a choice school. The school would be open to all students, including those from other counties, and district schools would receive $7,200 in state funds for every out-of-town student. If applications exceeded the space available, the school would defer to a lottery to determine which students could attend. An estimated 2,000 students would be enrolled in choice schools by the program's five-year mark, after which the program could be continued, expanded, or dissolved. The bill, however, also would limit the growth of charter schools by capping the number of students a district can lose to choice or charter schools. A compromise exempting all existing and approved charter schools from the cap was added to the final version of the bill, which ultimately failed to pass.

On May 17, 1999, a state appeals court rejected a series of legal claims that could have seriously hindered the growth of charter schools. In five separate rulings, the Appellate Division of the Superior Court dismissed legal challenges brought by public school officials in Highland Park, East Orange, Trenton, Matawan–Aberdeen, and Red Bank. The court rejected arguments that the state's charter schools adversely affect the quality of education, racial balance, and the financial condition of existing public schools. However, numerous bills that would limit the autonomy and funding of charter schools are still pending in the legislature and could loom again next year.

On April 22, 1999, the Children's Scholarship Fund announced the winners of the largest private scholarship program in the country. The recipients were selected randomly by computer-generated lottery. In Newark, 1,000 scholarship recipients were chosen from 9,018 applicants;

in Jersey City and Elizabeth, 400 recipients were chosen from 6,506 applicants.[4]

On November 30, 1999, the New Jersey Department of Education selected 10 school districts to take part in a pilot public school choice program. The program, scheduled to begin in September 2000, will allow the 10 school districts to accept students, tuition free, from any district in the state. The state will reimburse the districts $8,500 for each transfer student. The pilot program is slated to expand to 21 districts over a five-year period.

Developments in 2000

Legislation to establish a five-year tuition voucher pilot program has been introduced in each house.[5]

Position of the Governor/Composition of State Legislature

Governor Christine Todd Whitman, a Republican, campaigned as a strong supporter of full school choice. In 1995, however, concerned with potential budgetary constraints, the governor appointed an advisory panel to study the concept of school choice. Although she favors the panel's recommendations for a pilot voucher program, she has taken no further action. Both houses of the legislature are led by Republicans.

State Contacts

Jersey City Scholarship Fund
Dan Cassidy
Office of the Mayor
280 Grove Street
Jersey City, NJ 07302
Phone: (201) 547-5267
Fax: (201) 547-4288
E-mail: chpo.danielcemail.cityofjerseycity.com

Excellent Education for Everyone, Inc (E3)
Peter R. Denton, Founder
P.O. Box 528
Moorestown, NJ 08057
Phone: (856) 439-9100
Fax: (856) 235-0104
Web site: http://www.e-cubed.org
E-mail: mcardella@dentonvaccum.com

Lincoln Park Education Foundation, Inc.
Patricia A. Gray, Executive Director
9 Garden Street
Lincoln Park, NJ 07035
Phone: (973) 694-2492
Fax: (973) 694-2492

Newark Student–Partner Alliance
Frieda Zaffarese, Program Director
25 James Street
Newark, NJ 07102
Phone: (973) 621-2273
Fax: (973) 621-8120

New Jersey Department of Education
Phone: (609) 292-4469
Scott Mofitt, Office of Innovative Programs
Phone: (609) 292-5850
Fax: (609) 633-9825
Web site: http://www.state.nj.us/njded/
contact.htm

Scholarship Fund for Inner City Children
Kevin Moriarty, Executive Director
171 Clifton Avenue
Newark, NJ 07104-9500
Phone: (973) 497-4279
Fax: (973) 497-4282

Endnotes

1 For sources, see "An Explanation of the State Profile Categories."

2 See Children's Scholarship Fund Web site at *http://www.scholarshipfund.org.*

3 Nancy Parello, "School Choice Plan Advances; Some Districts Express Interest," Associated Press, January 21, 1999.

4 See Children's Scholarship Fund Web site at *http://www.scholarshipfund.org.*

5 See Education Commission of the States Web site at *http://www.ecs.org.*

New Mexico

State Profile[1]

School Choice Status
- Public school choice: Limited
- Charter schools: Established 1993
  - Strength of law: Weak
  - Number of charter schools in operation (winter 2000): 8
  - Number of students enrolled in charter schools (1998–1999): 4,642
- Publicly funded private school choice: N/A

K–12 Public and Private School Students and Schools
- Public school enrollment (fall 1998) and number of schools (1997–1998): 328,753 in 744 schools
- Private school enrollment and number of schools (1997–1998): 19,251 in 182 schools

K–12 Public and Private School Student Academic Performance
NAEP Test Results—percentage of students at each performance level for both public and private schools, with national percentages in parentheses

Performance Level	Reading 4th grade 1998	Reading 8th grade 1998	Math 4th grade 1996	Math 8th grade 1996	Science 8th grade 1996
Advanced	4% (6%)	1% (2%)	1% (2%)	2% (4%)	1% (3%)
Proficient	18 (23)	23 (28)	12 (18)	12 (19)	18 (24)
Basic	30 (31)	46 (41)	38 (42)	37 (38)	30 (33)
Below Basic	48 (39)	30 (28)	49 (38)	49 (39)	51 (40)

- SAT weighted rank (1999): N/A
- ACT weighted rank (1999): 23 out of 26 states

K–12 Public School Expenditures
- Current expenditures (1999–2000): $1,700,366,000
- Amount of revenue from the federal government (1998–1999): 13.2%
- Current per-pupil expenditures (1999–2000): $5,172

K–12 Public School Teachers (1998–1999)
- Number of teachers: 19,897
- Average salary: $32,398
- Students enrolled per teacher: 16.5
- Leading teachers union: NEA

Background

In 1993, New Mexico passed the Charter Schools Act, which authorized the state Board of Education to convert existing public schools in local school districts into charter schools, permit schools to restructure their curricula and encourage different and innovative teaching methods, and allow local school boards to allocate funds to individual schools for site-based budgeting and expenditures. Each charter is granted for a five-year period, after which it must pass a review process in order to be renewed. The original law allowed only five schools in the state to operate as charter schools, and only existing schools were eligible to apply.

The application for a charter requires the support of at least 65 percent of the school's teachers. The state Board of Education is responsible for approving charters, and there is no appeals process for rejected applications. Charter schools are not legally autonomous; they are under the control and authority of the local school boards.

The state Department of Education may contract with private firms to make educational alternatives available to students at risk of dropping out of high school. (Students are considered at risk if they fail three or more classes.)

In 1997, the superintendent of education signed an administrative directive to clarify the Charter Schools Act and the State Board of Education's Regulation 94–1 on Charter Schools. According to the directive, local school board policy will apply to charter schools unless the board decides otherwise. The charter school must have access to the local board to settle disputes with the district, and the district's administration must not deny the charter school's access to the local school board and its meetings.

The district must give a charter school, to the maximum extent possible, all revenue and expenditure information pertinent to the school's budget. The charter school must track revenue and expenditures and negotiate with the local school board to determine the degree of financial control that the school should have over these funding elements. The charter school may not have direct control over the allocation or utilization of transportation and student nutrition resources. Each school could amend its charter, through the State Board of Education, to give it more control over the budget or

to specify its relationship with the local board and school district.

On November 5, 1997, Governor Gary Johnson, a Republican, announced a new program of educational reforms, "For the Children's Sake." One of the components of this program was a comprehensive school choice plan for every child by 2002. Scholarships, phased in over a period of five years, would have been redeemable at a public, private, or religious school of choice. The proposal was not approved, but the governor re-introduced it during the 1999 legislative session.

Developments in 1999

Governor Gary Johnson vetoed the entire state budget twice because it did not include, among other provisions, a voucher plan. The governor advocates a voucher program that would provide 100,000 low-income students of the state's 328,000 schoolchildren vouchers worth approximately $3,000 to attend any public, charter, private, or religious school of choice. The program would first serve low-income students and then gradually expand to include all students within four years.

In an effort to resolve the exclusion of vouchers and tax cuts from the budget, Governor Johnson called a special legislative session. Finally he attempted to compromise with opponents of his voucher initiative by agreeing to a 12-year phase-in of a statewide voucher program. On May 10, the measure was voted down by margins of 50–20 in the House and 29–11 in the Senate. However, the House has agreed to create a task force on education to discuss problems in schools and possible reforms, including vouchers, before next year's legislative session.[2] As a result of the governor's diligence, support for school choice and statewide vouchers for every student has risen 58 percent.

The New Mexico legislature strengthened the state's charter school law by increasing the number of charter schools that may open in the state (currently, 75 new and 25 conversions are permitted).

Position of the Governor/Composition of State Legislature

Governor Gary Johnson, a Republican, is an avid supporter of vouchers and charter schools. He has identified education reform through school vouchers as his highest priority. Both houses of the legislature are led by Democrats.

State Contacts

Greater Educational Opportunities Foundation of New Mexico
Steve Wibarri, Director
803 Malachite Road, SW
Albuquerque, NM 87121
Phone: (505) 836-6533
Fax: (505) 836-6545
E-mail: ulibarrigeo@aol.com

New Mexico Department of Education
Brenda L. Suazo-Giles
Senior Executive Budget Analyst
School Budget and Finance Analysis Unit
300 Don Gaspar Avenue
Santa Fe, NM 87501-2786
Phone: (505) 476-0392
Fax: (505) 827-9931
E-mail: bgiles@sde.state.nm.us

New Mexico Independence Research Institute
Mr. Gene Aldridge, President/CEO
Dr. Harry Messenheimer, Senior Fellow
2401 Nieve Lane
Las Cruces, NM 88005
Phone: (505) 523-8800; (505) 268-2030
Web site: http://www.zianet.com/nmiri
E-mail: gsaldridge@zianet.com; hmessen@nmia.com

Endnotes

1 For sources, see "An Explanation of the State Profile Categories."

2 Loie Fecteau, "Vouchers Fall Flat in Voting: Dems Unanimous in Opposing Bill," *Albuquerque Journal*, May 11, 1999, at *http://www.albuquerquejournal.com/news/xgr99/1legis05-11.htm*.

New York

State Profile[1]

School Choice Status
- Public school choice: Limited
- Charter schools: Established 1998
    - Strength of law: Strong
    - Number of charter schools in operation (winter 2000): 5
    - Number of students enrolled in charter schools (winter 2000): 1,807
- Publicly funded private school choice: N/A

K–12 Public and Private School Students and Schools
- Public school enrollment (fall 1998) and number of schools (1997–1998): 2,838,554 in 4,204 schools
- Private school enrollment and number of schools (1997–1998): 467,520 in 1,924 schools

K–12 Public and Private School Student Academic Performance
NAEP Test Results—percentage of students at each performance level for both public and private schools, with national percentages in parentheses

Performance Level	Reading 4th grade 1998	Reading 8th grade 1998	Math 4th grade 1996	Math 8th grade 1996	Science 8th grade 1996
Advanced	5% (6%)	2% (2%)	2% (2%)	3% (4%)	2% (3%)
Proficient	24 (23)	32 (28)	18 (18)	19 (19)	25 (24)
Basic	33 (31)	44 (41)	44 (42)	39 (38)	30 (33)
Below Basic	38 (39)	22 (28)	36 (38)	39 (39)	43 (40)

- SAT weighted rank (1999): 17 out of 24 states and the District of Columbia
- ACT weighted rank (1999): N/A

K–12 Public School Expenditures
- Current expenditures (1999–2000): $25,440,055,000
- Amount of revenue from the federal government (1998–1999): 6.3%
- Current per-pupil expenditures (1999–2000): $8,924

K–12 Public School Teachers (1998–1999)
- Number of teachers: 201,168
- Average salary: $49,437
- Students enrolled per teacher: 14.1
- Largest teachers union: AFT (also known as New York State United Teachers)

Background

In January 1993, the New York City Board of Education adopted a proposal to broaden public school choice. In September 1993, the city's 700,000 elementary and junior high school students began attending schools outside their districts as long as space was available. This citywide policy applied only to out-of-district transfers; transfer policies within a district varied according to the policy of the receiving district. No provision was made for transportation, which posed a number of problems. Consequently, New York City's best public schools tend to be very crowded.

The state provides transportation to non-public schools as long as students use existing school bus routes.

One school district that gained vast recognition under this plan is East Harlem's District 4. Teachers in Harlem's junior high schools were allowed to redesign or create new schools, and parents were allowed to choose the schools their children would attend. Soon thereafter, reading scores began to soar; the district moved from last place among New York City's 32 school districts in 1973 to 15th in 1987. The plan also attracted white students to the largely minority school district.

A 1997 report by Paul Teske and Mark Schneider of the State University of New York examined the effects of public school choice in District 4 since its inception in 1974.[2] Released in January 1998, the study revealed widespread and significant improvements in the district's math and reading test scores, compared with scores in New York City's remaining 31 community school districts, where choice is not as available. These results stand up to econometric analysis, controlled for such factors as student demographics and district resources. The researchers found a direct correlation between the increase in the number of choice schools in District 4 and increases in math and reading scores. The report also points to a high level of parental satisfaction with the program.

In 1996, Mayor Rudolph Giuliani, a Republican, urged educators and lawmakers to use Catholic schools as models for reform and offered a proposal to allow students who were performing in the bottom 5 percent to attend a religious school. Cardinal John J. O'Connor repeated his offer to implement this proposal at no charge to the city in response to a challenge from Albert

Shanker, then president of the American Federation of Teachers. Faced with fierce opposition from the education establishment, Giuliani's proposal was not implemented. The city's Board of Regents rejected a similar plan by Regent Carlos Carballada to allow children in New York City's 87 failing schools the opportunity to choose a better school.

The city has several privately sponsored private school choice programs. In 1997, and again in 1999, philanthropist Virginia Gilder offered vouchers of up to 90 percent of the cost of private school tuition (up to $2,000 a year) to parents in Albany whose children attended Giffen Memorial Elementary School. Gilder's vouchers, known as "A Brighter Choice Scholarships (ABCS)," could be used for a minimum of three years and a maximum of six years for each student. The rationale for the program was simple: Giffen had the worst pupil performance scores of any school in the region and repeatedly had reported that over 50 percent of its students were not reading at state-set "minimum competency levels." In addition, 96 percent of Giffen Elementary's students were on the federal free-lunch program. By September 1999, more than 20 percent of the student body, including the child of the president of Giffen's Parent Teacher Association, had used the scholarships to attend a private school.

This exodus sent a much-needed wake-up call to Albany public school officials, who immediately took steps to reform Giffen Elementary. Lonnie Palmer, Albany's superintendent of schools, transferred Giffen's principal and replaced her with a new principal and two assistant principals, one of whom was charged specifically with overseeing and boosting academic performance. Palmer began to interview each of the school's teachers and found cause to remove 20 percent of them.

To help bring about faster change, the Albany Urban League provided a $100,000 grant to help Giffen students advance in reading. In 1998, the school scrapped its language arts program and replaced it with "Success for All," a Johns Hopkins University program that boasts particularly high success rates among low-income students.

Elsewhere, in New York City, the School Choice Scholarships Foundation (SCSF) guaranteed $11 million to send 2,200 students to schools of choice in 1997. The vast majority of recipients were from the 14 lowest-performing of the city's 32 school districts, which contain 87 percent of the city's lowest-performing schools. More than 40,000 children applied for scholarships during the foundation's first two years. All students eligible for the $1,400 annual scholarship were in the 1st through 6th grades and qualified for the federal free-lunch program.

According to a report published by Harvard University's Program on Education Policy and Governance and Mathematica Policy Research, Inc., low-income recipients of vouchers from New York's School Choice Scholarships Foundation scored higher on math and reading tests after only one year in the program.[3] Because the scholarships were awarded by lottery, evaluators were able to treat the comparison as a natural randomized experiment in which students were allocated randomly to scholarship and control groups. The study compared scholarship recipients in the 2nd through 5th grades to students with similar backgrounds who had applied for scholarships but did not receive one by lottery. Aggregated differences in test scores between the recipients and the control group for all grades were about two percentile points in both subjects. Among 4th and 5th graders, however, recipients scored four percentile points higher than the control group in reading and six points higher in math.

The study also reveals that parents of scholarship recipients were more satisfied with their children's education and with other aspects of school life than parents in the control group. Half the scholarship users gave their schools an "A" grade, compared with only one-eighth of the control group. More than half the parents of scholarship recipients were very satisfied with the academic quality of their child's new school, compared with one-sixth of the control group. Likewise, 58 percent of the scholarship parents expressed the highest satisfaction with "what's taught in school," compared with 18 percent of the control group.

Almost half the scholarship parents said they were satisfied with school safety, compared with only 22 percent of parents in the control group. Parents of scholarship students were more likely than control group parents to report that the following were not serious problems at their school: student destruction of property, being late for school, missing classes, fighting, cheating, and engaging in racial conflict.

Parent responses showed that scholarship students were asked to do more homework than were students in the control group: 55 percent reported that their child had at least one hour of homework each day, compared with only 36 percent of the control group parents; additionally, 16 percent of the control group parents rated their child's homework as too easy, compared with only 10 percent of the scholarship parents.

These scholarships also helped to reduce the racial isolation of minority students: 18 percent of scholarship parents, compared with only 11 percent of parents in the control group, reported that less than half the students in their child's classroom were of minority background. Conversely, 37 percent of the control group parents said that all the students in the classroom were minority, compared with just 28 percent of the scholarship parents.

On December 18, 1998, after several attempts, the New York State Senate and Assembly passed a strong charter school bill endorsed by Governor George Pataki. The bill allows for the establishment of 100 new charter schools and an unlimited number of conversion charter schools. Per-pupil operating funding follows the child to the charter school. The bill grants considerable autonomy to charter schools, including:[4]

- A blanket waiver of bureaucratic rules, regulations, and laws applicable to public schools, except for health, safety, and civil rights.

- Financial and administrative autonomy from local school districts.

- Freedom from certification requirements for non-instructional personnel, including principals.

- Moderate freedom from certification requirements for teachers. Up to 30 percent of all teachers or five teachers, whichever is less, may be non-certified. This does not include teachers with alternative certification.

- Freedom from state tenure laws and pre-existing collective bargaining agreements and freedom from mandated union representation. Only charter schools with more than 250 students in the first year of operation may be unionized. Ten of the charter schools, regardless of school size, will be exempt from unionization.

- Freedom to choose curriculum, uniform policy, number and length of school days, and school year.

- No provisions relevant to partnerships with private-sector groups and private educational firms.

Charter school accountability provisions in the bill include a five-year charter measured by how well the school performs; oversight by a chartering entity and the Board of Regents; use of exams that are the same as those administered by the state's public schools; and the requirement that students, at a minimum, meet state performance standards.

On September 28, 1988, Buffalo was named one of 40 "partner cities" for the Children's Scholarship Fund (CSF) challenge grant. The CSF matches funds raised by Buffalo residents to fund approximately 400 private scholarships for low-income students to attend a school of choice. A lottery in April 1999 determined who would receive the scholarships, which were awarded for at least four years to children entering kindergarten through 8th grade the following year.[5]

The CSF also selected New York City as a "partner city." At least 587,000 students—72 percent of New York's public school students in kindergarten through 8th grade—are eligible for scholarships. The CSF joined the School Choice Scholarships Foundation to administer the vouchers. The scholarships were awarded by lottery in mid-April 1999.[6]

Developments in 1999

In his State of the City address on January 14, 1999, Mayor Rudolph Giuliani once again proposed a pilot voucher program for New York City. Modeled after Milwaukee's voucher program, the pilot program would experiment with vouchers in one of the city's community school districts to determine whether it should be implemented citywide. The plan would need approval from the Schools Chancellor and the Board of Education, but not the state legislature.[7]

In an effort to appease then-Chancellor Rudy Crew, who threatened to resign if the pilot pro-

gram was funded through the education board, Giuliani offered to fund the $12 million program through the mayor's office. The $12 million will provide vouchers to low-income students over three years in one of the city's 32 community school districts. According to Mayor Giuliani, "we should not be afraid to basically turn the evaluation of schools over to the consumers, the parents and the children."[8] By the beginning of June, however, the mayor had postponed his plan to implement school vouchers in New York City. In a compromise with voucher opponents, he agreed instead to a study of the effectiveness of school vouchers. On December 23,1999, Crew's contract was not renewed, and he declined to serve out his term.

During the spring session, in an effort to encourage New Yorkers to become more involved in education, the Educational Tax Incentives Act was introduced in both the House and the Senate. The act would have offered a credit of up to $500 on state income tax returns for contributions to any private scholarship fund, to public schools, or for the purchase of materials used for home schooling. Although the bill had some bipartisan support, it never reached the floor in either house. Supporters of a tax credit provision introduced a new version during the 2000 legislative session.

On April 22, 1999, the Children's Scholarship Fund announced the winners of the largest private scholarship program in the country. The recipients were selected randomly by computer-generated lottery. In New York City, 2,500 scholarship recipients were chosen from 168,184 applicants, representing nearly 30 percent of the eligible student population; in Buffalo, where the CSF partnered with the BISON Scholarship Fund, 500 recipients were chosen from 5,560 applicants.[9]

On June 16, the State University of New York selected the first eight charter schools in New York State. Of the eight new schools, five will be located in New York City, one on Long Island, and two in upstate New York. Three of the schools began operation in fall 1999, and the remaining five are scheduled to open by fall 2000. On September 30, the State University of New York's Charter Schools Institute, a charter granting entity, received 90 applications to start charter schools in over 40 different communities.

Developments in 2000

A least 10 measures related to school choice have been introduced in the state legislature for 2000.

On January 11, New York Mayor Rudolph Giuliani called on the Board of Education to turn the operation of 10 to 20 of its most troubled schools over to private companies. The mayor, who has called for abolition of the Board of Education, hopes that such a move would force the board to compete with the private sector and do a better job of serving students. New York City currently has 96 of the state's 105 failing schools.

Position of the Governor/Composition of State Legislature

Governor George Pataki, a Republican, supports charter schools and was a major force in the passage of New York's charter school law in 1998. His plan to reduce property taxes for schools would lower school tax burdens for homeowners while maintaining steady funding of the school system. The House is led by Democrats; the Senate is led by Republicans.

State Contacts

Alliance for Parental Involvement in Education
P.O. Box 59
East Chatham, NY 12060
Phone: (518) 392-6900
Web site: www.croton.com/allpie/

American Family Association of New York
Frank Russo, State Director
7 Shoreview Road
Port Washington, NY 11050
Phone: (516) 767-9179
Fax: (516) 944-3544

Archdiocese of New York
James D. Mahoney, Associate Superintendent of Schools
1011 First Avenue
New York, NY 10022-4134
Phone: (212) 371-1000
Fax: (212) 371-1000, ext. 3481

BISON Scholarship Fund
Chris L. Jacobs, President
Cindy MacDonald, Program Director
220 Theater Place
Buffalo, NY 14202
Phone: (716) 854-0869
Fax: (716) 854-0877
Web site: http://www.bisonfund.com
E-mail: bisonfund@compuserve.com

A Brighter Choice Scholarships
Thomas Carroll, President
Susan Morales, Program Administrator
4 Chelsea Place
Clifton Park, NY 12185
Phone: (518) 383-2977
Fax: (518) 383-2841
E-mail: empire@capital.net

Children's Scholarship Fund–New York
Heather Lillian Hamilton, Associate Program Director
7 West 57th Street
New York, NY 10019
Phone: (212) 515-7133
Fax: (212) 750-4252
Web site: http://www.scholarshipfund.org

Empire Foundation for Policy Research
Thomas Carroll, President
4 Chelsea Park, 2nd Floor
Clifton Park, NY 12065
Phone: (518) 383-2877
Fax: (518) 383-2841
E-mail: empire@capital.net

Manhattan Institute
Lawrence Mone, President
Henry Olsen, Center for Civic Innovation
52 Vanderbilt Avenue
New York, NY 10017
Phone: (212) 599-7000
Fax: (212) 599-3494
Web site: http://www.manhattan-institute.org
E-mail: mi@manhattan-institute.org

New York Citizens for a Sound Economy
Michele Isele Mitola
P.O. Box 469
Port Chester, NY 10573
Phone: (914) 939-0067
Fax: (914) 939-0174
Web site: http://www.cse.org/cse
E-mail: nycse@cse.org

New Yorkers for Constitutional Freedoms
Rev. Duane Motley, Executive Director
P.O. Box 107
Spencerport, NY 14559
Phone: (716) 225-2340
Fax: (716) 225-2810
Web site: http://www.nyfrf.org
E-mail: family@cervtech.com

New York State Federation of Catholic School Parents
Marie Dolan, Legislative Chair
149–56 Delaware Avenue
Flushing, NY 11355-1319
Phone: (212) 575-7698
Fax: (212) 575-7669

Operation Exodus Inner City, Inc.
Luis Iza, Director
Caroline Miranda, Administrator
27 West 47th Street, Room 207
New York, NY 10036
Phone: (212) 391-8059
Fax: (212) 391-8077

Parents for School Choice
Jay Cohen
16 Court Street, Suite 1205
Brooklyn, NY 112411
Phone: (718) 596-0119
Fax: (718) 596-5967
Web site: http://www.parentchoice.org

School Choice Scholarships Foundation
1 Penn Plaza
250 West 34th Street
New York, NY 10119
Phone: (212) 333-8711; (800) 310- 5164
Fax: (212) 307-3230; (800) 688-0079
E-mail: scsf@worldnet.att.net

Student/Sponsor Partnership
Jane Martinez, Executive Director
420 Lexington Avenue, Suite 2930
New York, NY 10017
Phone: (212) 986-9575
Fax: (212) 986-9570
E-mail: jane@sspshp.org

Toussaint Institute Fund
Dr. Gail Foster
20 Exchange Place, 41st Floor
New York, NY 10005-3201
Phone: (212) 422-5338
Fax: (212) 422-0615

United New Yorkers for Choice in Education
Timothy Mulhearn, President
P.O. Box 4096
Hempstead, NY 11551-4096
Phone: (516) 292-1224
Fax: (516) 292-1607
E-mail: unyce@earthlink.net

Endnotes

1 For sources, see "An Explanation of the State Profile Categories."

2 Paul Teske, Mark Schneider, Melissa Marschall, and Christine Roch, *Evaluating the Effects of Public School Choice in District 4*, report prepared for the Manhattan Institute, New York, October 28, 1997.

3 Paul E. Peterson, David Myers, and William G. Howell, *An Evaluation of the New York City School Choice Scholarships Program: The First Year*, Harvard University Program on Education Policy and Governance and Mathematica Policy Research, October 28, 1998. See *http://data.fas.harvard.edu/pepg/NewYork-First.htm*.

4 From Gregg Birnbaum, "Senate OKs Charter Schools in 38% Pay-Raise Megadeal," *New York Post*, December 18, 1998, and information from the Empire Foundation.

5 See Children's Scholarship Fund Web site at *http://www.scholarshipfund.org*.

6 *Ibid.*

7 Abby Goodnough, "Mayor Proposes Voucher Experiment in Single School District," *New York Times Regional* on the Web, January 15, 1999.

8 Abby Goodnough, "Giuliani Altering School Voucher Plan," *The New York Times*, April 22, 1999, p. B3.

9 See Children's Scholarship Fund Web site at *http://www.scholarshipfund.org*.

North Carolina

State Profile[1]

School Choice Status

- Public school choice: N/A
- Charter schools: Established 1996
    Strength of law: Strong
    Number of charter schools in operation (fall 1999): 83
    Number of students enrolled in charter schools (1998–1999): 11,442
- Publicly funded private school choice: N/A

K–12 Public and Private School Students and Schools

- Public school enrollment (fall 1998) and number of schools (1997–1998): 1,245,608 in 2,048 schools
- Private school enrollment and number of schools (1997–1998): 88,127 in 550 schools

K–12 Public and Private School Student Academic Performance

NAEP Test Results—percentage of students at each performance level for both public and private schools, with national percentages in parentheses

Performance Level	Reading 4th grade 1998	Reading 8th grade 1998	Math 4th grade 1996	Math 8th grade 1996	Science 8th grade 1996
Advanced	6% (6%)	2% (2%)	2% (2%)	3% (4%)	2% (3%)
Proficient	22 (23)	29 (28)	19 (18)	17 (19)	22 (24)
Basic	34 (31)	45 (41)	43 (42)	36 (38)	32 (33)
Below Basic	38 (39)	24 (28)	36 (38)	44 (39)	44 (40)

- SAT weighted rank (1999): 22 out of 24 states and the District of Columbia
- ACT weighted rank (1999): N/A

K–12 Public School Expenditures

- Current expenditures (1999–2000): $7,636,976,000
- Amount of revenue from the federal government (1998–1999): 7.6%
- Current per-pupil expenditures (1999–2000): $6,042

K–12 Public School Teachers (1998–1999)

- Number of teachers: 78,627
- Average salary: $36,098
- Students enrolled per teacher: 15.8
- Largest teachers union: NEA

Background

In late 1996, the legislature passed a charter school law that requires charter schools to enroll at least 65 students and employ at least three teachers. Charter schools may choose to operate independently of the local board of education; if they do so, however, their employees will not receive state-funded benefits. All charter schools are required to be non-sectarian. Any individual, group, or nonprofit corporation may apply for a charter, and current public schools may convert to charter schools if the conversion has the support of a majority of the school's teachers and a significant number of parents. The number of charter schools is capped at five per district per year, with a maximum of 100 for the state, and each charter has a five-year term. Funding is set at the per-pupil cost for the district in which the school is located.

A provision to allow public school teachers who teach in charter schools to retain their retirement benefits was approved in 1997.

A 1998 survey of North Carolina business executives found that 77 percent strongly support the concept of charter schools and would like to see the state's charter school law broadened. The survey, conducted by the North Carolina Smart Schools Alliance, asked education-related questions of members of the largest statewide business organization, North Carolina Citizens for Business and Industry, and various local chambers of commerce throughout the state. About 72 percent of those surveyed said the state should consider a school successful if at least 90 percent of the students are performing at grade level. Nearly 66 percent favored scholarships or tax credits, and 77 percent said they favored tax deductions for parents who save money for their children's education (education savings accounts).[2]

Although the state does not have a publicly sponsored private school choice program, several private programs offer parents more choice. The Carolina Educational Opportunity Scholarship Fund (affiliated with the North Carolina Education Reform Network) offers scholarships of $1,000 to 200 low-income students in kindergarten through 8th grade who live in Durham, Wake, Forsyth, and Guilford Counties. The scholarships are awarded by lottery to parents whose children qualify for free or reduced price lunches and who can match the additional $1,000 estimated to cover the average private school tuition in those counties.[3]

On September 28, 1998, Charlotte was named one of 40 "partner cities" for the Children's Scholarship Fund (CSF) challenge grant. The CSF is a $100 million foundation underwritten by entrepreneurs Ted Forstmann and John Walton. It matches funds raised by Charlotte residents to fund private scholarships for low-income students to attend a school of choice. A lottery in April 1999 determined who would receive the scholarships, which were awarded for at least four years to children entering kindergarten through 8th grade the following year.[4]

Developments in 1999

On April 22, 1999, the Children's Scholarship Fund announced the winners of the largest private scholarship program in the country. The recipients were selected randomly by computer-generated lottery. In Charlotte, 534 scholarship recipients were chosen from 6,107 applicants.[5]

Position of the Governor/Composition of State Legislature

Governor James B. Hunt, a Democrat, does not support vouchers. He was part of a successful campaign against a 1996 proposed tuition tax credit of $200 for parents sending their children to private schools. Both houses of the legislature are led by Democrats.

State Contacts

Carolina Educational Opportunity Fund
Vernon Robinson, Executive Director
P.O. Box 272
Winston–Salem, NC 27102
Phone: (336) 768-3567
Fax: (336) 765-7655
E-mail: vrobinson@gte.net

CSF–Charlotte
Linda Hunt Williams, Executive Director
756 Tyvola Road, Suite 142
Charlotte, NC 28217
Phone: (704) 527-5437
Fax: (704) 583-2976

John Locke Foundation
John Hood, President
200 West Morgan Street, Suite 200
Raleigh, NC 27601
Phone: (919) 828-3876
Fax: (919) 821-5117
Web site: http://www.johnlocke.org
E-mail: jhood@johnlocke.org

North Carolina Alliance for Smart Schools
Doug Haynes, Executive Director
200 West Morgan Street, #200
Raleigh, NC 27601
Phone: (919) 828-3876
Fax: (919) 821-5117
E-mail: dhaynes@smartschools.org

North Carolina Christian School Association
Dr. Joe Haas, Executive Director
P.O. Box 231
Goldsboro, NC 27533
Phone: (919) 731-4844
Fax: (919) 731-4847
Web site: http://www.nccsa.org
E-mail: 1haas@nccsa.org

North Carolina Department of Public Instruction
Office of the State Superintendent
Education Building
301 North Wilmington Street
Raleigh, NC 27601-2825
Phone: (919) 715-1000
Fax: (919) 715-1278

North Carolina Family Policy Council
Bill Brooks, President
P.O. Box 2567
Raleigh, NC 27602
Phone: (919) 834-4090
Fax: (919) 834-0045

Endnotes

1 For sources, see "An Explanation of the State Profile Categories."

2 North Carolina Alliance for State Schools, press release, December 16, 1998.

3 Kelly Brewington, "Voucher Support Offers Matching Scholarship Plan," *The Herald–Sun*, January 14, 1999, p. C1.

4 See Children's Scholarship Fund Web site at *http://www.scholarshipfund.org*.

5 *Ibid.*

North Dakota

State Profile[1]

School Choice Status
- Public school choice: Statewide
- Charter schools: N/A
- Publicly funded private school choice: N/A

K–12 Public and Private School Students and Schools
- Public school enrollment (fall 1998) and number of schools (1997–1998): 114,597 in 565 schools
- Private school enrollment and number of schools (1997–1998): 7,332 in 60 schools

K–12 Public and Private School Student Academic Performance

NAEP Test Results—percentage of students at each performance level for both public and private schools, with national percentages in parentheses

Performance Level	Reading 4th grade 1998	Reading 8th grade 1998	Math 4th grade 1996	Math 8th grade 1996	Science 8th grade 1996
Advanced	n/a	n/a	2% (2%)	4% (4%)	3% (3%)
Proficient	n/a	n/a	22 (18)	29 (19)	38 (24)
Basic	n/a	n/a	51 (42)	44 (38)	37 (33)
Below Basic	n/a	n/a	25 (38)	23 (39)	22 (40)

- SAT weighted rank (1999): N/A
- ACT weighted rank (1999): 10 out of 26 states

K–12 Public School Expenditures
- Current expenditures (1999–2000): $498,832,000
- Amount of revenue from the federal government (1998–1999): 11.6%
- Current per-pupil expenditures (1999–2000): $4,428

K–12 Public School Teachers (1998–1999)
- Number of teachers: 7,955
- Average salary: $28,976
- Students enrolled per teacher: 14.4
- Largest teachers union: NEA

Background

North Dakota is among the best states on several national academic indicators, as shown in the above table. The legislature increased spending by 4.2 percent in the 2000 biennial budget without calling for any form of school choice in exchange.[2]

Developments in 1999

No developments were reported.

Position of the Governor/Composition of State Legislature

Governor Edward T. Schafer, a Republican, favors forms of public school choice but is opposed to vouchers. Both houses of the legislature are led by Republicans.

State Contact

North Dakota Family Alliance
4007 State Street North, Box 9
Bismarck, ND 58501
Phone: (701) 223-3575
Fax: (701) 223-3675

Endnotes

1   For sources, see "An Explanation of the State Profile Categories."

2   *Education Week, Quality Counts,* Vol. XIX, No. 18 (January 13, 2000), p. 144.

Ohio

State Profile[1]

School Choice Status
- Public school choice: Limited
- Charter schools: Established 1997
    Strength of law: Strong
    Number of charter schools in operation (fall 1999): 48
    Number of students enrolled in charter schools (1998–1999): 2,543
- Publicly funded private school choice: Voucher law in Cleveland since 1995
    Program description: This school choice program awards scholarships of up to $2,250 each to approximately 3,500 low-income children (in 1999–2000) to enable them to attend a K–8 public, private, or religious school of choice. During the 1998–1999 school year, 59 private schools participated in the program. The program is under litigation.

K–12 Public and Private School Students and Schools
- Public school enrollment (fall 1998) and number of schools (1997–1998): 1,842,067 in 3,841 schools
- Private school enrollment and number of schools (1997–1998): 251,543 in 991 schools

K–12 Public and Private School Student Academic Performance
NAEP Test Results—percentage of students at each performance level for both public and private schools, with national percentages in parentheses

Performance Level	Reading 4th grade 1998	Reading 8th grade 1998	Math 4th grade 1996	Math 8th grade 1996	Science 8th grade 1996
Advanced	n/a	n/a	n/a	n/a	n/a
Proficient	n/a	n/a	n/a	n/a	n/a
Basic	n/a	n/a	n/a	n/a	n/a
Below Basic	n/a	n/a	n/a	n/a	n/a

- SAT weighted rank (1999): N/A
- ACT weighted rank (1999): 15 out of 26 states

K–12 Public School Expenditures
- Current expenditures (1999–2000): $12,040,000,000
- Amount of revenue from the federal government (1998–1999): 5.8%
- Current per-pupil expenditures (1999–2000): $6,554

K–12 Public School Teachers (1998–1999)
- Number of teachers: 111,452
- Average salary: $40,566

- Students enrolled per teacher: 16.5
- Largest teachers union: NEA

Background

In 1990, Ohio became the fifth state to enact statewide open enrollment. Under the law, schools are required to accept students from within their district as long as space is available. Students may transfer between districts, with the state's share of funding following them to their new school; but districts can opt out of this program. Ohio also offers post-secondary enrollment options. High school students may enroll in college courses at nearby universities and community colleges.

Ohio is home to the nation's first publicly funded private school choice program that includes religious schools. On June 30, 1995, then-Governor George Voinovich, a Republican, signed a two-year budget package that created a $5 million pilot voucher program in Cleveland, where it was championed by Councilwoman Fannie Lewis (D). The Cleveland Pilot Project Scholarship Program, implementation of which began in September 1996, initially allowed the parents of 2,000 Cleveland elementary school students to use vouchers for tuition at a public, private, or religious school of choice.

The governor's Cleveland voucher plan offered:

- Broad eligibility for any student residing in the Cleveland city district and enrolled in kindergarten through 3rd grade.

- Broad eligibility for any state-chartered private school, whether religiously affiliated or non-religious.

- A scholarship of up to $2,500. Low-income students whose family income is below 200 percent of the poverty line would receive vouchers worth 90 percent of private school tuition cost or $2,250, whichever is less. All other students would receive vouchers worth 75 percent of tuition. Each year, a grade level would be added to the eligibility roll, up to and including the 8th grade.

- The opportunity for Cleveland's public schools to keep up to 55 percent of state aid per pupil each time a child took advantage of a voucher, even if parents accepted the maximum voucher amount—worth 45

percent of state aid, or $2,500—to spend on private school tuition.

The program took effect for the 1996–1997 school year. More than 6,800 parents applied for vouchers, and about 1,855 children were able to participate in the first year of the two-year pilot program. As of September 1999, nearly 3,500 students—approximately 5 percent of the public school enrollment—were using vouchers.

In January 1996, the American Federation of Teachers filed a lawsuit challenging the constitutionality of the Cleveland school choice plan and asking for an injunction. On July 31, 1996, Franklin County Common Pleas Judge Lisa Sadler ruled that the legislatively approved Cleveland plan violates neither Ohio's constitution nor the U.S. Constitution. She noted that the religion clauses of Ohio's constitution are no more restrictive than the First Amendment and that, because the "nonpublic sectarian schools participating in the scholarship program are benefited only indirectly, and purely as the result of the genuinely independent and private choices of aid recipients," including religious schools in a voucher program does not violate the First Amendment.

On May 1, 1997, however, by a vote of 3 to 0, the Ohio Court of Appeals struck down the Cleveland Pilot Scholarship Program, overturning Judge Sadler's decision. The court ruled that the program violated the religious establishment clauses of both constitutions, as well as a provision in Ohio's constitution requiring that general laws have statewide application.

Following this decision, the Ohio Supreme Court granted a motion to stay on July 24, 1997. This allowed the Cleveland scholarship program to continue operating while the appeals process proceeded. (See Developments in 1999 for update.)

Meanwhile, a fall 1997 study by Jay Greene of the University of Texas at Austin, William Howell of Stanford University, and Paul Peterson of Harvard University found that 63 percent of parents using the scholarships were "very satisfied" with the "academic quality" of their schools, whereas only 30 percent of those who applied but did not receive a voucher were happy with their public schools.[2]

In 1997, the legislature approved a provision in Governor Voinovich's budget to set up a pilot charter school program in Lucas County (in the Toledo area) and to allow conversions of public schools to charter schools throughout the state.

In May 1998, an amendment to the Cleveland voucher legislation by Representative Mike Wise (R–15) to require that the Cleveland School District provide transportation to students in the Cleveland scholarship program was approved by both houses of the legislature.[3] This measure significantly decreased the number of students who had to rely on taxicabs to get to a school of choice. For example, during the 1997–1998 school year, 565 of the 2,938 students enrolled took the yellow school buses to schools, while 1,084 were transported to school by taxi. However, during the 1998–1999 school year, 1,853 of the 3,744 students enrolled took the yellow school buses, while only 95 were transported to school by taxi.[4]

On September 28, 1998, Dayton, Toledo, and Cincinnati were named three of 40 "partner cities" for the Children's Scholarship Fund (CSF) challenge grant. The CSF is a $100 million foundation underwritten by entrepreneurs Ted Forstmann and John Walton. It matches funds raised by Dayton, Toledo, and Cincinnati residents to fund approximately 1,500 private scholarships for low-income students (750 in Dayton, 500 in Toledo, and 250 in Cincinnati) to attend a school of choice. A lottery in April 1999 determined who would receive the scholarships, which were awarded for at least four years to children entering kindergarten through 8th grade the following year. In Dayton, the CSF partnered with the city's existing private choice program, PACE, which expanded to serve at least 900 students in 1999–2000.[5]

Developments in 1999

On April 22, 1999, the Children's Scholarship Fund announced the winners of the largest private scholarship program in the country. The recipients were selected randomly by computer-generated lottery. In Dayton, 750 scholarship recipients were chosen from 5,824 applicants; in Toledo, 500 recipients were chosen from 6,606 applicants; in Cincinnati, 500 recipients were chosen from 12,468 applicants.[6]

A study released in September 1999 by Dr. Kim Metcalf of Indiana University finds that the Cleveland school choice program is beginning to reach its objectives.[7] Specifically:

- Scholarship students show a small but statistically significant improvement of achievement scores in two of five areas (language and science).

- The program effectively serves the population of families and children for which it was intended and developed.

- The majority of the children who participate in the program are unlikely to have enrolled in a private school without a scholarship.

- Scholarship parents' perceptions of and satisfaction with their children's schools are substantially improved.

- Among parents, the two most important factors for considering a new school are quality of education and safety.

On May 27, 1999, in the case *Simmons–Harris* v. *Goff*, the Ohio Supreme Court struck down (5–2) the Cleveland Scholarship and Tuitioning Program on procedural grounds. The court, however, emphasized in a separate ruling (4–0) that the program did not violate the First Amendment. The ruling notes that "whatever link between government and religion is created by the school voucher program is indirect, depending only on the genuinely independent and private choices of individual parents." The legislature was found to have violated a state constitutional requirement for "one-subject" legislative bills when it approved the Cleveland choice program as part of an appropriations bill. The ruling allowed the program to continue until the end of the school year and gave the legislature the opportunity to reauthorize the scholarship plan in a one-subject bill.[8]

On June 24, 1999, the legislature approved a two-year $17.2 billion state education budget that includes a provision reviving the Cleveland scholarship program. This new measure was signed into law on June 29.[9] Soon after the law had been passed, the Ohio Education Association, American Civil Liberties Union, and People for the American Way filed suit in federal court, challenging the program on First Amendment grounds and seeking a preliminary injunction (even though the Ohio Supreme Court had rejected an identical claim the previous year). On August 24, Federal Judge Solomon Oliver ruled that the Cleveland program was unconstitutional and granted a preliminary injunction because most parents were using the vouchers to send their children to religious schools. The ruling, handed down as the school year was about to begin, caused a huge public outcry and left some 3,800 voucher recipients scrambling to find appropriate public schools.

Judge Oliver modified his ruling several days later to allow current voucher recipients to remain in the program for one semester until a ruling on the program's constitutionality is handed down. On November 5, the U.S. Supreme Court granted a stay of an injunction against the Cleveland school choice program; but on December 20, Judge Oliver ruled that the program constitutes a form of "government-supported religious indoctrination" and therefore is unconstitutional. Judge Oliver based his ruling on the fact that 46 out of the 56 schools participating in the program are religious schools, arguing that this denied parents a "genuine choice" between religious and non-religious schools. This decision has been appealed to the U.S. Court of Appeals for the 6th Circuit. In the meantime the parties on both sides of the case have agreed to allow the 3,500 students in the program to remain in their schools until a final decision is reached.

Meanwhile, a June 1999 survey by Harvard University's John F. Kennedy School of Government, conducted by Paul Peterson, reveals that parents participating in Cleveland's voucher program are more satisfied with many aspects of the schools they chose than are parents with children still in public schools. Nearly half of all parents were "very satisfied," compared with less than 30 percent of public school parents. The study also reveals that voucher parents were much more satisfied with issues of discipline and safety at their schools than public school parents. The researchers surveyed 505 parents of students who received vouchers through the Cleveland Scholarship Program and 327 parents of students in Cleveland public schools.[10]

In addition, a study released on November 17, 1999, by the Columbus-based Buckeye Institute argues that school choice in Cleveland has provided better racial integration than the Cleveland public school system. The study, conducted by Dr. Jay P. Greene, research associate at Harvard University's Program on Education Policy and Governance and associate professor of government at the University of Texas, Austin, finds that 19 percent of Cleveland's voucher recipients attend private schools with a racial composition that resembles the average racial composition of the Cleveland area. Only 5.2 percent of Cleveland public school students are educated in comparably integrated schools. Furthermore, 61 percent of public school students attend schools that have almost entirely white or minority populations. Only 50 percent of voucher-receiving students are educated in a homogenous environment.

Developments in 2000

A new study of Dayton's PACE private scholarship program by Paul Peterson, Director of the Program on Education Policy and Governance at Harvard, William Howell of Stanford University, and Patrick Wolf of Georgetown University shows that African–American students in the program in grades 2–8 scored, on average, nearly seven percentile points higher in math than those who did not receive scholarships.[11]

Position of the Governor/Composition of State Legislature

Governor Robert Taft, a Republican, favors both public school choice and the use of vouchers. He supports Cleveland's voucher program and wants to expand the reach of Ohio's charter school system. Both houses of the legislature are led by Republicans.

State Contacts

Buckeye Institute for Public Policy Solutions
Rich Leonardi, President
4100 North High Street, Suite 200
Columbus, OH 43214
Phone: (614) 262-1593
Fax: (614) 262-1927
E-mail: buckeye@buckeinstitute.org

CSF–Greater Cincinnati
Lisa Claytor, Administrator
P.O. Box 361
33 West Walnut Street
Oxford, OH 45056
Phone: (513) 523-3816 or (888) 332-2408
Fax: (513) 984-2684

CSF–Toledo
Diocese of Toledo
Ricardo "Ric" Cervantes
1933 Spielbusch
Toledo, OH 43624
Phone: (419) 244-6711, ext. 375
Fax: (419) 255-8269

Governor's Commission on Educational Choice
David Brennan, Chairman
159 South Main Street, 6th Floor
Akron, OH 44308
Phone: (330) 996-0202
Fax: (330) 762-3938

Hope for Ohio's Children
Nancy Brennan
159 South Main Street
Akron, OH 44308
Phone: (330) 535-6868

Honorable Fannie Lewis
Councilwoman
601 Lakeside Avenue, #220
Cleveland, OH 44114
Phone: (216) 229-4277
Fax: (216) 229-4278

Ohio Department of Education
65 South Front Street
Columbus, OH 43215
Phone: (614) 466-3641
Web site: http://www.ode.ohio.us/

Ohio Roundtable–Freedom Forum
The School Choice Committee
David Zanotti, Chairman
Patty Hollo, Executive Director
Bert Holt, Co-Chairman
31005 Solon Road
Solon, OH 44139
Phone: (440) 349-3393
Fax: (440) 349-0154

Parents Advancing Choice in Education (PACE)
Theodore J. Wallace, Executive Director
110 North Main Street, Suite 1360
Dayton, OH 45402
Phone: (937) 264-4800
E-mail: twallace@erinet.com

Endnotes

1 For sources, see "An Explanation of the State Profile Categories."

2 The research can be found on the Internet at *http://www.data.fas.harvard.edu/pepg/*.

3 The Blum Center's *Educational Freedom Report*, No. 60, June 19, 1998.

4 *Ibid.*

5 See Children's Scholarship Fund Web site at *http://www.scholarshipfund.org*.

6 *Ibid.*

7 Dr. Kim Metcalf, "Evaluation of the Cleveland Scholarship and Tutoring Grant Program, 1996–99," Indiana Center for Evaluation, Indiana University, September 1999.

8 The Friedman–Blum *Educational Freedom Report*, No. 72, June 18, 1999.

9 The Friedman–Blum *Educational Freedom Report*, No. 73, July 23, 1999.

10 See Harvard University Web site at *http://data.fas.harvard.edu/pepg/*.

11 *Ibid.*

Oklahoma

State Profile[1]

School Choice Status
- Public school choice: Statewide
- Charter schools: Established 1999
    Strength of law: Strong
    Number of charter schools in operation (fall 1999): 0
    Number of students enrolled in charter schools: 0
- Publicly funded private school choice: N/A

K–12 Public and Private School Students and Schools
- Public school enrollment (fall 1998) and number of schools (1997–1998): 628,510 in 1,818 schools
- Private school enrollment and number of schools (1997–1998): 27,675 in 177 schools

K–12 Public and Private School Student Academic Performance
NAEP Test Results—percentage of students at each performance level for both public and private schools, with national percentages in parentheses

Performance Level	Reading 4th grade 1998	Reading 8th grade 1998	Math 4th grade 1996	Math 8th grade 1996	Science 8th grade 1996
Advanced	5% (6%)	1% (2%)	n/a	n/a	n/a
Proficient	25 (23)	28 (28)	n/a	n/a	n/a
Basic	36 (31)	51 (41)	n/a	n/a	n/a
Below Basic	34 (39)	20 (28)	n/a	n/a	n/a

- SAT weighted rank (1999): N/A
- ACT weighted rank (1999): 18 out of 26 states

K–12 Public School Expenditures
- Current expenditures (1999–2000): $3,311,591,000
- Amount of revenue from the federal government (1998–1999): 8.9%
- Current per-pupil expenditures (1999–2000): $5,266

K–12 Public School Teachers (1998–1999)
- Number of teachers: 40,559
- Average salary: $31,149
- Students enrolled per teacher: 15.5
- Largest teachers union: NEA

Background

In 1995, S.J.R. No. 17 was reintroduced to amend the state constitution to allow scholarships for children in elementary and secondary public or private schools. Under this bill, the legislature would have been authorized to develop a funding system that compiled all school operational funds into a single K–12 account, and the state treasurer would have determined appropriate scholarship amounts that were equal to or less than the state's per-pupil expenditure for parents who choose to send their children to public schools and 50 percent to 70 percent of that amount for parents who choose private schools. The bill was defeated. Despite several attempts, publicly funded private school choice programs have not succeeded in the state.

Developments in 1999

In June, the legislature passed the Oklahoma Charter Schools Act, making Oklahoma the 36th state to pass a charter school law. The law allows local school boards and vocational community colleges to charter public schools. It also allows charter schools to be chartered in school districts with 5,000 or more students (mainly Oklahoma City, Tulsa, and their surrounding communities and suburbs) and to have the option of collective bargaining.

The bill also included the Education Open Transfer Act, which allows inter-district public school choice.

Position of the Governor/Composition of State Legislature

Governor Frank Keating, a Republican, supports both public and private school choice. Both houses of the legislature are led by Democrats.

State Contacts

Committee for Oklahoma Educational Reform (COER)
John Hyde
7320 Rumsey Road
Oklahoma City, OK 73132-5331
Phone: (405) 721-4899
Web site: http://www.shaxberd.com/coer/
E-mail: jkhyd@cs.com

Oklahoma Christian Coalition
Kenneth Wood, Executive Director
5900 Mosteller Drive
Suite 1512, Founders Tower
Oklahoma City, OK 73112-4605
Phone: (405) 840-2156
Fax: (405) 840-2157

Oklahoma Council of Public Affairs
Brett Magbee, Executive Director
100 West Wilshire Boulevard, Suite C3
Oklahoma City, OK 73116
Phone: (405) 843-9212
Fax: (405) 843-9436
Web site: http://www.ocpathink.org

Oklahoma Family Policy Council
Mike Jestes, Executive Director
3908 North Peniel Avenue, Suite 100
Bethany, OK 73008-3458
Phone: (405) 787-7744
Fax: (405) 787-3900
E-mail: OKFamilyPC@aol.com

Oklahoma Scholarship Fund
Della Witter, Executive Director
3030 NW Expressway, Suite 1313
Oklahoma City, OK 73112
Phone: (405) 942-5489
Fax: (405) 947-4403
E-mail: dwitter@betterdays.org

Oklahoma State Department of Education
2500 North Lincoln Boulevard
Oklahoma City, OK 73105-4599
Phone: (405) 521-3333
Fax: (405) 521-6205
Web site: http://www.sde.state.ok.us/

Endnote

1 For sources, see "An Explanation of the State Profile Categories."

Oregon

State Profile[1]

School Choice Status
- Public school choice: Limited
- Charter schools: Established 1999
    Strength of law: Strong
    Number of charter schools in operation (fall 1999): 2
    Number of students enrolled in charter schools (fall 1999): 80
- Publicly funded private school choice: N/A

K–12 Public and Private School Students and Schools
- Public school enrollment (fall 1998) and number of schools (1997–1998): 542,809 in 1,252 schools
- Private school enrollment and number of schools (1997–1998): 44,290 in 327 schools

K–12 Public and Private School Student Academic Performance
NAEP Test Results—percentage of students at each performance level for both public and private schools, with national percentages in parentheses

Performance Level	Reading 4th grade 1998	Reading 8th grade 1998	Math 4th grade 1996	Math 8th grade 1996	Science 8th grade 1996
Advanced	5% (6%)	2% (2%)	2% (2%)	4% (4%)	3% (3%)
Proficient	23 (23)	31 (28)	19 (18)	22 (19)	29 (24)
Basic	33 (31)	45 (41)	44 (42)	41 (38)	36 (33)
Below Basic	39 (39)	22 (28)	35 (38)	33 (39)	32 (40)

- SAT weighted rank (1999): 2 out of 24 states and the District of Columbia
- ACT weighted rank (1999): N/A

K–12 Public School Expenditures
- Current expenditures (1999–2000): $3,626,160,000
- Amount of revenue from the federal government (1998–1999): 6.7%
- Current per-pupil expenditures (1999–2000): $6,641

K–12 Public School Teachers (1998–1999)
- Number of teachers: 29,317
- Average salary: $42,833
- Students enrolled per teacher: 18.5
- Largest teachers union: NEA

Background

A 1991 law contains two provisions for public school choice. The first permits parents of children who have not made progress at any grade level for at least one year to choose another school, provided the receiving school accepts the student. The second creates a 10th grade Certificate of Initial Mastery to indicate the attainment of a certain level of basic skills. A student earning this certificate may attend any public school or state community college to pursue vocational or college preparatory course work.

Several attempts to pass choice through the initiative and referendum process have failed. In 1990, the voters of Oregon rejected a ballot initiative introduced by Oregonians for School Choice, a grassroots parents' organization. The initiative, known as Measure 11, would have given parents a refundable tax credit worth up to $2,500 to send their children to the public or private school of choice or to pay for home schooling. Although the initiative was defeated by a 2–1 margin, the campaign galvanized a grassroots coalition promoting school choice.

In 1997, the Oregon School Choice Task Force spearheaded another proposal, which would have allowed state funding to go directly to parents to send their children to public, private, or religious schools of choice. The bill never cleared the House Education Committee. The task force also drafted a constitutional amendment to allow a tuition tax credit.

On September 28, 1998, Portland was named one of 40 "partner cities" for the Children's Scholarship Fund (CSF) challenge grant. The CSF is a $100 million foundation underwritten by entrepreneurs Ted Forstmann and John Walton. It matches funds raised by Portland residents to fund approximately 500 private scholarships for low-income students to attend a school of choice. A lottery in April 1999 determined who would receive the scholarships, which were awarded for at least four years to children entering kindergarten through 8th grade the following year.[2]

Developments in 1999

The Oregon House Education Committee approved H.B. 2597–2, which would have granted a $250 tax credit for contributions to K–12 public or private school scholarship foundations. However, the bill died in the House Revenue Committee. Supporters of school choice have filed an Arizona-like education tax credit initiative that they hope to place on the November 2000 ballot.

S.B. 100, a charter school bill, was signed into law by the governor on May 29, 1999.[3] According to James Spady, co-founder of the Education Excellence Coalition,[4] the bill allows charters—which must be nonprofit, 501(C)(3) public charities—to be fully autonomous. It allows an unlimited number of charters, but no more than 10 percent of the students in any district may attend a charter school (this restriction will be eliminated on January 1, 2003). The law also allows conversion of existing public schools with the consent of the local school board, as well as appeal and alternative sponsorship. Denials of charter applications may be appealed to the state board of education, the members of which are appointed by the governor. If the state board is unable to mediate the dispute, it may then grant the application and assume sponsorship of the charter school itself. If the state school board denies the application, the applicant may seek judicial review.

In addition, S.B. 100 allows charter schools to become separate bargaining units and permits charter school teachers to choose the same union, a new union, or no union. It also requires annual financial audits and sponsor site visits.

The law asks districts to pay charter schools their share of state funding within 10 days of the district's receipt of the funds from the state; allows charter schools to hire the most qualified teachers available, regardless of certification, as long as at least 50 percent of the faculty hold certificates; and allows a charter school to contract with a for-profit corporation (for example, a for-profit charter management company like the Edison Project) to operate the school. Finally, the law offers "performance-based" charter schools blanket waivers from most of the "compliance-based" Oregon Education Code, except those provisions directly related to health, safety, civil rights, public records, public meetings, and academic standards and testing. The law gives the state board of education the power to waive any requirement of the act if the board determines that the waiver would (among other things) "enhance the equitable access by under-served families to the public education of their choice."

Charter schools may not assume responsibility for a child's special education needs without permission from the child's school district. However, if the parents of special needs children enroll their children in a charter school, the child's school district retains the financial responsibility for providing all required special education services, unless the district specifically contracts with the charter school or some other service provider to assume that responsibility.

On April 22, 1999, the Children's Scholarship Fund announced the winners of the largest private scholarship program in the country. The recipients were selected randomly by computer-generated lottery. In Portland, 500 scholarship recipients were chosen from 6,639 applicants.[5]

Position of the Governor/Composition of State Legislature

Governor John A. Kitzhaber, a Democrat, supports charter schools. He is opposed to vouchers and tax credits. Both houses of the legislature are led by Republicans.

State Contacts

Cascade Policy Institute
Steve Buckstein, President
813 SW Alder, Suite 450
Portland, OR 97205
Phone: (503) 242-0900
Fax: (503) 242-3822
Web site: http://www.CascadePolicy.org
E-mail: steve@CascadePolicy.org

Children's Scholarship Fund–Portland
Tamar Hare, Executive Director
813 SW Alder, Suite 450
Portland, OR 97224
Phone: (503) 242-0900, ext. 15
Fax: (503) 242-3822
Web site: http://www.CascadePolicy.org/csf/enrolled.htm
E-mail: csf@CascadePolicy.org

Oregon Department of Education
255 Capitol Street, NE
Salem, OR 97310-0203
Phone: (503) 378-3569
Web site: http://www.ode.state.or.us/

Oregon Education Consumers Association (OECA)
171 NE 102nd Avenue
Portland, OR 97220
Phone: (503) 252-4999
Fax: (503) 252-4866
Web site: http://www.oregoneducation.org
E-mail: rob@oregoneducation.org

Oregon Charter School Service Center
171 NE 102nd Avenue
Portland, OR 97220
Phone: (503) 252-4999
Fax: (503) 252-4866
Web site: http://www.oregoncharters.org
E-mail: rob@oregoneducation.org

TAG Parent Network
Monique Lloyd
32870 Lake Creek Drive
Halsey, OR 97348
Phone: (541) 369-2515

School Choice Task Force
Lowell Smith, Ph.D., Chairman
1630 Hillwood Court South
Salem, OR 97302-3621
Phone: (503) 363-0899
Fax: (503) 585-4818
E-mail: lowellsmth@aol.com

Spencer Schock for State Superintendent
20310 Empire Avenue, Suite A–110
Bend, OR 97701
Phone: (541) 388-8229
Fax: (541) 388-8543
E-mail: schock@empnet.com

Endnotes

1   For sources, see "An Explanation of the State Profile Categories." Charter school data provided by the Cascade Institute.

2   See Children's Scholarship Fund Web site at *http://www.scholarshipfund.org*.

3   See Oregon Department of Education Web site at *http://www.Oregoncharters.org*.

4   E-mail memorandum from James Spady, May 20, 1999.

5   See Children's Scholarship Fund Web site at *http://www.scholarshipfund.org*.

Pennsylvania

State Profile[1]

School Choice Status
- Public school choice: N/A
- Charter schools: Established 1997
    Strength of law: Strong
    Number of charter schools in operation (fall 1999): 45
    Number of students enrolled in charter schools (1998–1999): 6,104
- Publicly funded private school choice: N/A

K–12 Public and Private School Students and Schools
- Public school enrollment (fall 1998) and number of schools (1997–1998): 1,816,566 in 3,115 schools
- Private school enrollment and number of schools (1997–1998): 343,191 in 1,989 schools

K–12 Public and Private School Student Academic Performance
NAEP Test Results—percentage of students at each performance level for both public and private schools, with national percentages in parentheses

Performance Level	Reading 4th grade 1998	Reading 8th grade 1998	Math 4th grade 1996	Math 8th grade 1996	Science 8th grade 1996
Advanced	n/a	n/a	1% (2%)	n/a	n/a
Proficient	n/a	n/a	19 (18)	n/a	n/a
Basic	n/a	n/a	48 (42)	n/a	n/a
Below Basic	n/a	n/a	32 (38)	n/a	n/a

- SAT weighted rank (1999): 21 out of 24 states and the District of Columbia
- ACT weighted rank (1999): N/A

K–12 Public School Expenditures
- Current expenditures (1999–2000): $13,159,359,000
- Amount of revenue from the federal government (1998–1999): 5.5%
- Current per-pupil expenditures (1999–2000): $7,240

K–12 Public School Teachers (1998–1999)
- Number of teachers: 111,065
- Average salary: $48,457
- Students enrolled per teacher: 16.4
- Largest teachers union: NEA

Background

Pennsylvania has come close to enacting vouchers at least three times in the past decade. In 1997, the legislature passed a charter school bill to permit an unlimited number of new charter schools to open once they receive approval from the school board. At least 75 percent of a charter school's teachers must be certified, and the school must comply with health, safety, and discrimination laws. All other regulations were waived. The bill sets aside approximately $1.4 million in state funds for planning and start-up costs, and up to $25,000 in grant money, for each charter school. It also allots $7.5 million over two years to cover "legitimate transition expenses."

In December 1997, the Legislative Commission on Restructuring Pennsylvania's Urban Schools, a bipartisan panel of 17 government, business, public education, and African–American leaders, recommended the adoption of a limited school choice pilot program for 3,000 children statewide and a program of "opportunity scholarships" for children from "academically-distressed" school districts.

In March 1998, in an effort to avoid expenditures related to a growing public school population and to provide parental choice, the Southeast Delco School District approved a program of tax benefits for families who relieve the district of public school expenses by sending their children to private schools or public schools in other districts. The program was challenged by the teachers union and others for allegedly violating the state constitution and statutes (but not on federal constitutional grounds). The state trial court ruled against the school district, holding that the program exceeds the district's statutory powers. Before the case went to trial, Judge Joseph F. Battle declared that nothing in Pennsylvania's public school code supports allowing districts to provide tuition reimbursements. The court addressed only statutory issues surrounding the plan, not its constitutionality. The case then was heard by the State Court of Appeals, which rejected the suit on similar grounds. Finally, in December 1999, the Commonwealth Court ruled that the plan conflicted with state law but again did not address the constitutionality of school choice. Therefore, this case has no implications for school choice beyond Pennsylvania, and conceivably could be trumped by state legislation declaring that districts may experiment with tuition reimbursement.[2]

On May 26, 1998, Cardinal Anthony Bevilacqua, Archbishop of Philadelphia, sent a letter to Philadelphia Mayor Edward Rendell and Philadelphia School District Superintendent David Hornbeck proposing a voucher plan to help alleviate several problems facing the school district. On June 5, he broadened his request for school choice in the Philadelphia area by sending similar letters to officials in 10 suburban school districts that suffered from overcrowding or money problems. His requests were greeted with silence.

On September 28, 1998, Philadelphia and Pittsburgh were named two of 40 "partner cities" for the Children's Scholarship Fund (CSF) challenge grant. The CSF is a $100 million foundation underwritten by entrepreneurs Ted Forstmann and John Walton. It matches funds raised by Philadelphia and Pittsburgh residents to fund approximately 1,750 private scholarships for low-income students (1,250 in Philadelphia and 500 in Pittsburgh) to attend a school of choice. A lottery in April 1999 determined who would receive the scholarships, which were awarded for at least four years to children entering kindergarten through 8th grade the following year.[3]

Developments in 1999

A survey conducted by the Annenberg Public Policy Center at the University of Pennsylvania found that 68.8 percent of Philadelphia residents support school choice.[4] The question asked of 1,820 residents was: "Do you favor or oppose the use of vouchers that allow a parent to send children to any school of their choice, whether public or private and receive a discount for tuition at that school?" Only 25 percent of respondents opposed vouchers, and 5.8 percent were undecided.

Of those polled who are parents with school-age children, a majority supported vouchers, regardless of religious affiliation. A breakdown of responses according to religious affiliation is as follows: Protestants favor vouchers by 82 percent to 15 percent; respondents who describe themselves as other Christians and non-Christians favor vouchers by a 3 to 1 ratio; and Jewish respondents favor vouchers by 50 percent to 43 percent.

A racial breakdown of all Philadelphia residents polled showed the following: Black residents favor vouchers by 72 percent to 22 percent; whites favor vouchers by 65 percent to 28 percent; and Hispanics favor vouchers by 79 percent to 16 percent.

On April 22, 1999, the Children's Scholarship Fund announced the winners of the largest private scholarship program in the country. The recipients were selected randomly by computer-generated lottery. In Philadelphia, 1,500 scholarship recipients were chosen from 41,054 applicants; in Pittsburgh, 500 recipients were chosen from 10,308 applicants.[5]

In March, Governor Tom Ridge introduced the Academic Recovery Act. The act would identify eight troubled school districts in the state and offer educators in those districts greater flexibility in the management of their districts, allowing them to create charter schools, privatize services, and hire teachers without certification. It also would provide a voucher to parents in the struggling districts to send their children to the public, private, or religious school of choice. The plan would empower the state to take over failing school districts that are declared "academically bankrupt."[6]

The act was later reconfigured to a plan that included restructuring distressed school districts, education recovery grants for students in failing schools, and a local option opportunity grant program. In the end, the plan was scaled down to one that would immediately assist 7,500 students in Delaware County and place the rest of the state under a two-year delay warning system (making failing districts eligible for extra services and funds under the bill) before vouchers kick in. Without any certainty that it had sufficient votes to pass the state House of Representatives, the plan was withdrawn from consideration on June 17.[7] The governor, however, has vowed to continue pushing for these reforms.

The two-year moratorium on appeals of charter applications that were denied by local school boards (which was included in the 1997 charter school law) expired in 1999. The legislature adopted a plan to create a charter school appeals board. As a result, charter schools whose applications were rejected by school boards will have the chance to be reheard by the Appeals Board, which has the authority to approve the application and allow the school to open. Of the first nine cases considered by the Appeals Board, three were decided in favor of the local school boards and six were decided in favor of the charter schools, reversing the actions of the local school boards.

The 1999 Philadelphia mayoral race was won by John Street (D), who opposes vouchers.[8]

A study by the Pennsylvania Department of Education, released on March 13, 2000, reported that "charter schools are proving themselves as innovative and effective educational opportunities for Pennsylvania students." [9]

Position of the Governor/Composition of State Legislature

Governor Tom Ridge, a Republican, strongly supports vouchers and charter schools. Both houses of the legislature are led by Republicans.

State Contacts

Allegheny Institute for Public Policy
Garry Bowyer, President
David Kirkpatrick, Senior Fellow and Director, School Reform Project
835 Western Avenue, #300
Pittsburgh, PA 15233
Phone: (412) 231-6020
Fax: (412) 231-6027

Archdiocese of Philadelphia
Guy Ciarrocchi, Public Affairs Director
222 North 17th Street
Philadelphia, PA 19103
Phone: (215) 587-3677
Fax: (215) 587-0515

CEO America, Lehigh Valley
Sharon Recchio, Executive Director
33 South Seventh Street, Suite 250
Allentown, PA 18101
Phone: (610) 776-8740
Fax: (610) 776-8741

CSF–Philadelphia
Cathy Westcott, Executive Director
Matti White, Administrator
718 Arch Street, Suite 402 North
Philadelphia, PA 19106
Phone: (215) 925-4328
Fax: (215) 925-4342

Commonwealth Foundation for Public Policy Alternatives
Sean Duffy, President
3544 North Progress Avenue, Suite 101
Harrisburg, PA 17110

Phone: (717) 671-1901
Fax: (717) 671-1905
Web site: http://www.commonwealth
foundation.org
E-mail: info@commonwealthfoundation.org

Pennsylvania Catholic Conference
Frederick Cabell
P.O. Box 2835
223 N Street
Harrisburg, PA 17105
Phone: (717) 238-9613
Fax: (717) 238-1473

Pennsylvania Department of Education
Dr. Eugene Hickock, Secretary of Education
333 Market Street
Harrisburg, PA 17126
Phone: (717) 783-9780
Fax: (717) 787-7222

Pennsylvania Family Institute
Michael Geer, President
1240 North Mountain Road
Harrisburg, PA 17112
Phone: (717) 545-0600
Fax: (717) 545-8107
Web site: http://www.pafamily.org

Pennsylvania Leadership Council
223 State Street
Harrisburg, PA 17101
Phone: (717) 232-5919
Fax: (717) 232-1186

Pittsburgh Urban Scholarship Help (PUSH)
Carolyn Curry, Program Director
425 Sixth Street, Room 570
Pittsburgh, PA 15219
Phone: (412) 394-3695
Fax: (412) 394-1173

REACH (Road to Educational Achievement Through Choice) Alliance
Chris Bravacos, President
P.O. Box 1283
Harrisburg, PA 17108-1283
Phone: (717) 238-1878
Fax: (717) 234-2286

The Urban League Partnership Program
Brian Young, Administrator
251 South 24th Street
Philadelphia, PA 19103-5529
Phone: (215) 731-4103
Fax: (215) 731-4112

Endnotes

1 For sources, see "An Explanation of the State Profile Categories."

2 Deidre Shaw, "School Vouchers Are Ruled Illegal," *The Philadelphia Inquirer*, October 16, 1998.

3 See Children's Scholarship Fund Web site at *http://www.scholarshipfund.org*.

4 W. Russel G. Byers, "Solid Poll Position for School Vouchers in City," *Philadelphia Daily News*, April 22, 1999.

5 See Children's Scholarship Fund Web site at *http://www.scholarshipfund.org*.

6 The Friedman–Blum *Educational Freedom Report*, No. 67, January 22, 1999.

7 The Friedman–Blum *Educational Freedom Report*, No. 72, June 18, 1999.

8 Susan Snyder, "Board Postpones Action on Charters. Mayor Street Wants His New School Board to Vote on Charter School Applications. The Current Board Agreed," *The Philadelphia Inquirer*, February 23, 2000.

9 Pennsylvania Department of Education, press release, "Study Finds Overwhelming Majority of Teachers, Parents Believe Charter Schools Meet Their Mission," March 13, 2000.

Rhode Island

State Profile[1]

School Choice Status

- Public school choice: N/A
- Charter schools: Established 1995
  - Strength of law: Weak
  - Number of charter schools in operation (fall 1999): 2
  - Number of students enrolled in charter schools (1998–1999): 393
- Publicly funded private school choice: N/A

K–12 Public and Private School Students and Schools

- Public school enrollment (fall 1998) and number of schools (1997–1998): 153,710 in 314 schools
- Private school enrollment and number of schools (1997–1998): 25,597 in 130 schools

K–12 Public and Private School Student Academic Performance

NAEP Test Results—percentage of students at each performance level for both public and private schools, with national percentages in parentheses

Performance Level	Reading 4th grade 1998	Reading 8th grade 1998	Math 4th grade 1996	Math 8th grade 1996	Science 8th grade 1996
Advanced	7% (6%)	2% (2%)	1% (2%)	3% (4%)	2% (3%)
Proficient	25 (23)	28 (28)	16 (18)	17 (19)	24 (24)
Basic	33 (31)	44 (41)	44 (42)	40 (38)	33 (33)
Below Basic	35 (39)	26 (28)	39 (38)	40 (39)	41 (40)

- SAT weighted rank (1999): 14 out of 24 states and the District of Columbia
- ACT weighted rank (1999): N/A

K–12 Public School Expenditures

- Current expenditures (1999–2000): $1,196,133,000
- Amount of revenue from the federal government (1998–1999): 5.6%
- Current per-pupil expenditures (1999–2000): $7,754

K–12 Public School Teachers (1998–1999)

- Number of teachers: 11,859
- Average salary: $50,322
- Students enrolled per teacher: 13.0
- Largest teachers union: NEA

Background

On June 30, 1995, Governor Lincoln Almond signed the state's first charter school bill, the Act to Establish Charter Schools, into law. This legislation restricts charters to existing public schools and allows them to convert to charter schools only with approval of two-thirds of their teachers and a majority of parents. All teachers and administrators in a charter school must be certified by the state, and teachers remain employees of the school district.

Developments in 1999

No developments were reported.

Position of the Governor/Composition of State Legislature

Governor Lincoln Almond, a Republican, supports school choice. Both houses of the legislature are led by Democrats.

State Contact

Rhode Island Department of Education
Steve Nardelli, Charter Schools Division
255 Westminster Street
Providence, RI 02903
Phone: (401) 222-4600, ext. 2015
Fax: (401) 351-7874

Endnote

1   For sources, see "An Explanation of the State Profile Categories."

South Carolina

State Profile[1]

School Choice Status
- Public school choice: N/A
- Charter schools: Established 1996
    Strength of law: Strong
    Number of charter schools in operation (fall 1999): 10
    Number of students enrolled in charter schools (1998–1999): 467
- Publicly funded private school choice: N/A

K–12 Public and Private School Students and Schools
- Public school enrollment (fall 1998) and number of schools (1997–1998): 654,993 in 1,055 schools
- Private school enrollment and number of schools (1997–1998): 56,169 in 316 schools

K–12 Public and Private School Student Academic Performance
NAEP Test Results—percentage of students at each performance level for both public and private schools, with national percentages in parentheses

Performance Level	Reading 4th grade 1998	Reading 8th grade 1998	Math 4th grade 1996	Math 8th grade 1996	Science 8th grade 1996
Advanced	4% (6%)	1% (2%)	1% (2%)	2% (4%)	1% (3%)
Proficient	18 (23)	21 (28)	11 (18)	12 (19)	16 (24)
Basic	33 (31)	43 (41)	36 (42)	34 (38)	28 (33)
Below Basic	45 (39)	35 (28)	52 (38)	52 (39)	55 (40)

- SAT weighted rank (1999): 25 out of 24 states and the District of Columbia
- ACT weighted rank (1999): N/A

K–12 Public School Expenditures
- Current expenditures (1999–2000): $3,932,824,000
- Amount of revenue from the federal government (1998–1999): 8.1%
- Current per-pupil expenditures (1999–2000): $6,015

K–12 Public School Teachers (1998–1999)
- Number of teachers: 42,202
- Average salary: $34,506
- Students enrolled per teacher: 15.5
- Largest teachers union: NEA

Background

In 1996, the legislature passed the Charter Schools Act to allow local school boards to sponsor charter schools. The legislation does not establish a cap on the number of charter schools and is considered a strong law, according to the Center for Education Reform.[2]

In April 1997, Attorney General Charles Condon issued an informal opinion that a provision in the Charter Schools Act requiring the schools to recruit a student body whose racial makeup is roughly proportional to the racial makeup of the school district was unconstitutional.

The 1998 General Assembly passed an Education Oversight Act that called for the evaluation and grading of all public schools in South Carolina. The original bill contained provisions enabling parents with a child enrolled in a failing public school to transfer to a school of choice, provided there was enough space. This provision was removed during conference proceedings.

Developments in 1999[3]

Partners Advancing Choice in Education (PACE), a new private scholarship program, plans to award scholarships to low-income students in grades 1 through 6. The scholarships will cover between 30 percent and 60 percent of private school tuition, up to $2,000.

The South Carolina General Assembly passed H. 3082, the Alternative School Law, that allows school districts to begin developing alternative schools beginning with the 1999–2000 school year.

Representative Lewis Vaughn (R–Greenville) introduced the Open Enrollment Act of 1999 for students in K–12. The legislation would permit public funds to be used at private schools. However, the chairman of the House Education and Public Works Committee, Representative Ronald Townsend (R–Anderson), who opposes open enrollment, introduced legislation to create an Open Enrollment Task Force that would study the school choice–open enrollment concept. Some legislators believe the task force is a ploy to quell the school choice debate until after the November 2000 elections.

During the summer of 1999, House Speaker David Wilkens (R–Greenville) appointed a bipartisan committee to study school choice in South Carolina. The committee held six hearings at which members of the public were invited to share their opinions. A majority of those who spoke in support of school choice were parents, while the most vocal opponents were union members, ACLU, political organizations, and the League of Women Voters.

Several South Carolina lawmakers are hoping to introduce legislation during the 2000 session that will amend South Carolina's charter school law. Specifically they would like to amend the racial quotas structured into the law that have kept charter schools from opening in urban and minority neighborhoods. Legislators also are looking at the possibility of stripping charter school jurisdiction from the local school boards, which have continued to deny charter applications, and empower an independent state board to review these applications.

Developments in 2000

On February 16, the House of Representatives passed (65–43) legislation introduced by Representative Bobby Harrell (R–Charleston) to eliminate the racial quota provision in the state's charter school law.

Position of the Governor/Composition of State Legislature

Governor Jim Hodges, a Democrat, is opposed to school choice and any voucher–tuition scholarship program. The House is led by Republicans; the Senate is led by Democrats.

State Contacts

Partners Advancing Choice in Education (PACE) Foundation
Jonathan Hudgens, Executive Director
1323 Pendleton Street
Columbia, SC 29201
Phone: (803) 254-1201
Fax: (803) 779-4953

South Carolina Department of Education
Rutledge Building
1429 Senate Street
Columbia, SC 29201
Phone: (803) 734-8500
Fax: (803) 734-8624
Web site: http://www.state.sc.us/sde/

South Carolina Policy Council
Edward McMullen, President
1323 Pendleton Street
Columbia, SC 29201-3708
Phone: (803) 779-5022
Fax: (803) 779-4953
E-mail: etm@scpolicycouncil.com

Endnotes

1   For sources, see "An Explanation of the State Profile Categories."

2   Angela Dale and Dave DeSchryver, eds., *The Charter School Workbook: Your Roadmap to the Charter School Movement* (Washington, D.C.: Center for Education Reform, 1997). Updates available at *http://www.edreform.com/pubs/chglance.htm.*

3   Information provided by the South Carolina Policy Council.

South Dakota

State Profile[1]

School Choice Status
- Public school choice: Statewide
- Charter schools: N/A
- Publicly funded private school choice: N/A

K–12 Public and Private School Students and Schools
- Public school enrollment (fall 1998) and number of schools (1997–1998): 131,764 in 814 schools
- Private school enrollment and number of schools (1997–1998): 9,794 in 91 schools

K–12 Public and Private School Student Academic Performance
NAEP Test Results—percentage of students at each performance level for both public and private schools, with national percentages in parentheses

Performance Level	Reading 4th grade 1998	Reading 8th grade 1998	Math 4th grade 1996	Math 8th grade 1996	Science 8th grade 1996
Advanced	n/a	n/a	n/a	n/a	n/a
Proficient	n/a	n/a	n/a	n/a	n/a
Basic	n/a	n/a	n/a	n/a	n/a
Below Basic	n/a	n/a	n/a	n/a	n/a

- SAT weighted rank (1999): N/A
- ACT weighted rank (1999): 17 out of 26 states

K–12 Public School Expenditures
- Current expenditures (1999–2000): $670,454,000
- Amount of revenue from the federal government (1998–1999): 9.8%
- Current per-pupil expenditures (1999–2000): $5,061

K–12 Public School Teachers (1998–1999)
- Number of teachers: 9,070
- Average salary: $28,552
- Students enrolled per teacher: 14.5
- Largest teachers union: NEA

Background

Although South Dakota has a statewide public school choice program, it is not enthusiastically supported because of the lack of multiple public schools within an area. The distance between existing schools forces students to attend the closest school.

Developments in 1999

No developments were reported.

Developments in 2000

A plan to pass charter schools and a plan to offer students $1,200 scholarships to attend a school of choice were approved by the House State Affairs Committee, but both were defeated on the floor.[2]

Position of the Governor/Composition of State Legislature

The positions of Governor William J. Janklow, a Republican, on vouchers and charter schools are not known. When he served as governor from 1979 to 1987, he instituted an open enrollment program. Both houses of the legislature are led by Republicans.

State Contacts

Citizens for Choice in Education
Kay Glover, Founder
411 Glover Street
Sturgis, SD 57785
Phone: (605) 347-2495
Fax: (605) 347-4485

Great Plains Public Policy Institute
Ronald Williamson
P.O. Box 88138
Sioux Falls, SD 57109
Phone: (605) 332-2641
Fax: (605) 338-3458

Representative Hal Wick
3009 Donahue Drive
Sioux Falls, SD 57105
Phone: (605) 332-1360
Fax: (605) 332-4365

South Dakota Family Policy Council
Nathan Schock
Research and Project Director
3500 South First Avenue, #210
Sioux Falls, SD 57105
Phone: (605) 335-8100
Fax: (605) 335-4029
E-mail: sdfamily@aol.com

Endnotes

1 For sources, see "An Explanation of the State Profile Categories."

2 Information provided by the South Dakota Family Policy Council.

Tennessee

State Profile[1]

School Choice Status
- Public school choice: Statewide
- Charter schools: N/A
- Publicly funded private school choice: N/A

K–12 Public and Private School Students and Schools
- Public school enrollment (fall 1998) and number of schools (1997–1998): 903,319 in 1,522 schools
- Private school enrollment and number of schools (1997–1998): 84,651 in 513 schools

K–12 Public and Private School Student Academic Performance
NAEP Test Results—percentage of students at each performance level for both public and private schools, with national percentages in parentheses

Performance Level	Reading 4th grade 1998	Reading 8th grade 1998	Math 4th grade 1996	Math 8th grade 1996	Science 8th grade 1996
Advanced	5% (6%)	1% (2%)	1% (2%)	2% (4%)	2% (3%)
Proficient	20 (23)	25 (28)	16 (18)	13 (19)	20 (24)
Basic	33 (31)	45 (41)	41 (42)	38 (38)	31 (33)
Below Basic	42 (39)	29 (28)	42 (38)	47 (39)	47 (40)

- SAT weighted rank (1999): N/A
- ACT weighted rank (1999): 24 out of 26 states

K–12 Public School Expenditures
- Current expenditures (1999–2000): $4,771,068,000
- Amount of revenue from the federal government (1998–1999): 8.0%
- Current per-pupil expenditures (1999–2000): $5,255

K–12 Public School Teachers (1998–1999)
- Number of teachers: 53,593
- Average salary: $36,500
- Students enrolled per teacher: 16.9
- Largest teachers union: NEA

Background

Tennessee law allows students to attend public schools outside their district, but there are bureaucratic restrictions. For example, transferring students must obtain permission from the receiving district's school board to ensure that the transfer does not harm state desegregation efforts.

On March 31, 1998, a House subcommittee halted Republican Governor Don Sundquist's charter school legislation (H.B. 2553 and S.B. 2693) and referred it to the Education Oversight Committee for study over the summer. Opponents of the bill disagreed with provisions that would allow for-profit organizations to charter a school but would not require licensing of charter school teachers.[2] The measure, which the Tennessee Education Association opposed, ultimately failed.

Though the state is void of choice laws, several private programs offer parents more options. In January 1998, a new private scholarship program, the Memphis Opportunity Scholarship Trust (MOST), began operations. During the 1998–1999 school year, MOST awarded 165 scholarships to low-income children living in Shelby County. Scholarships worth up to 60 percent of private school tuition were capped at $1,500.

The Children's Educational Opportunity Foundation (CEO) started a private scholarship program in Chattanooga in 1998 as well. CEO Chattanooga will award scholarships for up to 50 percent of tuition, with a maximum of $1,500, to 200 low-income elementary students living in Hamilton County. The program also will establish three "Safe Haven" private elementary schools over the next two years for 150 students. This program will be studied by researchers at the University of Tennessee at Chattanooga.

On September 28, 1998, Memphis and Chattanooga were named two of 40 "partner cities" for the Children's Scholarship Fund (CSF) challenge grant. The CSF is a $100 million foundation underwritten by entrepreneurs Ted Forstmann and John Walton. It matches funds raised by Memphis and Chattanooga residents to fund approximately 1,250 private scholarships for low-income students (750 in Memphis and 500 in Chattanooga) to attend a school of choice. A lottery in April 1999 determined who would receive the scholarships, which were awarded for at least four years to children entering kindergarten through 8th grade the following year.[3]

Developments in 1999

Governor Don Sundquist again proposed charter school legislation. This time, Jane Walters, a lifetime member of the Tennessee Education Association, served as point person for the legislation. Walters rewrote the bill to satisfy all the concerns of the Tennessee Education Association. Despite these efforts, TEA came up with a whole new list of concerns and voted to oppose the bill. As a result, on April 20, 1999, the bill stalled in the House K–12 Subcommittee in a tie vote with one member absent.

A strong new charter bill written with the assistance of the Charter School Resource Center of Tennessee likely will be introduced in the early part of the 2000 legislative session, which began on January 11, 2000.[4]

On April 22, 1999, the Children's Scholarship Fund announced the winners of the largest private scholarship program in the country. The recipients were selected randomly by computer-generated lottery. In Memphis, 750 scholarship recipients were chosen from 9,211 applicants; in Chattanooga, 500 recipients were chosen from 2,910 applicants.[5] As of October 28, 1999, 625 new private scholarships had been awarded. The average scholarship amount in Tennessee was $1,276.

Position of the Governor/Composition of State Legislature

Governor Don Sundquist, a Republican, supports charter schools. His views on vouchers are unknown. Both houses of the legislature are led by Democrats.

State Contacts

CSF–Chattanooga
J. C. Bowman, President
Gail Tryon, Administrator
102 Walnut Street
Chattanooga, TN 37403
Phone: (423) 756-0410 x105
Fax: (423) 756-8250
E-mail: gail@resourcefoundation.org

CEO Knoxville
Mike McClamroch, President
Pam Ricketts, Administrator
P.O. Box 10459

Knoxville, TN 37939-0459
Phone: (423) 637-7020
Fax: (423) 986-1563

Charter School Resource Center of Tennessee
Dale Berryhill, Executive Director
6363 Poplar Avenue, Suite 410
Memphis, TN 38119
Phone: (910) 844-0046
E-mail: TNCharters@aol.com

Memphis Opportunity Scholarship Trust (MOST)
Trent Williamson, Executive Director
850 Ridge Lake Boulevard, Suite 220
Memphis, TN 38120
Phone: (901) 767-7005
Fax: (901) 818-5260
E-mail: trentwilliamson@rfshotel.com

Tennessee Department of Education
Andrew Johnson Tower, 6th Floor
710 James Robertson Parkway
Nashville, TN 37243-0375
Phone: (615) 741-2731
Web site: http://www.state.tn.us/education/homepage.htm

Tennessee Family Institute
Michael Gilstrap, President
A. Roger Abramson, Research and Policy Analyst
1808 West End Avenue, Suite 1214
P.O. Box 23348
Nashville, TN 37202-3348
Phone: (615) 327-3120
Fax: (615) 327-3126
E-mail: fouryou@tennesseefamily.org

Endnotes

1 For sources, see "An Explanation of the State Profile Categories."

2 Rebecca Ferrar, "Governor Allows Charter School Plan to Die for Session, Move to Study Group," *The Knoxville News–Sentinel*, April 1, 1998, p. A3.

3 See Children's Scholarship Fund Web site at *http://www.scholarshipfund.org.*

4 E-mail correspondence from state contact Dale Berryhill, Charter School Resource Center of Tennessee, received January 10, 2000.

5 See Children's Scholarship Fund Web site at *http://www.scholarshipfund.org.*

Texas

State Profile[1]

School Choice Status
- Public school choice: Limited
- Charter schools: Established 1995
    Strength of law: Strong
    Number of charter schools in operation (fall 1999): 168
    Number of students enrolled in charter schools (1998–1999): 16,841
- Publicly funded private school choice: N/A

K–12 Public and Private School Students and Schools
- Public school enrollment (fall 1998) and number of schools (1997–1998): 3,971,267 in 7,053 schools
- Private school enrollment and number of schools (1997–1998): 223,294 in 1,329 schools

K–12 Public and Private School Student Academic Performance
NAEP Test Results—percentage of students at each performance level for both public and private schools, with national percentages in parentheses

Performance Level	Reading 4th grade 1998	Reading 8th grade 1998	Math 4th grade 1996	Math 8th grade 1996	Science 8th grade 1996
Advanced	5% (6%)	1% (2%)	3% (2%)	3% (4%)	1% (3%)
Proficient	24 (23)	27 (28)	22 (18)	18 (19)	22 (24)
Basic	34 (31)	48 (41)	44 (42)	38 (38)	32 (33)
Below Basic	37 (39)	24 (28)	31 (38)	41 (39)	45 (40)

- SAT weighted rank (1999): 20 out of 24 states and the District of Columbia
- ACT weighted rank (1999): N/A

K–12 Public School Expenditures
- Current expenditures (1999–2000): $23,706,640,000
- Amount of revenue from the federal government (1998–1999): 8.4%
- Current per-pupil expenditures (1999–2000): $5,970

K–12 Public School Teachers (1998–1999)
- Number of teachers: 261,275
- Average salary: $35,041
- Students enrolled per teacher: 15.2
- Largest teachers union: Association of Texas Professional Educators (independent teachers organization)

Background

In 1995, the legislature rewrote the Texas Education Code to offer two types of charter schools as well as to set up home rule school districts. The state Board of Education is authorized to grant up to 20 open enrollment charters to institutions of higher education, nonprofit organizations, or governmental entities. Open enrollment charter schools generally are free from most state and local laws, rules, and regulations. School district boards of trustees may grant an unlimited number of charters to parents and teachers who present a petition showing sufficient support for a charter.

The conversion of a district to home rule may be initiated either by a school board resolution or by a petition signed by a fair number of registered voters in a district. Except for provisions to ensure accountability, the new code permits an unlimited number of communities to make rules for their districts. Like open enrollment charters, both charter school programs and home rule school district charters relieve the burden of abiding by all state laws, rules, and regulations. The revised code allows a student enrolled in a consistently low-performing school to transfer to another school.

The 1997 legislative session brought significant improvement in the state's charter school bill, raising the cap on open enrollment charters to 120 and allowing for an unlimited number of charters for schools serving at-risk students.

A report to the state Board of Education found that the state's existing charter schools primarily served minority and low-income students.[2] Charter school enrollments are comprised, on average, of 26 percent African–American students (compared with 14 percent in the state's public schools); 52 percent Hispanic students (compared with 36 percent in state public schools); and 19 percent white students (compared with 47 percent in state public schools).

In June 1993, the Texas Justice Foundation filed suit on behalf of Guadalupe and Margie Gutierrez and their children, Lupita and Vanessa, claiming that the state's monopoly on public education funding would never produce a "suitable" and "efficient" system with a "general diffusion of knowledge," as the Texas constitution requires. The lawsuit requested that the plaintiffs' school district be ordered to contract with a private entity chosen by the family to educate their children. On January 30, 1995, the Texas Supreme Court ruled against the plaintiffs on the grounds that the relief they sought was a "political question." The court held, however, that the state constitution does not require that education be provided by districts or a state agency; the legislature may decide whether education should be administered by a state agency, by the districts, or by any other means. This finding validates to some extent the constitutionality of vouchers in Texas.

In May 1996, Houston's voters rejected a $390 million bond measure to build 15 new schools and renovate 84 existing ones. As a result, Superintendent Rod Paige offered to place students from some 65 overcrowded schools into area private schools at district expense instead of busing them to a distant public school. Shortly thereafter, the Houston School Board trustees voted unanimously to approve Paige's innovative plan, despite opposition from the education establishment.

On April 22, 1998, CEO America launched the nation's first fully funded voucher program offered to every family in a school district. CEO Horizon (the brainchild of CEO America, CEO San Antonio, and San Antonio business leaders) made $50 million available over the next 10 years to allow every low-income child in the predominantly Hispanic Edgewood Independent School District to attend a school of choice. For every 15 scholarships awarded to a child currently enrolled in public school, one will go to a child in a non-public school in proportion to current school enrollment (93.7 percent of students attend public schools, and 6.3 percent attend non-public schools).

During the 1998–1999 school year (the program's first year), 700 of the 13,000 eligible students elected to leave Edgewood public schools for private schools. The Edgewood Independent School District responded by instituting intra-district public school choice and commissioning a $120,000 management study to improve its administrative efficiency.

CEO Horizon scholarship students enrolled in schools within the district receive $3,600 annually for kindergarten through 8th grade and $4,000 for the 9th through 12th grades. Students living in the district but enrolled in an existing school outside the district are eligible for 100 percent of tuition reimbursement, up to $2,000 for kindergarten through 8th grade and $3,500 for the 9th through 12th grades.

On May 21, 1998, the Houston Independent School District Board of Education passed (by a vote of 5 to 4) a plan allowing the district to pay the costs of transferring failing students from low-performing public schools to a district-approved private school. To qualify, a student must have failed the Texas Assessment of Academic Skills (TAAS) in reading and math. The student must also be attending a public school ranked as "low performing" by the district, which ranked no schools as such in 1997, or by the Texas Education Agency, which ranked three schools as "low performing" in 1997. The student will have the option to transfer to any private school that meets the district's criteria. The school must be non-religious, meet state accreditation standards, be willing to accept a maximum yearly tuition of $3,575 per student, abide by state laws governing public schools, and accept all students regardless of conduct and academic track record.

The Texas Poll, conducted in October 1998 by Scripps Howard, found that 51 percent of Texans surveyed supported legislation to create a voucher program to allow students in low-performing public schools to attend private schools.[3]

On September 28, 1998, Dallas, Fort Worth, and Houston were named three of 40 "partner cities" for the Children's Scholarship Fund (CSF) challenge grant. The CSF is a $100 million foundation underwritten by entrepreneurs Ted Forstmann and John Walton. It matches funds raised by Dallas and Fort Worth residents to fund approximately 3,150 private scholarships for low-income students (1,250 in Dallas, 500 in Fort Worth, and 1,400 in Houston) to attend a school of choice. A lottery in April 1999 determined who would receive the scholarships, which were awarded for at least four years to children entering kindergarten through 8th grade the following year.[4]

Developments in 1999

On March 24, 1999, the Texas Senate Education Committee approved a bill for a small-scale voucher program for about 149,000 low-income students in the state's six most urban counties. The bill, championed by Senator Teel Bivins (R), had the backing of Governor George W. Bush and Lieutenant Governor Rick Perry. After an uphill battle in the Democrat-controlled Texas House, the bill failed to pass.[5]

In the House, Representative Kent Grusendorf (R–94) introduced HB 2118, a pilot program that would allow up to 10 percent of children in any low-performing school in one of Texas's seven largest school districts to attend a school of choice. The student would receive from the residence district a scholarship worth up to 80 percent of per-pupil funding (excluding funds dedicated to school facilities). The district would retain the remaining 20 percent of per-pupil expenditures and 100 percent of the debt service taxes. In this way, the bill provides for an increase in per-pupil funding for children in public schools. No school would be required to participate; but once a school did elect to participate, it would have to accept all applicants. Participating private schools would not be bound to public school regulations, but participating students would be required to take the state evaluation (TAAS) exam.[6] HB 2118 also failed.

In March, CEO America released its findings on San Antonio's Horizon program, the nation's first fully funded private voucher program offered to all parents in an entire district. The study, conducted by Paul Peterson of Harvard, found that the program did not lead to an exodus from the public schools, thus draining the district's budget. Only 800 students left the public schools, reducing the budget by only 3.5 percent. However, after the inception of the Horizon program, the Edgewood Independent School District implemented an inter-district choice program that allowed 200 students from other districts to transfer to Edgewood schools, bringing with them $775,000 that otherwise would have gone to their home districts. In addition, nearly every scholarship applicant was accepted to his or her school of choice, thus refuting arguments that private schools would cherry-pick the best students.[7]

In September 1999, Peterson also concluded that Texas's voucher program does not "cream" the best students out of the public school system for its program. The multiyear study found that there was no significant academic or economic difference between the students who entered the Horizon program and those who remained in the public school system.

On April 22, 1999, the Children's Scholarship Fund announced the winners of the largest private scholarship program in the country. The recipients were selected randomly by computer-generated lottery. In Dallas, 900 scholarship recipients were chosen from 17,761 applicants;

in Fort Worth, 491 recipients were chosen from 9,338 applicants; in Houston, 250 recipients were chosen from 19,187 applicants.[8]

Position of the Governor/Composition of State Legislature

Governor George W. Bush, a Republican, supports vouchers and charter schools. The House is led by Democrats; the Senate is led by Republicans.

State Contacts

Charter School Resource Center of Texas
Patsy O'Neill, Executive Director
40 NE Loop 410, Suite 408
San Antonio, TX 78216
Phone: (210) 348-7890
Fax: (210) 348-7899
E-mail: oneillp@texas.net

CEO Austin
Jane Kilgore, Program Administrator
111 Congress Avenue, Suite 3000
Austin, TX 78701
Phone: (512) 472-0153
Fax: (512) 310-1688
E-mail: austinceo@aol.com

CEO Midland
Andrea Catania, Chairman
6 Desta Drive, Suite 6440
Midland, TX 79705
Phone: (915) 682-4422
Fax: (915) 683-1988
E-mail: rba@onr.com

CEO San Antonio
Robert Aguirre, Managing Director
Teresa Treat, Program Director
8122 Datapoint Drive, Suite 804
San Antonio, TX 78229
Phone: (210) 614-0037
Fax: (210) 614-5730
E-mail: tftreat@aol.com

Children's Education Fund
Patricia J. Broyles, Executive Director
Fran Sauls, Administrator
P.O. Box 225748
Dallas, TX 75214
Phone: (972) 298-1811
Fax: (972) 298-6369
Web site: http://www.todayfoundation.org
E-mail: today@todayfoundation.org

Children's Education Fund
1701 North Hampton, Suite B
Desoto, TX 75115
Phone: (972) 298-1811
E-mail: edutyler@aol.com

Every Church a School Foundation
A Choice for Every Child
Martin Tyler Angell, Executive Director
9805 Walnut Street, #C206
Dallas, TX 75243
Phone/Fax: (972) 699-3446
E-mail: martinangell@mymail.net

Free Market Foundation
Kelly Shackelford, Executive Director
Deborah Muse, Vice Chairman
P.O. Box 740367
Dallas, TX 75374
Phone: (972) 423-8889
Fax: (972) 680-9172

Houston CEO Foundation
Herb Butrum, Executive Director
Stacy Bandfield, Administrator
952 Echo Lane, Suite 350
Houston, TX 77024
Phone: (713) 722-7444
Fax: (713) 722-7442
Web site: http://www.hern.org/ceo
E-mail: staceyb@hern.org

STAR Sponsorship Program
Patty Myers, Executive Director
Frances Hauss, Administrator
316 Bailey Avenue, Suite 109
Fort Worth, TX 76107
Phone: (817) 332-8550
Fax: (817) 332-8825
E-mail: Starsponsorship@mailcity.com

Texas Citizens for a Sound Economy
Peggy Venable, Director
1005 Congress Avenue, Suite 910
Austin, TX 78701
Phone: (512) 476-5905
Fax: (512) 476-5906
Web site: http://www.cse.org/cse
E-mail: venable@cse.org

Texas Coalition for Parental Choice in Education (TCPCE)
Pam Benson
107 Ranch Road, 620 South, #34D
Austin, TX 78734
Phone: (512) 266-9012
E-mail: jbarmadilo@aol.com

Texas Education Agency
1701 North Congress Avenue
Austin, TX 78701-1494
Phone: (512) 463-9734
Web site: http://www.tea.state.tx.us/

Texas Justice Foundation
Allan Parker, President
8122 Datapoint Drive, Suite 812
San Antonio, TX 78229
Phone: (210) 614-7157
Fax: (210) 614-6656
Web Site: http://www.txjf.org
E-mail: aparker@stic.net

Texas Public Policy Foundation
Jeffrey M. Judson, President
P.O. Box 40519
San Antonio, TX 78229
Phone: (210) 614-0080
Fax: (210) 614-2649
Web site: http://www.tppf.org
E-mail: jmjudson@txdirect.net

Endnotes

1 For sources, see "An Explanation of the State Profile Categories."

2 Dr. Delbert Table *et al.*, "Texas Open Enrollment Charter Schools; Year One Evaluation: A Research Report to Be Presented to the Texas State Board of Education," December 1997.

3 The Fall 1998 Texas Poll, conducted by Scripps Howard and the Office of Survey Research, University of Texas, October 1998.

4 See Children's Scholarship Fund Web site at *http://www.scholarshipfund.org*.

5 The Friedman–Blum *Educational Freedom Report*, No. 69, March 19, 1999.

6 Correspondence from the Texas Justice Foundation, December 1999.

7 CEO America, "First Semester Report," March 1999.

8 See Children's Scholarship Fund Web site at *http://www.scholarshipfund.org*.

Utah

State Profile[1]

School Choice Status
- Public school choice: Statewide
- Charter Schools: Established 1998
    - Strength of law: Weak
    - Number of charter schools in operation (fall 1999): 8
    - Number of students enrolled in charter schools (1998–1999): N/A
- Publicly funded private school choice: N/A

K–12 Public and Private School Students and Schools
- Public school enrollment (fall 1998) and number of schools (1997–1998): 477,061 in 759 schools
- Private school enrollment and number of schools (1997–1998): 14,543 in 139 schools

K–12 Public and Private School Student Academic Performance
NAEP Test Results—percentage of students at each performance level for both public and private schools, with national percentages in parentheses

Performance Level	Reading 4th grade 1998	Reading 8th grade 1998	Math 4th grade 1996	Math 8th grade 1996	Science 8th grade 1996
Advanced	5% (6%)	2% (2%)	2% (2%)	3% (4%)	2% (3%)
Proficient	23 (23)	29 (28)	21 (18)	21 (19)	30 (24)
Basic	43 (31)	46 (41)	46 (42)	46 (38)	38 (33)
Below Basic	38 (39)	23 (28)	31 (38)	30 (39)	30 (40)

- SAT weighted rank (1999): N/A
- ACT weighted rank (1999): 11 out of 26 states

K–12 Public School Expenditures
- Current expenditures (1999–2000): $1,863,753,000
- Amount of revenue from the federal government (1998–1999): 6.6%
- Current per-pupil expenditures (1999–2000): $3,889

K–12 Public School Teachers (1998–1999)
- Number of teachers: 21,585
- Average salary: $32,950
- Students enrolled per teacher: 22.1
- Largest teachers union: NEA

Background

In 1991, Utah enacted a voluntary open enrollment program to allow students in participating school districts to transfer to schools in other participating districts. Funding would follow the student, and the balance of the student's educational costs in the new district would be split between the sending and receiving districts. However, incentives to participate were lacking, and no district agreed to participate during the 1991–1992 school year. The law was amended in 1992 to make open enrollment mandatory as of September 1993.

In 1997, a tuition tax credit was defeated in the legislature. The bill offered state income tax credits to parents who chose to send their children to non-public schools. The amount would have been phased in over several years until the credit reached a value of $2,000 per child.

A survey conducted in 1997 by R. T. Nielsen for the Utah Coalition for Freedom in Education found that 79 percent of Utah voters support parental choice in education that includes public, private, and parochial schools.[2]

In 1998, the legislature approved a relatively weak charter school law under which any non-parochial school may apply to the state Board of Education for a charter. For conversion schools, the school must show evidence of support from two-thirds of the parents and certified teachers. On average, 75 percent of per-pupil funding would follow the child to the charter school. The law caps the number of charter schools at eight.[3]

Developments in 1999

No developments were reported.

Developments in 2000

A school choice bill was introduced in the 2000 legislative session. H.B. 401, Income Tax—Private Investment in Education, sponsored by Representative John Swallow, would provide a dollar-for-dollar tax credit to parents who transfer their children to private schools rather than rely on the public system. In addition to parents, any taxpayer (individual or business) could contribute to the tuition of a child in private school and receive the credit. The legislation also would allow taxpayers to receive a tax credit for contributions to private scholarship organizations that provide private school scholarships to low-income children. The program would be the first statewide school choice program of its kind in the nation. Although the legislature adjourned without fully considering the bill, prospects for passage next year look very promising.

Independent of the school choice legislation, a private scholarship organization, the Utah Children's Scholarship Fund, has been announced. It will raise private money to provide scholarships to low-income children to attend a private school of choice. The grants will provide partial tuition or, in some cases, full tuition for students in grades K–12. To apply, families must qualify as low-income based on the federal free–reduced lunch program criteria. There are about 140 private and parochial schools in Utah, and a majority are expected to receive some students as a result of this program. The scholarships will be usable at any private school in Utah. Currently, contributions to the Utah Children's Scholarship Fund will be tax deductible.[4]

Position of the Governor/Composition of State Legislature

Governor Michael Leavitt, a Republican, favors choice within the public school system but strongly opposes private school choice. Both houses of the legislature are led by Republicans.

State Contacts

Sutherland Institute
David Salisbury, President
111 East 5600 South Street, Suite 208
Murray, UT 84107
Phone: (801) 281-2081
Fax: (801) 281-2414
Web site: http://www.sutherlandinstitute.org
E-mail: sutherland@utah-inter.net

Utah Children's Scholarship Fund
Jordan Clements, President
c/o Peterson Ventures
111 East Broadway, Suite 1080
Salt Lake City, UT 84111
Phone: (801) 359-8880
E-mail: jordan@petersonventures.com

Utah State Office of Education
Pat O'Hara, Director of School Finance
250 East 500 South
Salt Lake City, UT 84111
Phone: (801) 538-7665
Fax: (801) 538-7729

Endnotes

1 For sources, see "An Explanation of the State Profile Categories." Private school data provided by the Sutherland Institute.

2 The Blum Center's *Educational Freedom Report*, No. 58, April 24, 1998.

3 See Center for Education Reform Web site at *http://www.edreform.com/laws/Utah.htm*.

4 E-mail correspondence from David Salisbury of the Sutherland Institute, received March 2, 2000.

Vermont

State Profile[1]

School Choice Status

- Public school choice: N/A
- Charter schools: N/A
- Publicly funded private school choice: Tuitioning law since 1869

    Program description: Parents who live in districts without high schools (grades 7–12) or elementary schools are reimbursed for the cost of sending their children to a non-religious private school or a public school in a neighboring district or state of choice; boarding schools are not included. In some areas, union districts have been created to centralize high school attendance from small rural towns in which families do not have the option of being reimbursed for private school costs. The program initially included religious as well as non-religious schools; in 1961, however, a ruling by the Vermont Supreme Court prohibited the inclusion of religiously affiliated schools. In 1998–1999, about 400 students attended private schools under the program.

K–12 Public and Private School Students and Schools

- Public school enrollment (fall 1998) and number of schools (1997–1998): 106,691 in 355 schools
- Private school enrollment and number of schools (1997–1998): 10,823 in 101 schools

K–12 Public and Private School Student Academic Performance

NAEP Test Results—percentage of students at each performance level for both public and private schools, with national percentages in parentheses

Performance Level	Reading 4th grade 1998	Reading 8th grade 1998	Math 4th grade 1996	Math 8th grade 1996	Science 8th grade 1996
Advanced	n/a	n/a	3% (2%)	4% (4%)	3% (3%)
Proficient	n/a	n/a	20 (18)	23 (19)	31 (24)
Basic	n/a	n/a	44 (42)	45 (38)	36 (33)
Below Basic	n/a	n/a	33 (38)	28 (39)	30 (40)

- SAT weighted rank (1999): 7 out of 24 states and the District of Columbia
- ACT weighted rank (1999): N/A

K–12 Public School Expenditures

- Current expenditures (1999–2000): $729,877,000
- Amount of revenue from the federal government (1998–1999): 4.9%
- Current per-pupil expenditures (1999–2000): $6,836

K–12 Public School Teachers (1998–1999)

- Number of teachers: 8,084
- Average salary: $36,800

- Students enrolled per teacher: 13.2
- Largest teachers union: NEA

Background

Since 1869, Vermont has had an educational choice system for students who reside in towns that do not have their own public high school and do not belong to a union high school district and parents in towns which do not offer all elementary grades. Tuition town students in the 7th through 12th grades may attend an approved public or non-sectarian school located within or outside Vermont. Their town school boards pay their tuition expenses. If the student chooses an independent school, the voters of the town school district can decide whether to pay an amount equal to the state's average union high school tuition, with parents required to make up the difference if this amount is below the actual tuition charged.

For towns that have no elementary schools, Act 271 of 1990 provides for similar tuitioning by school boards to both public and independent schools. Parents of these students do not have the legal right to have the tuition paid for their children to attend an independent school of choice, but it would be highly unusual for a school board to refuse a parent's request.

Until 1962, towns were allowed to pay tuition at Catholic high schools. Then the Vermont Supreme Court ruled that using public money to pay tuition at a parochial school violated the state's constitution.

In 1996, the school board of Chittenden, a tuition town, sought to pay the tuition of 14 students to Mt. St. Joseph Academy, a nearby Catholic high school. The state responded by withholding the town's state education aid. On August 29, 1996, the town filed a lawsuit (*Chittenden Town School District* v. *Vermont Department of Education*) to force the state to release the aid. On June 27, 1997, Rutland County Superior Court Judge Alden Byran struck down Chittenden's efforts to include religious schools in its tuitioning options. An appeal was filed in the Vermont Supreme Court in early July 1997. Oral arguments were presented before the court on March 10, 1998, on whether the town of Chittenden should be permitted to allow religious schools in its tuitioning options. A decision excluding these schools was handed down in June 1999.

In 1997, a group of state House members led by Representative Howard Crawford (R–Burke) sponsored a bill to create "Education Freedom Districts." Under H. 393, the voters of a school district essentially could have designed their own school system, including options for vouchers, charter schools, an exemption from teacher certification, subject matter examination for teachers, merit pay, termination of union dues checkoffs, and privatization. No action was taken, but the bill will be resubmitted in 2000.

In 1997, the legislature passed the controversial Equal Education Opportunity Bill (Act 60). Under this legislation, the state will collect all local school taxes and distribute the money to all towns equally. Some jurisdictions will receive less than they had been spending per pupil. As part of this major revision in education financing, the Senate, by a vote of 18 to 12, passed an amendment to allow parents to use the state block grant ($5,000 per pupil) to send their child to any approved non-sectarian school beginning in 2003. The provision was dropped at the insistence of House conferees. An identical amendment offered in 1998 by Senator Vincent Illuzzi (R–Essex, Orleans) was rejected by a vote of 12 to 17.

Developments in 1999

In the March 1999 school board elections, one member of the Chittenden school board was replaced, and the new board voted 2–1 to stop funding the tuition of students at St. Joseph's (a religious school) at public expense.

The Vermont Supreme Court issued its ruling in *Chittenden Town School District* v. *Vermont Department of Education*. The ruling, released on June 11, 1999, stated that school districts may not make tuition payments to sectarian schools "in the absence of adequate safeguards against the use of such funds for religious worship." The ruling was based almost exclusively on Vermont's constitution, specifically its "compelled support" clause (Chapter I, Article 3), making resort to the federal appeals process difficult. Nevertheless, on October 9, 1999, the case was appealed to the U.S. Supreme Court, which on December 13, 1999, declined to hear the Vermont case, thereby allowing the lower court ruling to stand and excluding sectarian schools from the program.

A new private scholarship program, Vermont S.O.S., awarded 135 three-year scholarships to low-income students entering kindergarten through 8th grade in fall 1999. The scholarships cover 50 percent of tuition up to $2,000 a year. Students already attending private school at the time of receiving the scholarship will receive 25 percent of the scholarship, awarded annually.

Senate bill 203 was passed by the Senate during the 1999 legislative session. It is an extremely weak public high school choice bill and threatens to undermine Vermont's traditional tuitioning system. Although school choice activists were supportive as the bill was being drafted in the Senate Education Committee, they plan to withdraw their support in 2000.

Several bills promoting publicly funded private school choice were introduced in 1999 but were carried over to the 2000 legislative session.[2]

Position of the Governor/Composition of State Legislature

Governor Howard Dean, a Democrat, favors public school choice. In his state of the state message in 1998, Governor Dean declared himself in favor of "empowering parents" to choose a public school of choice; legislation to bring this about (S 203) has not yet been approved by the House Education Committee. Both houses of the legislature are led by Democrats.

State Contacts

Ethan Allen Institute
John McClaughry, President
4836 Kirby Mountain Road
Concord, VT 05824
Phone: (802) 695-1448
Fax: (802) 695-1436

Vermonters for Better Education
Libby Sternberg, Executive Director
170 North Church Street
Rutland, VT 05701
Phone: (802) 773-3740
E-mail: lsternberg@aol.com

Vermonters for Educational Choice
Jerry Smiley, President
3343 River Road
New Haven, VT 05472
Phone: (802) 388-2133

Vermont S.O.S. Fund
Ruth Stokes, Executive Director
P.O. Box 118
Burlington, VT 05402
Phone: (802) 879-7460
Fax: (802) 879-2550

Vermont Independent Schools Association
Web site: http://www.vtedresources.org

Endnotes

1   For sources, see "An Explanation of the State Profile Categories."

2   E-mail from Libby Sternberg, Vermonters for Educational Choice, May 20, 1999.

Virginia

State Profile[1]

School Choice Status
- Public school choice: N/A
- Charter schools: Established 1998
    Strength of law: Weak
    Number of charter schools in operation (fall 1999): 0
    Number of students enrolled in charter schools (1998–1999): N/A
- Publicly funded private school choice: N/A

K–12 Public and Private School Students and Schools
- Public school enrollment (fall 1998) and number of schools (1997–1998): 1,124,022 in 1,811 schools
- Private school enrollment and number of schools (1997–1998): 98,307 in 591 schools

K–12 Public and Private School Student Academic Performance
NAEP Test Results—percentage of students at each performance level for both public and private schools, with national percentages in parentheses

Performance Level	Reading 4th grade 1998	Reading 8th grade 1998	Math 4th grade 1996	Math 8th grade 1996	Science 8th grade 1996
Advanced	6% (6%)	3% (2%)	2% (2%)	3% (4%)	2% (3%)
Proficient	24 (23)	30 (28)	17 (18)	18 (19)	25 (24)
Basic	34 (31)	45 (41)	43 (42)	37 (38)	32 (33)
Below Basic	36 (39)	22 (28)	38 (38)	42 (39)	41 (40)

- SAT weighted rank (1999): 13 out of 24 states and the District of Columbia
- ACT weighted rank (1999): N/A

K–12 Public School Expenditures
- Current expenditures (1999–2000): $6,927,452,000
- Amount of revenue from the federal government (1998–1999): 5.3%
- Current per-pupil expenditures (1999–2000): $6,153

K–12 Public School Teachers (1998–1999)
- Number of teachers: 79,803
- Average salary: $37,475
- Students enrolled per teacher: 14.1
- Largest teachers union: NEA

Background[2]

In 1991, the Secretary of Education under former Democratic Governor Douglas Wilder asked the state Board of Education to study school choice developments around the country and evaluate the feasibility of implementing school choice in Virginia. A sample survey of Virginians conducted in conjunction with this study revealed broad support for the general concept, and great support when the question included religious schools among the choices available to parents.

When Governor George Allen, a Republican, took over in 1994, he showed a strong interest in education alternatives. His "Blue Ribbon Strike Force" Commission on Government Reform recommended in 1994 that the state provide "all parents with maximum choice possible in the determination of the education of their children" and called for school choice to "increase the competitive behavior among schools and school districts."

Governor Allen's Commission on Champion Schools examined primary and secondary education around the state, and the recommendations in its final report became the basis for numerous statewide education reforms designed to promote higher academic standards and greater accountability. The commission also examined educational alternatives and noted in its final report that the "most discredited idea in economics is that a government monopoly is the best way to deliver services." The commission called for a variety of school choice options, including charter schools, both intra-district and inter-district school choice, educational opportunity grants, and tuition tax credits, and suggested providing vouchers to the parents of students whose schools lose their accreditation under the state's Standards of Accreditation.

In 1998, State Delegate Jay Katzen (R–31) introduced a bill requesting a study of the feasibility of granting state or local tax credits for private school tuition payments and home instruction. The bill died in committee.

After several attempts, charter school legislation was finally passed in 1998. Virginia's charter schools, like ordinary public schools, must adhere to most regulations covering school operations, including state curriculum standards and testing as well as requirements governing pupil-staff ratios, licensing, and much more.

Virginia's law also stipulates that charter schools must be a part of a local school division and must be approved by the local school board, with no appeals process. Charters in Virginia are limited to two per school division until July 1, 2000, at which time a school division may have up to 10 percent of its schools as charter schools.

Under Virginia's new Standards of Accreditation for public schools, advocated by former Governor Allen and approved in 1997, a public school will lose its accreditation if sufficient numbers of its students do not meet state standards for academic achievement.

Developments in 1999

H.B. 1740, the Virginia Children's Educational Opportunity (CEO) Act of 1999, was introduced in the Virginia House on January 13, 1999. The companion bill in the Senate was S.B. 866. Championed by the Virginia-based Family Foundation, the bill would have phased in a tax credit of up to $500 for individuals or businesses making donations to scholarship organizations that support the education of low-income children in kindergarten through 12th grade. The bill also proposed another credit of 80 percent to 100 percent for parents who have paid certain costs for their children's education in private, parochial, or home-schooling situations as well as other public schools besides the child's free, assigned school. These credits would be phased in over a period of five years. The bill never cleared the education committee of either the House of Delegates or the Senate.[3]

Late in 1999, the Virginia Institute for Public Policy proposed a Universal Tuition Tax Credit plan. Under this proposal, parents would receive a dollar-for-dollar reduction in their Virginia state income tax liability for every dollar they spend on tuition, up to one-half of the state's per-pupil expenditure in the public school system or 80 percent of the private school tuition, whichever is smaller. (If the student's family fell below the federal poverty level, the full amount of the tuition would be allowable up to the maximum of 50 percent of the public school system's per-pupil expenditure.) Individuals who pay others' tuition would be eligible to receive the same tax credit, and corporations would receive a 100 percent tax credit for money donated for school scholarships.

Following negotiations with the U.S. Department of Education in 1998, Virginia has received a three-year federal grant to support charter school planning and implementation. The state will receive $631,000 the first two years and $842,000 the third year.

To date, there are no charter schools in Virginia; as of December 1999, 14 school districts were accepting applications for charter schools.

Developments in 2000

The Virginia Children's Educational Opportunity Act was reintroduced in modified form in both houses of the General Assembly. HB 68 provides state tax credits of up to $2,500 for each child to defray the costs of qualifying educational expenses, including private school tuition, textbooks, and tutoring. HB 68 also would provide up to a $550 tax credit for each home-schooled child and give $500 tax credits for donors to a scholarship fund—called a School Tuition Organization—to benefit low-income families. On the opening day of the session, hundreds of supporters attended a rally to push the legislation at the state capitol. The bill again failed to clear the House or Senate Finance Committees, but school choice advocates have a good chance of reintroducing choice in upcoming years.

In the meantime, a new private scholarship program, Children First Virginia, will begin helping low-income students in Northern Virginia and Richmond to attend a school of choice starting in the fall of 2000.

Position of the Governor/Composition of State Legislature

Governor James Gilmore, a Republican, campaigned on maintaining the education reforms initiated by Governor George Allen and on reducing public school class size by increasing the number of public school teachers. In his first press conference after the election, Governor Gilmore noted his willingness to consider innovative measures to improve children's education, including school choice. He did not, however, voice support for the school choice proposals that were introduced in the General Assembly. Both houses of the legislature are led by Republicans.

State Contacts

Children First Virginia
c/o Clare Boothe Luce Policy Institute
Michelle Easton, President
112 Elden Street, Suite P
Herndon, VA 22170
Phone: (703) 318-0730
Fax: (703) 318-8867

Clare Boothe Luce Policy Institute
Michelle Easton, President
112 Elden Street, Suite P
Herndon, VA 22170
Phone: (703) 318-0730
Fax: (703) 318-8867

Family Foundation
John Whitlock, President
Martin Brown, Executive Vice Director
Robyn DeJarnette, Government Relations Director
6767 Forest Hill Avenue, Suite 270
Richmond, VA 23225
Phone: (804) 330-8331
Fax: (804) 330-8337
Web Site: www.familyfoundation.org
E-mail: vafamily@familyfoundation.org

David W. Garland
1322 Nottoway Avenue
Richmond, VA 23227
Phone: (804) 422-1760
E-mail: dwgjd@mindspring.com

Home School Legal Defense Association
Doug Domenech, Executive Director
P.O. Box 3000
Purcellville, VA 20134
Phone: (540) 338-1835
Fax: (540) 338-2733
Web site: http://www.hslda.org

Landmark Legal Foundation
Mark Levin, President
Peter Hutchison, General Counsel
457–B Carlisle Drive
Herndon, VA 20170
Phone: (703) 689-2370
Fax: (703) 689-2373

Lexington Institute
Bob Holland, Senior Fellow
Don Soifer, Vice President
1655 North Fort Myer Drive, #325
Arlington, VA 22209
Phone: (703) 522-5828
Fax: (703) 522-5837
Web site: http://www.lexingtoninstitute.org

Office of the Secretary of Education
200 North Ninth Street
Ninth Street Office Building
Richmond, VA 23212
Phone: (804) 786-1151
Fax: (804) 371-0154

Rutherford Institute
Ron Rissler, Legal Coordinator
P.O. Box 7482
Charlottesville, VA 22906-7482
Phone: (804) 978-3888
Fax: (804) 978-1789
Web site: http://rutherford.org

Thomas Jefferson Institute for Public Policy
Michael Thompson, President
9035 Golden Sunset Lane
Springfield, VA 22153
Phone: (703) 455-9447
Fax: (703) 455-1531

Virginia Department of Education
P.O. Box 2120
Richmond, VA 23218-2120
Phone: (804) 780-7000
Web site: www.pen.K12.va.us/html

Virginia Institute for Public Policy
John Taylor, President
20461 Tappahannock Place
Potomac Falls, VA 20615-4791
Phone: (703) 421-8635
Fax: (703) 421-8631
Web site: http://www.virginiainstitute.org
E-mail: TrtimQuids@aol.com

Endnotes

1 For sources, see "An Explanation of the State Profile Categories."

2 Based on information provided by state contact David W. Garland, December 1999.

3 See *http://www/vachoice.home.mindspring.com.*

Washington

State Profile[1]

School Choice Status
- Public school choice: Statewide
- Charter schools: N/A
- Publicly funded private school choice: N/A

K–12 Public and Private School Students and Schools
- Public school enrollment (fall 1998) and number of schools (1997–1998): 999,616 in 2,016 schools
- Private school enrollment and number of schools (1998–1999): 81,057 in 468 schools

K–12 Public and Private School Student Academic Performance
NAEP Test Results—percentage of students at each performance level for both public and private schools, with national percentages in parentheses

Performance Level	Reading 4th grade 1998	Reading 8th grade 1998	Math 4th grade 1996	Math 8th grade 1996	Science 8th grade 1996
Advanced	6% (6%)	2% (2%)	1% (2%)	4% (4%)	2% (3%)
Proficient	23 (23)	30 (28)	20 (18)	22 (19)	25 (24)
Basic	34 (31)	45 (41)	46 (42)	41 (38)	34 (33)
Below Basic	37 (39)	23 (28)	33 (38)	33 (39)	39 (40)

- SAT weighted rank (1999): 1 out of 24 states and the District of Columbia
- ACT weighted rank (1999): N/A

K–12 Public School Expenditures
- Current expenditures (1999–2000): $6,152,966,000
- Amount of revenue from the federal government (1998–1999): 6.7%
- Current per-pupil expenditures (1999–2000): $6,126

K–12 Public School Teachers (1998–1999)
- Number of teachers: 49,500
- Average salary: $38,692
- Students enrolled per teacher: 20.2
- Largest teachers union: NEA

Background

Washington offers post-secondary enrollment options to allow 11th and 12th grade students to take courses, free of charge, for high school or college credit at community or technical colleges. Students enrolled in a private school or in home schooling also may take advantage of this option.

The state has been in the spotlight in recent years because of several campaign finance violations by its teachers union. In 1997, Attorney General Christine Gregoire filed a lawsuit against the Washington Education Association (WEA), charging that it had committed multiple violations of campaign finance law in the 1996 campaign to oppose statewide charter school and voucher initiatives.

Among the violations that the state penalized were failures to correctly report hundreds of thousands of dollars in campaign contributions, concealing the fact that highly paid political operatives were employed by the National Education Association and that the NEA had funneled $410,000 through the WEA to oppose the 1996 ballot initiatives on charter schools and vouchers. For these violations, the WEA and some officials were fined more than $108,300 and WEA members each were to receive a share of a $330,000 repayment.

One charge that was raised but not addressed by state action was that the WEA's actions violated Washington State's "paycheck protection" statute requiring annual written authorization before a payroll deduction can be diverted for political contributions. Instead, the Attorney General prepared guidelines interpreting the paycheck protection statute so as not to apply to labor organizations using general dues for election campaign contributions.

The permissive guidelines came to the financial rescue of an ailing teachers union. Contributions to the WEA's PAC had dropped off dramatically after the campaign finance violations came to light: The WEA reported that more than 85 percent of the state's public school teachers had refused to contribute to its PAC. The state's guidelines now allow the WEA to supplement PAC contribution losses with mandatory dues from its members.

Washington's Evergreen Freedom Foundation and Teachers for a Responsible Union have filed a lawsuit against the WEA, charging the union

with violating the paycheck protection statute by diverting employee payroll deductions to political campaigns without permission. The lawsuit also claims that the WEA's political activities are so extensive that the union has violated public disclosure laws that govern political action committees.

In August 1999, a lower court ruled that, although the WEA spent more money on campaigns than nearly all political action committees, the union was not obligated to disclose financial activity as a political action committee. This decision is being appealed by the foundation and the teachers.

In an earlier ruling, the court affirmed the state's position, articulated in the Attorney General's guidelines, that the paycheck protection statute did not apply to unions' general dues. The foundation was allowed an accelerated appeal of this question, and the Supreme Court heard arguments in November of 1999.

A ruling on whether the WEA must secure permission before using general fund dues for campaign contributions is expected in 2000. If the Supreme Court overturns the lower court, the WEA could be required to fund its campaign activities from voluntary sources.[2]

The Senate Education Committee held a hearing on House Bill 2019, a charter school proposal, at the end of the 1998 legislative session. For the fourth consecutive year, however, the legislature failed to pass a charter school bill. S.B. 7901 died in the Senate Ways and Means Committee despite broad support from Governor Gary Locke, the Superintendent of Public Instruction, a majority of House Democrats, and a majority of House and Senate Republicans. Not one of the nine Democrats on the Senate Ways and Means Committee voted to send the bill to the Senate floor. Although Governor Locke supported the bill, his fiscal 1999 education budget proposal did not make passage of a charter school bill a priority. He has promised to sign any bipartisan bill that reaches his desk.

On September 28, 1998, Seattle was named one of 40 "partner cities" for the Children's Scholarship Fund (CSF) challenge grant. The CSF is a $100 million foundation underwritten by entrepreneurs Ted Forstmann and John Walton. It matches funds raised by Seattle residents to fund approximately 250 private scholarships for low-income students to attend a school of choice. A lottery in April 1999 determined who would receive the scholarships, which were awarded for at least four years to children entering kindergarten through 8th grade the following year.[3]

Developments in 1999
On April 22, 1999, the Children's Scholarship Fund announced the winners of the largest private scholarship program in the country. The recipients were selected randomly by computer-generated lottery. In Seattle and Tacoma, 250 scholarship recipients were chosen from 8,259 applicants.[4]

Developments in 2000
Charter advocates introduced House Bill 2415 with the support of a new advocate: Senator Julia Patterson (D). The new proposal allowed for the creation of 20 charter schools and was limited to districts in which enrollment is above 2,000. Aside from these two limitations, the charters were given vast fiscal and legal autonomy; were given 100 percent of per-pupil funding; and had access to start-up grants and were eligible for local and state matching funds for facilities.[5]

Under a procedural rule of the state legislature, however, all bills must have been passed by the House or Senate by 5:00 p.m. on February 15, 2000. Although the charter bill had been on the floor calendar for several days, it was never brought up for a vote. Thus, for the fifth consecutive year, the legislature failed to pass charter schools. Charter advocates will now try to place charter schools on the state's 2000 ballot.

Position of the Governor/Composition of State Legislature
Governor Gary Locke, a Democrat, supports charter schools. The Senate is led by Democrats; power is shared in the House because of a 49–49 tie.

State Contacts
CSF–Seattle-Tacoma
Bob Hurlbut, Administrator
1401 East Jefferson, Suite 300
Seattle, WA 98122
Phone: (206) 329-7305
Fax: (206) 329-7415

Education Excellence Coalition
Jim and Fawn Spady
4426 2nd Avenue, NE
Seattle, WA 98105-6191
Phone: (206) 634-0589
Fax: (206) 633-3561
E-mail: JimSpady@aol.com

Evergreen Freedom Foundation
Bob Williams, President
P.O. Box 552
Olympia, WA 98507
Phone: (360) 956-3482
Fax: (360) 352-1874
Web site: http://www.effwa.org
E-mail: effwa@effwa.org

Washington Federation of Independent Schools
Daniel Sherman
P.O. Box 369
DuPont, WA 98327-0369
Phone: (253) 912-5808
Fax: (253) 912-5809
Web site: www.WFIS.org

Washington Institute Foundation
Dick Derham, President
4025 Delridge Way, SW, Suite 210
Seattle, WA 98106
Phone: (206) 937-9691
Fax: (206) 938-6313
Web site: http://www.wips.org
E-mail: wif@wips.org

Washington Office of Superintendent of Public Instruction
Old Capitol Building
P.O. Box 47200
Olympia, WA 98504
Phone: (360) 753-6738
Web site: http://www.ospi.wednet.edu/

Washington Research Council
Richard S. Davis, President
1085 Washington Street, Suite 406
Seattle, WA 98104
Phone: (206) 467-7088
Fax: (206) 467-6957

Endnotes
1 For sources, see "An Explanation of the State Profile Categories."

2 E-mail correspondence from Jami Lund, Evergreen Freedom Foundation, March 5, 2000.

3 See Children's Scholarship Fund Web site at *http://www.scholarshipfund.org.*

4 *Ibid.*

5 For the text of this bill, see *http://www.leg.wa.gov.*

West Virginia

State Profile[1]

School Choice Status

- Public school choice: Limited
- Charter schools: N/A
- Publicly funded private school choice: N/A

K–12 Public and Private School Students and Schools

- Public school enrollment (fall 1998) and number of schools (1997–1998): 296,562 in 819 schools
- Private school enrollment and number of schools (1997–1998): 14,640 in 159 schools

K–12 Public and Private School Student Academic Performance

NAEP Test Results—percentage of students at each performance level for both public and private schools, with national percentages in parentheses

Performance Level	Reading 4th grade 1998	Reading 8th grade 1998	Math 4th grade 1996	Math 8th grade 1996	Science 8th grade 1996
Advanced	6% (6%)	1% (2%)	2% (2%)	1% (4%)	1% (3%)
Proficient	23 (23)	26 (28)	17 (18)	13 (19)	20 (24)
Basic	33 (31)	47 (41)	44 (42)	40 (38)	35 (33)
Below Basic	38 (39)	26 (28)	37 (38)	46 (39)	44 (40)

- SAT weighted rank (1999): N/A
- ACT weighted rank (1999): 21 out of 26 states

K–12 Public School Expenditures

- Current expenditures (1999–2000): $2,042,531,000
- Amount of revenue from the federal government (1998–1999): 10.8%
- Current per-pupil expenditures (1999–2000): $6,878

K–12 Public School Teachers (1998–1999)

- Number of teachers: 20,623
- Average salary: $34,244
- Students enrolled per teacher: 14.4
- Largest teachers union: NEA

Background

West Virginia has no school choice or charter school programs.

Developments in 1999

No developments were reported.

Developments in 2000

On January 12, 2000, an education tax credit bill was filed in the House Education Committee.[2]

Position of the Governor/Composition of State Legislature

Governor Cecil Underwood, a Republican, has not stated a position on school choice or charter schools. Both houses of the legislature are led by Democrats.

State Contacts

CPR for the Family
c/o Mary Ann Rohr
Route 1, Box 103
Walker, WV 26180
Phone: (304) 489-2132

West Virginia Department of Education
1900 Kanawha Boulevard East
Charleston, WV 25305
Phone: (304) 558-2546
Web site: http://www.wvde.state.wv.us/

Endnotes

1 For sources, see "An Explanation of the State Profile Categories."

2 See Education Commission of the States Web site at *http://www.ecs.org*.

Wisconsin

State Profile[1]

School Choice Status
- Public school choice: Statewide
- Charter schools: Established 1993
    Strength of law: Strong
    Number of charter schools in operation (fall 1999): 45
    Number of students enrolled in charter schools (1998–1999): 2,530
- Publicly funded private school choice: Milwaukee Parental choice Program since 1990
    Program description: The Milwaukee plan offers families whose income is at or below 1.75 percent of the poverty level to attend a private or religious school of choice. The vouchers are limited to 15 percent of the district's public school enrollment (a maximum of about 15,000 scholarships a year); due to popular demand, the students are selected by lottery. In 1999–2000, the plan provided more than 8,000 students with scholarships of up to $5,000 each to attend 91 private or religious schools of choice.

K–12 Public and Private School Students and Schools
- Public school enrollment (fall 1998) and number of schools (1997–1998): 879,535 in 2,112 schools
- Private school enrollment and number of schools (1997–1998): 143,577 in 1,073 schools

K–12 Public and Private School Student Academic Performance
NAEP Test Results—percentage of students at each performance level for both public and private schools, with national percentages in parentheses

Performance Level	Reading 4th grade 1998	Reading 8th grade 1998	Math 4th grade 1996	Math 8th grade 1996	Science 8th grade 1996
Advanced	6% (6%)	2% (2%)	3% (2%)	5% (4%)	4% (3%)
Proficient	28 (23)	31 (28)	24 (18)	27 (19)	35 (24)
Basic	38 (31)	46 (41)	47 (42)	43 (38)	34 (33)
Below Basic	28 (39)	21 (28)	26 (38)	25 (39)	27 (40)

- SAT weighted rank (1999): N/A
- ACT weighted rank (1999): 1 out of 26 states

K–12 Public School Expenditures
- Current expenditures (1999–2000): $6,708,569,000
- Amount of revenue from the federal government (1998–1999): 4.4%
- Current per-pupil expenditures (1999–2000): $7,588

K–12 Public School Teachers (1998–1999)

- Number of teachers: 56,592
- Average salary: $40,657
- Students enrolled per teacher: 15.5
- Largest teachers union: NEA

Background

In April 1990, Governor Tommy Thompson, a Republican, signed legislation spearheaded by State Representative Annette "Polly" Williams (D–Milwaukee) to give low-income Milwaukee parents the opportunity to send their children to a private non-sectarian school of choice at state expense. After surviving a grueling round of constitutional challenges, participation in the Milwaukee Parental Choice Program (MPCP) has expanded every year since its inception.

The first five annual evaluations (1991–1995) of the Milwaukee choice program were conducted for the Wisconsin Department of Public Instruction by John F. Witte, a professor of political science at the University of Wisconsin in Madison. His survey revealed high levels of parent and student satisfaction with the program, as well as increased parental involvement at participating schools and improved discipline and attendance. But because Witte compared the children in the choice program with the general student population of Milwaukee rather than with children from similar socioeconomic backgrounds, he found no rise in academic test scores for choice students and stated that no firm conclusion could be drawn from the results. Yet nearly all parents participating in the program reported that their children were improving academically, that their children's attitudes toward school were improving, and that they planned to stick with the schools they had chosen.[2] (Witte has since endorsed the voucher program in a book that was released in early 2000.[3])

Witte released his data for peer review after the fifth-year evaluation. A secondary analysis of his data, which compared students in the choice program to those who had applied but were randomly rejected, showed significant improvements in academic achievement. This analysis was conducted by Paul Peterson of the John F. Kennedy School of Government and Department of Government at Harvard University and Jay Greene of the Center for Public Policy at the University of Houston. Their study revealed that the reading scores of students in their third and fourth years in Milwaukee's choice program

were, on average, three to five percentile points higher, and math scores were five to 12 percentile points higher, than those of students who were unable to get a scholarship.[4] The significance of these results led the researchers to conclude that "If similar success could be achieved for all minority students nationwide, it could close the gap separating white and minority test scores by somewhere between one-third and more than one-half."[5]

A later study by Cecilia Rouse of Princeton University also found that the Milwaukee choice program significantly increased the mathematical achievement of students who had participated in the program.[6]

Backed by such strong popular support, Governor Thompson proposed an expansion of the choice program in his fiscal 1995–1997 budget and included religious schools in the range of schools from which parents could choose. On July 26, 1995, Governor Thompson signed the expanded program into law. The major provisions of Wisconsin's expanded choice program are as follows:[7]

- Eligibility is limited to Milwaukee families with incomes at or below 175 percent of the federal poverty level. An estimated 65,000 to 70,000 children are eligible under this guideline.

- Participation is limited to 15 percent of enrollment in the MPS system, or about 15,700 students. In the original program, participation was limited to 1.0 percent of MPS enrollment; this was increased to 1.5 percent in 1993. The legislature approved expanding the program to include up to 7,250 students in the first year.

- Students may attend any participating private K–12 school in Milwaukee, including religious schools. For the 1999–2000 school year, the voucher amount is set at $5,106 per student or the school's cost per student, whichever is less. Private schools in the program are paid for operating costs and debt service.

- As payment, the state issues a check made payable to the school and the parent or guardian of a participating student, and mails it to the private school; the check is then endorsed by the parent and used by the school for that student's expenses.

From the fall of 1995 until June 1998, the education establishment and its allies prevented Milwaukee's low-income children from taking advantage of the expanded Milwaukee choice program. The American Civil Liberties Union and Wisconsin affiliates of the National Education Association, joined by the National Association for the Advancement of Colored People (NAACP), challenged the constitutionality of the expanded Wisconsin program in state court. In August 1995, they succeeded in temporarily blocking implementation of the program.

The 1995 injunction came as approximately 2,000 newly eligible students were beginning classes at religious schools. The day the injunction was handed down, plans were launched for a fund-raising campaign to enable these students to stay at the schools their parents had chosen. By mid-September 1995, about $2 million had been raised. Hundreds of contributions from individuals and employers were matched by a $1 million grant from the Lynde and Harry Bradley Foundation. With the in-kind contributions from schools and personal sacrifices made by parents of choice students, nearly all the children who had enrolled in the expanded program were able to stay in their school of choice.

Under the leadership of Parents Advancing Values in Education (PAVE), millions of dollars in additional funds were raised for the 1996–1997 and 1997–1998 school years. As a result, while litigation proceeded, the number of low-income children benefiting from school choice increased to about 6,000. This included roughly 1,500 students at non-sectarian schools in the tax-supported program and about 4,500 students with PAVE scholarships, most of whom attended religious schools.

The 1995 injunction was the first step in a protracted legal battle over the expanded choice program that did not end until 1998. In a historic June 10, 1998, ruling, by a vote of 4 to 2, the Wisconsin Supreme Court sustained all aspects of Wisconsin's expanded choice program, holding that it complied with both the U.S. Constitution and the state constitution. The court found that the program does not violate the separation clauses of the Constitution because it is neutral between religious and secular options, and parents or children direct the funds. The court also ruled that the program does not violate the state constitution because it operates primarily to the benefit of children, not religious schools. The court dismissed NAACP claims that the program would segregate Milwaukee school students. In addition, students who were eligible in 1995 but who enrolled in private schools using PAVE scholarships were still eligible for the approved program.

This decision weakens allegations by opponents of school choice that the program violates the Establishment Clause of the U.S. Constitution. Citing a 1971 U.S. Supreme Court ruling, the Wisconsin court's majority opinion, written by Justice Donald W. Steinmetz, declared, "The simplistic argument that every form of financial aid to church-sponsored activity violates the Religion Clauses was rejected long ago." Moreover, "Not one cent flows from the state to a sectarian private school under the [plan] except as a result of the necessary and intervening choices of individual parents." The one-paragraph dissenting opinion addressed only the state constitution's religious establishment provision. This means that the First Amendment issue was settled by a vote of 4 to 0 in favor of choice.

Opponents then appealed this decision to the U.S. Supreme Court, which decided on November 11, 1998, not to review the case, thus effectively upholding the Milwaukee choice program.

The momentum for educational reform in Wisconsin received another boost in 1997 when the legislature approved Governor Thompson's plan to expand and strengthen the state's charter school law. The most significant change affects Milwaukee, where charter schools now may operate independently of affiliation or approval of the city's public school system. Instead, chartering authority has been extended to the city of Milwaukee, the University of Wisconsin–Milwaukee, and the Milwaukee Area Technical College. As with the choice program, the expanded charter program began modestly in 1998–1999 with two schools operating under a city of Milwaukee charter. For the 1999–2000 school year, many schools have shown an interest in participating, including several seeking a charter from the University of Wisconsin–Milwaukee.

Meanwhile, a report by the Greater Milwaukee Education Trust, released on February 16, 1998, found that even though spending in the Milwaukee public school system had increased by 66 percent over the past 10 years, there had been no improvement in graduation rates, attendance rates, or the overall grade-point average during the same period.[8]

Developments in 1999

In the 1999 Milwaukee School Board elections, touted by the local teachers union as a referendum on school choice, all five union-supported candidates, including three incumbents, were defeated. The Milwaukee Teachers Education Association had endorsed the five candidates who lost.

More than 8,000 choice students are attending 91 parochial and private schools thanks to the voucher program and public support for choice, which is at an all-time high. An October 1999 poll of 800 people in the Milwaukee area conducted by the *Milwaukee Journal Sentinel* showed that 60 percent of the people in the area support the private school voucher program. The strongest support was among African–Americans and Hispanics with 74 percent and 77 percent, respectively, in favor of current school choice programs. Among people with incomes below $11,000 a year, 81 percent support the current school choice programs.

Developments in 2000

The official evaluator of the Milwaukee school choice program, John Witte, whose reports have been used to show that school choice does not work, endorsed the Milwaukee choice program in a new book released in early 2000. *The Market Approach to Education: An Analysis of America's First Voucher Program* finds choice to be a "useful tool to aid low-income families."[9]

A report by the state's Legislative Audit Bureau finds that, despite fears of "creaming" and segregation, school choice is serving a student population identical to that of the Milwaukee public school system. The report also finds that most of the schools participating in the Milwaukee parental choice program provide high-quality academic programs and tests.[10]

Position of the Governor/Composition of State Legislature

The leadership of Governor Tommy Thompson, a Republican, has helped to create and expand Wisconsin's school choice and charter reforms. His reforms have been enacted despite sustained opposition from teachers unions and other opponents of choice. Governor Thompson also has been a strong supporter of higher standards in public schools and has sponsored and signed legislation that substantially increases financial support for K–12 education. The House is led by Republicans; the Senate is led by Democrats.

State Contacts

American Education Reform Council
Susan Mitchell
2025 North Summit Avenue
Milwaukee, WI 53202
Phone: (414) 319-9160
Fax: (414) 765-0220

Institute for the Transformation of Learning
Office of Research
2025 North Summit Avenue, Suite 101
Milwaukee, WI 53202
Phone: (414) 765-0691
Fax: (414) 765-1271

Parents for School Choice
Zakiya Courtney, Executive Director
2541 North 46th Street
Milwaukee, WI 53210
Phone: (414) 933-7778; (414) 258-4810, ext. 307

Partners Advancing Values in Education (PAVE)
Daniel McKinley, Executive Director
1434 West State Street
Milwaukee, WI 53233
Phone: (414) 342-1505
Fax: (414) 342-1988; (414) 342-1513
Web site: http://www.pave.org
E-mail: paveorg@yahoo.com

Representative Annette "Polly" Williams
P.O. Box 8953
Madison, WI 53708
Phone: (608) 266-0960
Fax: (414) 871-6112

Wisconsin Department of Public Instruction
Milwaukee Parental School Choice Program
Charlie Toulmin, Administrator
125 South Webster Street, Box 7841
Madison, WI 53707-7841
Phone: (608) 266-2853
Fax: (608) 266-2840
Web site: http://www.dpi.state.wi.us/dpi/dfm/
sms/choice.html
E-mail: charles.toulmin@dpi.state.wi.us

Wisconsin Policy Research Institute
James Miller, President
P.O. Box 487
Thiensville, WI 53092
Phone: (414) 241-0514
Fax: (414) 241-0774
Web site: http://www.wpri.org
E-mail: wpri@mail.execpc.com

Endnotes

1 For sources, see "An Explanation of the State Profile Categories."

2 For copies of annual evaluations of the Milwaukee Parental Choice Program, contact the Wisconsin Department of Public Instruction, P.O. Box 7841, Madison, WI 53707-7841, (608) 266-1771.

3 Joe Williams, "Ex-Milwaukee Evaluator Endorses School Choice," *The Sunday Journal Sentinel*, January 9, 2000, p.1.

4 Jay P. Greene and Paul E. Peterson, "The Effectiveness of School Choice in Milwaukee: A Secondary Analysis of Data from the Program's Evaluation," American Political Science Association Panel on the Political Analysis of Urban School Systems, August–September 1996. See also Jay P. Greene, Paul E. Peterson, and Jiangtao Du, "School Choice in Milwaukee: A Randomized Experiment," in Paul E. Peterson and Bryan Hassel, eds., *Learning from School Choice* (Washington, D.C: Brookings Institution, 1998).

5 Greene and Peterson, "The Effectiveness of School Choice in Milwaukee: A Secondary Analysis of Data from the Program's Evaluation," p. 4.

6 Cecilia E. Rouse, "Private School Vouchers and Student Achievement: An Evaluation of the Milwaukee Parental Choice Program," Department of Economics, Princeton University, December 1996.

7 From information provided by American Education Reform Council, Milwaukee, Wisconsin.

8 The Blum Center's *Educational Freedom Report*, No. 57, March 20, 1998.

9 Williams, "Ex-Milwaukee Evaluator Endorses School Choice."

10 See *www.legis.state.wi.us/lab/windex.htm*.

Wyoming

State Profile[1]

School Choice Status
- Public school choice: Limited
- Charter schools: Established 1995
    - Strength of law: Weak
    - Number of charter schools in operation (fall 1999): 0
    - Number of students enrolled in charter schools (1998–1999): N/A
- Publicly funded private school choice: N/A

K–12 Public and Private School Students and Schools
- Public school enrollment (fall 1998) and number of schools (1997–1998): 94,420 in 412 schools
- Private school enrollment and number of schools (1997–1998): 2,593 in 43 schools

K–12 Public and Private School Student Academic Performance
NAEP Test Results—percentage of students at each performance level for both public and private schools, with national percentages in parentheses

Performance Level	Reading 4th grade 1998	Reading 8th grade 1998	Math 4th grade 1996	Math 8th grade 1996	Science 8th grade 1996
Advanced	6% (6%)	2% (2%)	1% (2%)	2% (4%)	2% (3%)
Proficient	24 (23)	27 (28)	18 (18)	20 (19)	32 (24)
Basic	35 (31)	47 (41)	45 (42)	46 (38)	37 (33)
Below Basic	35 (39)	24 (28)	36 (38)	32 (39)	29 (40)

- SAT weighted rank (1999): N/A
- ACT weighted rank (1999): 13 out of 26 states

K–12 Public School Expenditures
- Current expenditures (1999–2000): $650,000,000
- Amount of revenue from the federal government (1998–1999): 6.2%
- Current per-pupil expenditures (1999–2000): $6,913

K–12 Public School Teachers (1998–1999)
- Number of teachers: 6,646
- Average salary: $33,500
- Students enrolled per teacher: 14.2
- Largest teachers union: NEA

Background

Wyoming does not have a school choice program. Because the state is largely rural, many believe that instituting school choice programs statewide would present many practical problems.

Wyoming's first charter school law was passed on March 6, 1995. It allows for the establishment of public charter schools across the state, but it also restricts the ability of private schools to apply for charter status and mandates minimum state standards. The law places no limit on the number of charters that can be granted (although each charter is limited to a period of five years) and allows charter schools some freedom from the regulatory requirements and laws governing public schools.

Natrona County School District No. 1 allows 11th and 12th grade students to take courses for high school and college credit at nearby Casper College.

Developments in 1999

An amendment to offer parents vouchers was introduced in the Senate in 1999 but failed by two votes.

Developments in 2000

State Senator Mike Massie introduced a two-year, $1,000,000 pilot plan to provide seed funding for start-up costs for schools of choice and charter schools across Wyoming.[2] The measure was rejected.

An amendment to the budget bill to allow a two-year voucher pilot program for 50–100 students also failed to pass.[3]

Position of the Governor/Composition of State Legislature

Governor Jim Geringer, a Republican, is pursuing innovative options to reform education. These options include charter schools, combined home school–public school accommodations, and broader opportunities for religious educational choice. Both houses of the legislature are led by Republicans.

State Contacts

Wyoming Citizens for Educational Choice
Nancy Hamilton
1055 Hidalgo Drive
Laramie, WY 82072
Phone: (307) 721-9541
E-mail: Treyham@vwyo.edu

Fort Caspar Academy
Norm Carrell, Principal
2000 Casper Street
Casper, WY 82604
Phone: (307) 577-4531
E-mail: norm_carrell@ncsd.k12.wy.us

Endnotes

1   For sources, see "An Explanation of the State Profile Categories."

2   Wyoming Citizens for Educational Choice Communicator, e-mail correspondence, January 10, 2000.

3   Wyoming Citizens for Educational Choice Communicator, e-mail correspondence, February 27, 2000.

Mariana Islands

Background

The legislature of the Commonwealth of the Northern Mariana Islands (CNMI) considered a comprehensive voucher program in 1996–1997. The islands' public schools suffer from many of the same problems that afflict public schools on the mainland. Public schools are overcrowded and generally unsatisfactory, causing many parents who live near the worst ones to misrepresent where they live in order to avoid sending their children to those schools. There are no teachers unions, and support for school choice is nearly unanimous.

In 1997, then-Governor Froilan Tenorio, a Democrat, and State Representative Heinz Hofschneider, an Independent, introduced the Parental Choice Scholarship Program. Under this program, the 12,000 students on the Mariana Islands would have received scholarships of up to $1,500 to redeem at a school chosen by their parents.[1] A watered-down version of this plan was approved by the education committee in late 1997, but after the governor failed to win reelection, the plan was never debated again.

Developments in 1999

The recently elected speaker of the CNMI House, Ben Fital, is a school choice advocate.

Position of the Governor

The position of Governor Pedro P. Tenorio, a Republican, on vouchers is unknown.

Contacts

Speaker Ben Fital
CNMI Legislature
P.O. Box 586
Saipan, MP 96950

Office of the Resident Representative of the CNMI
Pete Torres
2121 R Street, NW
Washington, DC 20008
Phone: (202) 673-5869

Endnote

1 The Blum Center's *Educational Freedom Report*, No. 49, July 25, 1997.

Puerto Rico

Background

Governor Pedro Rosello, a Democrat, signed a pilot voucher plan into law in September 1993. The $10 million project enabled parents with annual incomes of less than $18,000 to receive vouchers for up to $1,500 toward tuition at public or private schools of choice, including religious schools. The law also allowed all parents choice among the Commonwealth's public schools. In addition, 40 public schools were transformed into self-governing "community schools" that function like charter schools. The vouchers were portable between public schools and between private and public schools.

Preliminary evidence belies assertions that a voucher program would ruin the public school system. In the fall of 1993, 1,809 vouchers were awarded. Students used 1,181 of these vouchers to transfer from one public school to another; 317 used them to move from private to public schools; and 311 used them to shift from public to private schools. A total of 16,889 students chose their own schools in 1994, and nearly 15,000 of them chose to go to public schools.

In 1994, the teachers unions filed a lawsuit claiming that Puerto Rico's new school choice law was unconstitutional. The Washington, D.C.-based Institute for Justice represented a group of parents and children who supported the pilot voucher program. On November 30, 1994, by a vote of 5 to 2, the Puerto Rico Supreme Court ruled in *Asociacion de Maestros de P.R.* v. *Arsenio Torres* that the scholarship program allowing poor children to attend a school of choice violated the commonwealth's constitution. The court permitted the program to continue until the end of the 1994–1995 school year, and the public school choice provision was allowed to continue indefinitely. During that year, 14,101 vouchers were awarded, of which 10,598 were used for public school choice, 1,793 were used for transfers from private to public schools, and 1,710 were used for transfers from public to private schools.[1]

Because the decision was based solely on Puerto Rico's constitution, the case has not been appealed to the U.S. Supreme Court. The ruling does not establish a precedent for school choice programs in other states or jurisdictions.

Developments in 1999

The commonwealth enacted a program to provide low-income parents funds for non-tuition, education-related expenses at a public, private, or religious school of choice. A governing board would decide the amount of the fund for parents. The plan has been halted by an injunction.[2]

Position of the Governor

Governor Pedro Rosello, a Democrat, spearheaded Puerto Rico's school choice plan.

Contacts

Governor Pedro Rossello
Puerto Rico Federal Affairs Administration
Office of the Governor
1100 17th Street, NW, Suite 800
Washington, DC 20036

Puerto Rico Federal Affairs Administration
Honorable Victor Fajardo
1100 17th Street, NW, Suite 800
Washington, DC 20036

Endnotes

1 "What We Know About Vouchers," WestEd Policy Program, September 1999.

2 *Ibid.*

APPENDIX A

Select List of National Organizations That Promote School Choice

Alexis de Tocqueville Institution
1611 North Kent Street, Suite 901
Arlington, VA 22209
Phone: (703) 351-4969
Fax: (703) 351-0090
Web site: www.adti.net

American Education Reform Council
2025 North Summit Avenue, Suite 103
Milwaukee, WI 53202
Phone: (414) 319-9160
Fax: (414) 765-0220

American Enterprise Institute
1150 17th Street, NW
Washington, DC 20036
Phone: (202) 862-5800
Fax: (202) 862-7178
Web site: www.aei.org

American Legislative Exchange Council
910 17th Street, NW, 5th Floor
Washington, DC 20006
Phone: (202) 466-3800
Fax: (202) 466-3801
Web site: www.alec.org

Cato Institute
1000 Massachusetts Avenue, NW
Washington, DC 20001
Phone: (202) 842-0200
Fax: (202) 842-3490
Web site: www.cato.org

Center for Education Reform
1001 Connecticut Avenue, NW, Suite 204
Washington, DC 20036
Phone: (202) 822-9000
Fax: (202) 822-5077
Web site: www.edreform.com

CEO America
P.O. Box 330
901 McClain Road, Suite 802
Bentonville, AR 72712-0330
Phone: (501) 273-6957
Fax: (501) 273-9362
Web site: www.ceoamerica.org

Children's Scholarship Fund (CSF)
7 West 57th Street
New York, NY 10019
Phone: (212) 752-8555
Fax: (212) 750-4252
Web site: www.scholarshipfund.org

Christian Coalition
1801–L Sara Drive
Chesapeake, VA 23320
Phone: (757) 424-2630
Fax: (757) 424-9068
Web site: www.cc.org

Citizens for a Sound Economy
1250 H Street, NW, Suite 700
Washington, DC 20005
Phone: (202) 783-3870
Fax: (202) 783-4687
Web site: www.cse.org

Citizens for Educational Freedom
9333 Clayton Road
St. Louis, MO 63124
Phone: (314) 997-6361
Fax: (314) 997-6321
Web site: www.Educational-Freedom.org

The Claremont Institute
250 West First Street, Suite 330
Claremont, CA 91711
Phone: (909) 621-6825
Fax: (909) 626-8724
Web site: www.claremont.org

Andrew Coulson
19045 State Highway 305
Suite 220, PMB 123
Poulsbo, WA 98370
Phone: (360) 394-9535
Fax: (360) 394-9517
Web site: www.schoolchoices.org

The Edison Project
521 5th Avenue, 15th Floor
New York, NY 10175
Phone: (212) 309-1600

Fax: (212) 309-1604
Web site: www.edisonproject.com

Education Leaders Council
1001 Connecticut Avenue, Suite 204
Washington, DC 20036
Phone: (202) 822-9000
Fax: (202) 822-5077
Web site: www.edreform.com/elc

Education Policy Institute
4401–A Connecticut Avenue, NW
Box 294
Washington, DC 20008
Phone: (202) 244-7535
Fax: (202) 244-7584
Web site: www.educationpolicy.org

Empower America
1701 Pennsylvania, Avenue, NW, Suite 900
Washington, DC 20006
Phone: (202) 452-8200
Fax: (202) 833-0388
Web site: www.empower.org

Family Research Council
801 G Street, NW
Washington, DC 20001
Phone: (202) 393-2100
Fax: (202) 393-2134
Web site: www.frc.org

Greater Educational Opportunities Foundation
1800 North Meridian Street, Suite 506
Indianapolis, Indiana 46202
Phone: (317) 283-4711
Fax: (317) 283-4712
Web site: www.geofoundation.org

John F. Kennedy School of Government
T308 Harvard University
Cambridge, MA 02138
Phone: (617) 495-7976
Fax: (617) 496-4428
Web site: www.data.fas.harvard.edu/pepg/

The Heartland Institute
19 South LaSalle, Suite 903
Chicago, IL 60603
Phone: (312) 377-4000
Fax: (312) 377-5000
Web site: www.heartland.org

The Heritage Foundation
214 Massachusetts Avenue, NE
Washington, DC 20002-4999
Phone: (202) 546-4400
Fax: (202) 546-8328
Web site: www.heritage.org/schools

The Hudson Institute
Herman Kahn Center
5395 Emerson Way
Indianapolis, IN 46226
Phone: (317) 545-1000
Fax: (317) 545-9639
Web site: www.hudson.org

Institute for the Transformation of Learning
Marquette University
P.O. Box 1881
Milwaukee, WI 53201-1881
Phone: (414) 288-5775
Fax: (414) 288-6199

Institute for Justice
1717 Pennsylvania Avenue, NW, Suite 200
Washington, DC 20006
Phone: (202) 955-1300
Fax: (202) 955-1329
Web site: www.instituteforjustice.org

Landmark Legal Foundation
3100 Broadway, Suite 515
Kansas City, MO 64111
Phone: (816) 931-5559
Fax: (816) 931-1115
Web site: www.landmarklegal.org

The Lexington Institute
1655 North Fort Myer Drive, Suite 325
Arlington, VA 22209
Phone: (703) 522-5828
Fax: (703) 522-5837
Web site: www.lexingtoninstitute.org

Manhattan Institute
52 Vanderbilt Avenue
New York, NY 10017
Phone: (212) 599-7000
Fax: (212) 599-3494
Web site: manhattan-institute.org

Milton and Rose D. Friedman Foundation
P.O. Box 82078
One American Square, Suite 2440
Indianapolis, IN 46282
Phone: (317) 681-0745
Fax: (317) 681-0945
Web site: www.friedmanfoundation.org

National Center for Neighborhood Enterprise
1424 16th Street, NW
Washington, DC 20036
Phone: (202) 518-6500
Fax: (202) 588-0314
Web site: www.ncne.com

National Center for Policy Analysis
12655 North Central Expressway, Suite 720
Dallas, TX 75243
Phone: (972) 386-6272
Fax: (972) 386-0924
Web site: www.ncpa.org

National Right to Work Legal Defense
Foundation, Inc.
8001 Braddock Road
Springfield, VA 22160
Phone: (703) 321-8510
Fax: (703) 321-9613
Web site: www.nrtw.org

Pacific Research Institute for Public Policy
755 Sansome Street, Suite 450
San Francisco, CA 94111
Phone: (415) 989-0833
Fax: (415) 989-2411
Web site: www.pacificresearch.org

Reason Public Policy Institute
3415 South Sepulveda Boulevard, Suite 400
Los Angeles, CA 90034-6064
Phone: (310) 391-2245
Fax: (310) 391-4395
Web site: www.reason.org

State Policy Network
13101 Preston Road, Suite 403
Dallas, TX 75240
Phone: (972) 233-6676
Fax: (972) 233-6696
Web site: www.spn.org

Thomas B. Fordham Foundation
1627 K Street, NW, Suite 600
Washington, DC 20006
Phone: (202) 223-5452
Fax: (202) 223-9226
Web site: www.edexcellence.net

Toussaint Institute
20 Exchange Place, 41st Floor
New York, NY 10005-3201
Phone: (212) 422-5338
Fax: (212) 422-0615

APPENDIX B

Home School Laws of the United States

The following table was assembled by the Home School Legal Defense Association. Copyright 2000 (last revised January 13, 2000—most current information posted at *http://www.hslda.org/central/state*). May be reproduced only by permission. Home School Legal Defense Association, P.O. Box 3000, Purcellville, Virginia 20134.

Home School Laws of the United States

	Compulsory School Age	Legal Options to Home School	Attendance Required
Alabama			
	"between the ages of 7 and 16"	Establish and/or enroll in a church school	None specified (175 days required for the public schools)
		Use a private tutor	140 days per year, 3 hours per day between the hours of 8 a.m. and 4 p.m.
Alaska			
	"between 7 and 16"	Establish and operate a home school	None
		Use a private tutor	180 days per year
		Enroll in a state department of education-approved full-time correspondence program	180 days per year
		Request school board approval to provide an equal alternate educational experience	180 days per year
		Qualify as a religious or other private school	180 days per year
Arizona			
	"between 6 and 16"; by noting so in affidavit (see *Notice Required*) instruction in a home school setting may be delayed until eight years of age	Establish and operate a home school	None
Arkansas			
	"5 through 17 on or before September 15 of that year"; a child under age 6 on September 15 may be waived from kindergarten with submission of a state-provided form	Establish and operate a home school	None

Home School Laws of the United States

Subjects Required	Teacher Qualifications and Testing Requirements	Notice Required	Recordkeeping Required
None	None	File a notice of enrollment and attendance with the local superintendent on a provided form (not required annually)	Maintain a daily attendance register
Reading, spelling, writing, arithmetic, English, geography, history of the United States, science, health, physical education, and Alabama history	Teacher certification No Testing	File a statement showing children to be instructed, the subjects taught, and the period of instruction with the local superintendent	Maintain a register of the child's work
None	None	None	None
Comparable to those offered in the public schools	Teacher certification No Testing	None	None
Comparable to those offered in the public schools	None	None	None
Comparable to those offered in the public schools	None	None	None
None, but standardized testing must cover English grammar, reading, spelling, and math	No Teacher certification Must Administer a standardized test in grades 4,6, and 8	File a "Private School Enrollment Reporting Form" with the local superintendent by the first day of public school; also file a "Private and Denominational Schools Enrollment Report" and a "School Calendar" with the state department of education by October 15 each year	Maintain monthly attendance records; also maintain records on immunization, courses, standardized testing, academic achievement, and physical exams
Reading, grammar, math, social studies, and science	None	File a affidavit of intent with the local superintendent within 30 days of the start (even if instruction will be delayed until age 8) or end of home schooling	None
None	No teacher certification Must participate in same state-mandated norm-referenced tests given to public school students (in grades 5, 7, and 10); no cost to parent unless alternate testing procedures are approved	File written notice of intent with the local superintendent by August 15 (for those starting in fall semester), December 15 (for those starting in spring semester), or 14 days prior to withdrawing child mid-semester from public school; re-file annually thereafter at beginning of school year	None

Home School Laws of the United States

	Compulsory School Age	Legal Options to Home School	Attendance Required
California	"between the ages of 6" by December 2 and "under 18 years of age"	Qualify as a private school	None
		Use a private tutor	175 days per year, 3 hours per day
		Enroll in an independent study program through the public school	As prescribed by the program
		Enroll in a private school satellite program, taking "independent study"	As prescribed by the program
Colorado	"7 and under the age of 16." Also "appl[ies] to a six-year-old child who has been enrolled in a public school in the first [or higher] grade," unless the "parent or legal guardian chooses to withdraw such child."	Establish and operate a home school	172 days per year, averaging four hours per day
		Enroll in a private school that allows home instruction	None
		Use a private tutor	None
Connecticut	"five years of age and over and under sixteen years of age"; five- or six-year-olds can opt out when the parent goes to the school district and signs an option form	Establish and operate a home school	Generally, 180 days per year
Delaware	"between 5 years of age and 16 years of age"; can delay start (if "in best interests of the child") with school authorization	Establish and operate a home school providing "regular and thorough instruction" to the satisfaction of the local superintendent and the state board of education	180 days per year

Home School Laws of the United States

Subjects Required	Teacher Qualifications and Testing Requirements	Notice Required	Recordkeeping Required
Same as the public schools and in the English language	Must be "capable of teaching" No Testing	File an annual affidavit with the local superintendent between October 1 and October 15	Maintain an attendance register
Same as the public schools and in the English language	Teacher certification No Testing	None	None
As prescribed by the program	No teacher certification Testing as prescribed by the program	A de facto part of the enrollment process	As prescribed by the program
As prescribed by the program	Must be "capable of teaching" Testing as prescribed by the program	None	As prescribed by the program
Constitution of the United States, reading, writing, speaking, math, history, civics, literature, and science	No teacher certification Must Administer a standardized test for grades 3, 5, 7, 9, and 11 or have the child evaluated by a "qualified person… selected by parent"	File notice of intent with the local superintendent 14 days prior to start of home school and annually thereafter	Maintain attendance records, test and evaluation results, and immunization records
As prescribed by the program	None	None	None
Constitution of the United States, reading, writing, speaking, math, history, literature, and science	Teacher certification No testing	None	None
Reading, writing, spelling, English, grammar, geography, arithmetic, United States history, and citizenship, including a study of the town, state, and federal governments	None	None, but parents may voluntarily comply with State Dept. of Education guidelines by filing a "Notice of Intent" form with the local superintendent within 10 days of the start of home school	Maintain a portfolio indicating that instruction in the required courses has been given
Same as the public schools	No teacher certification Must administer a written examination as prescribed during the approval process	Report enrollment, student ages, and attendance to Dept. of Education on or before July 31 each year; also submit annual statement of enrollment as of last school day in September in form prescribed by Dept. of Education	None

Home School Laws of the United States

	Compulsory School Age	Legal Options to Home School	Attendance Required
Delaware (Con't)		Establish and/or enroll in a home school association or organization	180 days per year
D.C.	"age of 5 years by December 31 of current school year until minor reaches the age of 18"	Provide private instruction not affiliated with an educational institution	During the period that the public schools are in session
Florida	"attained the age of 6 years by February 1…but have not attained the age of 16 years"	Establish and operate a home school	None specified (180 days required for the public schools)
		Qualify and operate as part of a private school corporation (a legally incorporated group of home school families)	None specified (180 days required for the public schools)
Georgia	"between 7th and 16th birthdays"; a child under 7 who has attended public school for more than 20 days is also subject to the compulsory attendance law	Establish and conduct a home study program	180 days per year, 4½ hours per day
Hawaii	"have arrived at the age of at least 6 years and…not…at the age of 18 years" by January 1	Establish and operate a home school	None

Home School Laws of the United States

Subjects Required	Teacher Qualifications and Testing Requirements	Notice Required	Recordkeeping Required
Same as the public schools	None	Association or organization must register with the Dept. of Education; report enrollment, student ages, and attendance to Dept. of Education on or before July 31 each year; and submit annual statement of enrollment as of last school day in September in form prescribed by Dept. of Education	None
None	None	None, unless the child is being removed from the public school	None
None	No teacher certification Must annually, either: (1) administer any standardized test or a state student assessment test (must be given by a certified teacher); (2) have child evaluated by a certified teacher or (3) be evaluated by a licensed psychologist; or (4) have child evaluated by another valid tool that is mutually agreed upon	File notice of intent with the local superintendent within 30 days of establishment for home school (not required annually)	Maintain a portfolio of records and materials (log of texts and sample work sheets)
None	None	None	None
Reading, language arts, math, social studies, and science	High school diploma or GED for a teaching parent; baccalaureate degree for any private tutor used Must administer and retain the results of a standardized test every 3 years beginning at the end of the 3rd grade	File a declaration of intent with the local superintendent within 30 days of commencing the home study program and by September 1 annually thereafter	Maintain attendance records and submit monthly to the superintendent; write and retain an annual progress report
Curriculum must "be structured and based on educational objectives as well as the needs of the child, be cumulative and sequential, provide a range of up-to-date knowledge and needed skills, and take into account the interests, needs, and abilities of the child"	No teacher certification Must administer standardized achievement test of parent's choice in grades 3, 6, 8, and 10; submit annual report (of child's progress) to local principal comprised of either: (1) standardized test results, or (2) written evaluation by certified teacher, or (3) written evaluation by parent	File a notice of intent with the principal of the public school the child would otherwise be required to attend before starting to home school (not required annually); notify this same principal within 5 days after ending home school	Maintain a record of the planned curriculum

Home School Laws of the United States

	Compulsory School Age	Legal Options to Home School	Attendance Required
Hawaii (Con't.)		Enroll in a superintendent-approved appropriate alternative educational program	As prescribed during the approval process (approximately 3 hours per day)
Idaho	"attained the age of 7 years, but not the age of 16 years"	Provide an alternate educational experience for the child that "is otherwise comparably instructed"	Same as the public schools
Illinois	"between the ages of 7 and 16 years"	Operate a home school as a private school	Generally, 176 days per year (but not mandated for private or home schools)
Indiana	"Earlier of the date on which the child officially enrolls in a school or reaches the age of 7 until the date on which he reaches the age of 18."	Operate a home school as a private school	Same as the public schools; generally, 180 days per year
Iowa	"age 6 by September 15 until age 16"	Establish and operate a home school	148 days per year (37 days each quarter)
		Establish and operate a home school that is supervised by a licensed teacher	148 days per year (37 days each quarter)
		Use a private tutor	148 days per year (37 days each quarter)

Home School Laws of the United States

Subjects Required	Teacher Qualifications and Testing Requirements	Notice Required	Recordkeeping Required
As prescribed during the approval process	Baccalaureate degree to teach Must participate in statewide testing program at the public schools	None	None
Same as the public schools	None	None	None
Language arts, biological and physical science, math, social sciences, fine arts, health and physical development, honesty, justice, kindness, and moral courage	None	None	None
None	None	None, unless specifically requested by the state superintendent of education	Maintain attendance records
None	No teacher certification Must complete by May 1 and submit to the local school district by June 30: (1) test results from an acceptably administered standardized test, or (2) a portfolio for review	Complete an annual "Competent Private Instruction Report Form"; file 2 copies with the local school district by 1st day of school or within 14 days of withdrawal from school	None
None	No certification for teaching parent; license for the supervising teacher No testing requirement; however, must meet with supervising teacher twice per quarter (one may be conducted by telephone)	Complete an annual "Competent Private Instruction Report Form"; file 2 copies with the local school district by 1st day of school or within 14 days of withdrawal from school	None
None	Teaching license No testing	Complete an annual "Competent Private Instruction Report Form"; file 2 copies with the local school district by 1st day of school or within 14 days of withdrawal from school	None

Home School Laws of the United States

	Compulsory School Age	Legal Options to Home School	Attendance Required
Kansas	"reached the age of 7 and under the age of 18 years"	Operate a home school as a non-accredited private school	"substantially equivalent to...the public schools" (i.e., 186 days per year or 1,116 hours per year; 1,086 hours for 12th grade)
		Operate a home school as a satellite of an accredited school	As prescribed by the supervising private school
		Qualify for a state board of education approved religious exemption in the high school grades	As prescribed during the approval process
Kentucky	"has reached the 6th birthday and has not passed the 16th birthday"	Qualify a home school as a private school	185 days per year, or the equivalent of 175 six-hour days
Louisianna	"from the child's 7th birthday until his 17th birthday"	Establish and operate a home school as approved by the board of education	180 days per year
		Operate a home school as a private school	180 days per year
Maine	"7 years of age or older and under 17 years"	Establish and operate a home school as approved by the local school board and the commissioner of the state department of education	175 days per year

Home School Laws of the United States

Subjects Required	Teacher Qualifications and Testing Requirements	Notice Required	Recordkeeping Required
None	Must be a "competent" teacher (however, local school board has no authority to define or evaluate "competence" of private school teachers) No testing	Register name and address of school with the state board of education (not subject to approval)	None
As prescribed by the supervising private school	Must be a "competent" teacher (however, local school board has no authority to define or evaluate "competence" of private school teachers) Testing as prescribed by the supervising private school	Register name and address of school with the state board of education (not subject to approval)	As prescribed by the supervising private school
As prescribed during the approval process	Teacher certification as prescribed during the approval process Testing as prescribed during the approval process	A defacto part of the approval process	As prescribed during the approval process
Reading, writing, spelling, grammar, history, mathematics, and civics	None	Notify the local board of education of those students in attendance within two weeks of start of school year	Maintain an attendance register and scholarship reports
At least equal to the quality of that in the public schools including the Declaration of Independence and the Federalist Papers	No teacher certification Must submit with renewal application documents showing satisfactory evidence that the program is at least equal to that offered by the public schools	File an application and a copy of the child's birth certificate, with board of education, within 15 days after start of home school and annually thereafter	Whatever form(s) of documentation is (are) planned to satisfy the testing requirement
At least equal to the quality of that in the public schools including the Declaration of Independence and the Federalist Papers	None	Submit notification to the state department of education within the first 30 days of the school year	None
English, language arts, math, science, social studies, physical and health education, library skills, fine arts, Maine studies (in one grade between grade 6 and grade 12), and computer proficiency (in one grade between grade 7 and grade 12)	No teacher certification Must annually, either: (1) administer a standardized test, or (2) take a local test, or (3) have child's progress reviewed by a certified teacher, a superintendent-selected local advisory board, or a home school support group that includes a certified teacher	Complete a state-provided "Application for Equivalent Instruction Through Home Instruction" form; submit a copy to both the local school board and the commissioner of the state department of education 60 days prior to start of home school	None

Home School Laws of the United States

	Compulsory School Age	Legal Options to Home School	Attendance Required
Maine (Con't.)		Operate a home school as a non-approved private school that teaches at least two unrelated students	175 days per year
Maryland	"5 years old or older and under 16" with one-year exemption available for 5-year-olds	Establish and operate a qualified home school	Must be of "sufficient duration to implement the instructional program"
		Provide supervised home instruction through a church school or a state-approved correspondence course	As prescribed by the supervising program
Massachusetts	"6 to 16 years of age"	Establish and operate a home school as approved in advance by the local school committee or superintendent	None specified, though 900 hours at elementary level and 990 hours at secondary level are expected
Michigan	"age of 6 to the child's 16th birthday"	Establish and operate a home education program	None
		Operate a home school as a nonpublic school	None
Minnesota	"between 7 and 16 years of age"; extends to 18 years old in the year 2000	Establish and operate a qualified home school	None

Home School Laws of the United States

Subjects Required	Teacher Qualifications and Testing Requirements	Notice Required	Recordkeeping Required
None	None	None	None
Must provide "regular, thorough instruction" in the same subjects as the public schools including English, math, science, social studies, art, music, health, and physical education	None	File a notice of intent with the state department of education at least 15 days before the start of home school	Maintain a portfolio of "relevant materials," reviewable by the local superintendent up to 3 times per year
As prescribed by the supervising program	No teacher certification Testing as prescribed by the supervising program	File a notice of intent with the state department of education at least 15 days before the start of home school	As prescribed by the supervising program
Reading, writing, English language and grammar, geography, arithmetic, drawing, music, history, and Constitution of United States, duties of citizenship, health (including CPR), physical education, and good behavior	No teacher certification Must annually, either: (1) administer a standardized test (must be administered by a neutral party), or (2) submit progress reports to the school district	A de facto part of the approval process	None
Reading, spelling, mathematics, science, history, civics, literature, writing, and English grammar	None	None	None
Must be "comparable to those taught in the public schools"	Teacher certification (unless claiming a religious exemption) No testing	Submit, to the local superintendent, at start of each school year a statement of enrollment	Maintain records of enrollment, courses of study, and qualifications of teachers (must be submitted to the Dept. of Education upon request)
Reading, writing, literature, fine arts, math, science, history, geography, government, health, and physical education	No teacher certification Must administer an annual standardized test as agreed to by the local superintendent	File with the local superintendent by October 1 of each school year the name, age, and address of each child taught	If teaching parent is not at least a college graduate, submit a quarterly report to the local superintendent showing the achievement of each child in the required subjects

Home School Laws of the United States

	Compulsory School Age	Legal Options to Home School	Attendance Required
Mississippi	"age of 6 on or before September 1…and has not attained the age of 17 on or before September 1"	Establish and operate a home school	Whatever "number of days that each [home] school shall require for promotion from grade to grade"
Missouri	"between the ages of 7 and 16 years"	Establish and operate a home school	1,000 hours per year; at least 600 hours in the five required subjects; 400 of these 600 hours must occur at "the regular home school location"
Montana	"7 years of age or older prior to the first day of school" and "the later of the following dates: the child's 16th birthday; the day of completion of the work of the 8th grade"	Establish and operate a home school	180 days per year, 4 hours per day for grades 1–3 and 6 hours per day for grades 4–12
Nebraska	"not less than 7 nor more than 16 years of age"	Establish and operate a home school as a private school	1,032 hours per year for elementary grades, 1,080 hours per year for high school grades
Nevada	"between the ages of 7 and 17 years"	Establish and operate a home school	180 days per year; 240 minutes per day for grades 1 and 2; 300 minutes per day for grades 3–6; 330 minutes per day for grades 7–12
New Hampshire	"at least 6 years of age [on September 30] and under 16 years of age"	Establish and operate a home school	None

Home School Laws of the United States

Subjects Required	Teacher Qualifications and Testing Requirements	Notice Required	Recordkeeping Required
None	None	File a "certificate of enrollment" by September 15 of each school year to the district's attendance officer	None
Reading, math, social studies, language arts, and science	None	None required; parents *may* "provide" a notice of intent within 30 days of establishment and on September 1 each year thereafter	Maintain records of subjects taught, activities engaged in, samples of the child's academic work and evaluations or a credible equivalent
Same "basic instructional program" as the public schools	None	File annual notice of intent with the county superintendent	Maintain attendance and immunization records; must be available for inspection by local superintendent upon request
Language arts, math, science, social studies, and health	No teacher certification, unless the teacher is "employed" by the family No testing	File an annual notice of intent with the state commissioner of education by August 1 (or 30 days prior to the start of home school)	None
Parents must provide the local school board with "satisfactory written evidence" that "the child is receiving at home... equivalent instruction of the kind and amount approved by the state board of education," including U.S. and Nevada constitutions	Either: (1) possess a teaching certificate for grade level taught, or (2) consult with a licensed teacher or 3-year home school veteran, or (3) use an approved correspondenc course, or (4) obtain a waiver; options 1, 2, and 3 are waived after 1st year No testing	File, with the local school board, annual "satisfactory written evidence" that the "child is receiving at home... equivalent instruction of the kind and amount approved by the state board of education"	None
Science, mathematics, language, government, history, health, reading, writing, spelling, U.S. and New Hampshire constitutional history, and art and music appreciation	No teacher certification Must by July 1, file either: (1) results from a standardized test, or (2) results from a state student assessment test used by the local school district, or (3) a written evaluation by a certified teacher, or (4) results of another measure agreeable to the local school board	Within 30 days of withdrawing from public school or moving into the school district, file a notice of intent with a private school principal, the state commissioner of education, or the local superintendent	Maintain a portfolio of records and materials including a log of reading materials used, samples of writings, worksheets, workbooks or creative materials used or developed by the child

Home School Laws of the United States

	Compulsory School Age	Legal Options to Home School	Attendance Required
New Jersey	"between the ages of six and 16 years"	Establish and operate a home school	None specified (180 days required for the public schools)
New Mexico	"at least five years of age prior to 12:01am on September 1 of the school year...to the age of majority...unless the person has graduated from high school"; children under 8 can be excused	Establish and operate a home school	Same as public schools
New York	"a minor who becomes six years of age on or before the first of December in any school year...until the last day of session in the school year in which the minor becomes sixteen years of age" or completes high school	Establish and operate a home school	Substantial equivalent of 180 days per year; 900 hours per year for grades 1–6; 990 hours per year for grades 7–12
North Carolina	"between the ages of seven and 16 years"	Establish and operate a home school	At least nine calendar months per year, excluding reasonable holidays and vacations

Home School Laws of the United States

Subjects Required	Teacher Qualifications and Testing Requirements	Notice Required	Recordkeeping Required
U.S. and New Jersey history, citizenship, civics, geography, sexual assault prevention*, health*, safety, and physical education *may opt out	None	None	None
Reading, language arts, mathematics, social studies, and science	High school diploma or equivalent to teach Testing in grades 4, 6, and 8 either: (1) take the district-administered state achievement test, or (2) participate in the Bob Jones University Press Testing Service *(must notify the school board of intent by January 15)*	File notice of intent with the school district superintendent within 30 days of establishing the home school and by April 1 of each subsequent year	Maintain attendance and immunization records
Grades K–12: patriotism and citizenship, substance abuse, traffic safety, fire safety *Grades 1–6:* arithmetic, reading, spelling, writing, English, geography, U.S. history, science, health, music, visual arts, and physical education *Grades 7–8:* English, history and geography, science, mathematics, physical education, health, art, music, practical arts, and library skills *At least once in grades 1–8:* U.S. and New York history and constitutions *Grades 9–12:* English, social studies—including American history, participation in government, and economics, math, science, art or music, health, physical education, and electives	Teachers must be "Competent" Testing: Must file, with the local superintendent, an annual assessment by June 30; must be from a standardized test every other year in grades 4–8, and every year in grades 9–12; other years can be satisfied by either another standardized test or a written narrative evaluation prepared by a certified teacher, a home instruction peer review panel, or other person chosen by the parent with the consent of the superintendent	File annual notice of intent with the local superintendent by July 1 or within 14 days if starting home schooling mid-year; complete and submit an Individualized Home Instruction Plan (form provided by district)	Maintain attendance records (must make available for inspection upon request of the local superintendent); file, with the local superintendent, quarterly reports listing hours completed, material covered, and a grade or evaluation in each subject
None, but annual standardized tests must cover English grammar, reading, spelling, and mathematics	High school diploma or GED to teach Must administer an annual standardized test measuring achievement in English grammar, reading, spelling, and mathematics, the results of which must be available for inspection	File notice of intent with the state division of non-public education upon starting home school	Maintain attendance and immunization records and results of standardized tests

Home School Laws of the United States

Compulsory School Age	Legal Options to Home School	Attendance Required
North Dakota		
"any educable child of an age of seven years to sixteen years"	Establish and operate a home school	175 days per year, four hours per day
	Operate a home school as a county- and state-approved private school	Same as the public schools

Home School Laws of the United States

Subjects Required	Teacher Qualifications and Testing Requirements	Notice Required	Recordkeeping Required
Elementary: spelling, reading, writing, arithmetic, language, English grammar, geography, U.S. history, civil government, nature, elements of agriculture, physiology and hygiene, effects of alcohol, prevention of contagious diseases, U.S. Constitution *High school level:* English, math, science, social studies, health and physical education, music, combination of business, economics, foreign language, industrial arts, or vocational education	To teach, must possess either: (1) a teaching certificate, or (2) a baccalaureate degree, (3) a high school diploma or GED and be monitored by a certified teacher during first two years or until child completes 3rd grade, whichever is later; monitoring must continue thereafter if child scores below the 50th percentile on required standardized achievement test, or (4) proof of meeting or exceeding the cut-off score of the national teacher exam Must take a standardized achievement test in grades 3, 4, 6, 8, and 11; must be administered by a certified teacher; results must be provided to the local superintendent; a composite score below the 30th percentile requires a professional assessment for learning problems and submission of a plan of remediation to the local superintendent	File annual notice of intent with the local superintendent 14 days prior to the start of the home school or within 14 days of establishing residency inside the district *For autistic children:* In addition to above, file a copy of the child's diagnosis from a licensed psychologist along with an individualized education program developed and followed by the child's school district and parent or by a team selected and compensated by the parent	Maintain an annual record of courses and each child's academic progress assessments, including standardized achievement test results *For autistic children:* Also file with the local superintendent progress reports from an individualized education program team selected by the parent on or before November 1, February 1, and May 1of each school year
Elementary: spelling,reading, writing, arithmetic, language, English grammar, geography, U.S. history, civil government, nature, elements of agriculture, physiology and hygiene, effects of alcohol, prevention of contagious diseases, U.S. Constitution *High school level:* English, math, science, social studies, health and physical education, music, combination of business, economics, foreign language, industrial arts, or vocational education	Teacher certification No testing	A de facto part of the approval process	None

Home School Laws of the United States

Compulsory School Age	Legal Options to Home School	Attendance Required
Commonwealth of the Northern Mariannas Islands		
"between the ages of six and sixteen"	Seek approval to operate a home school	180 days per year with at least "300 minutes of secular instruction daily"
	Seek approval to operate a home school as an chartered non-public school	180 days per year with at least "300 minutes of secular instruction daily"
Ohio		
"between six and eighteen years of age"	Establish and operate a home school	900 hours per year
Oklahoma		
"over age of five (5) years and under the age of eighteen (18) years"	Establish and operate a home school as an "other means of education" expressed in the state constitution	None
Oregon		
"between the ages of 7 and 18 years who have not completed the twelfth grade"	Establish and operate a home school	None

Home School Laws of the United States

Subjects Required	Teacher Qualifications and Testing Requirements	Notice Required	Recordkeeping Required
Same as the public schools	None	Submit a waiver application to the commissioner at least 60 days prior to start of school year	Submit to the commissioner monthly, quarterly, and annual reports on program progress
As prescribed by the board in issuing a charter	None	Submit to the board of education an application for a charter	As prescribed by the board in issuing a charter
Language arts, geography, U.S. and Ohio history, government, math, health, physical education, fine arts, first aid and science	To teach, need a high school diploma, GED, test scores showing high school equivalence, or work under a person with a baccalaureate degree until child's test scores show proficiency or parent earns diploma or GED Testing: must submit with renewal notification either: (1) standardized test scores, or (2) a written narrative showing satisfactory academic progress, or (3) an approved alternative assessment	Submit an annual notice of intent to the local superintendent	None
Reading, writing, math, science, citizenship, U.S. constitution, health, safety, physical education, conservation	None	None	None
None	No teacher certification Testing: Must participate in an approved comprehensive test in grades 3, 5, 8, and 10 administered by "a qualified neutral person"; if child was withdrawn from public school, the first test must be administered at least 18 months after child was withdrawn; children with disabilities are to be evaluated as per their individualized education plan	Notify education service district in writing when child starts being taught at home; when moving, notify new district in same manner	None

Home School Laws of the United States

	Compulsory School Age	Legal Options to Home School	Attendance Required
Pennsylvania	From time the child enters school, "which shall not be later than the age of eight (8) years, until the age of seventeen (17) years"	Establish and operate a home education program	180 days per year or 900 hours at the elementary level or 990 hours at the secondary level
		Establish and/or operate a home school as an extension or satellite of a private school	180 days per year or 900 hours at the elementary level or 990 hours at the secondary level
		Use a private tutor who: (1) is teaching one or more children who are members of a single family, (2) provides the majority of instructiuon, and (3) is receiving a fee or other consideration for the instruction	180 days per year or 900 hours at the elementary level or 990 hours at the secondary level
Puerto Rico	"between six and eighteen years of age"	Establish and operate a home school as a non-governmental school	Same as the public schools
Rhode Island	"completed six (6) years of life on or before December 31 of any school year and not completed sixteen (16) years of life"	Establish and operate a home school as approved by the local school board	"Substantially equal" to that of the public schools

Home School Laws of the United States

Subjects Required	Teacher Qualifications and Testing Requirements	Notice Required	Recordkeeping Required
Elementary level: English, spelling, reading, writing, arithmetic, U.S. and Pennsylvania history, civics, health and physiology, physical education, music, art, geography, science, safety and fire prevention *Secondary level:* English language, literature, speech and composition, science, geography, civics, world, U.S., and Pennsylvania history, algebra and geometry, art, music, physical education, health, safety, and fire prevention	High school diploma or equivalent to teach Testing: Must administer standardized tests in grades 3, 5, and 8; submit results as part of portfolio	File a notarized affidavit with the local superintendent prior to start of home school and annually by August 1st thereafter	Maintain a portfolio of materials used, work done, standardized test results in grades 3, 5, and 8, and a written evaluation completed by June 30 of each year
Elementary level: Same as home education program *Secondary level:* Same as home education program, plus biology, chemistry, a foreign language, general mathematics and statistics	None	School principal must file a notarized affidavit with the department of education	None
Same as satellite of private school	Teacher ceritication needed No testing	File copy of certification and criminal history record with the local superintendent	None
Same as the public schools	None	None	None
Reading, writing, geography, arithmetic, U.S. and Rhode Island history, principles of American government, English, health and physical education; U.S. and R.I. constitution in high school	None Testing as prescribed during the approval process; may require report cards	A de facto part of the approval process	Maintain an attendance register

Home School Laws of the United States

	Compulsory School Age	Legal Options to Home School	Attendance Required
South Carolina	"five years of age before September first until…seventeenth birthday or" graduation from high school; five-year-olds may be excused from kindergarten with submission of written notice to the school district	Establish and operate a home school as approved by the local school board	180 days per year, 4½ hours per day
		Establish and operate a home school under the membership auspices of the South Carolina Association of Independent Home Schools (SCAIHS)	180 days per year
		Establish and operate a home school under the membership auspices of an association for home schools with no fewer than 50 members	180 days per year
South Dakota	"six years old by the first day of September and who has not exceeded the age of sixteen years"; children under age 7 can be excused	Establish and operate a home school	Similar to that of the public schools; generally 175 days per year
Tennessee	"between the ages of six (6) and seventeen (17) years, both inclusive"; also applicable to children under age 6 who have enrolled in any public, private, or parochial school for more than six weeks; a parent of a six-year-old may make application for a one-semester or one-year deferral with the principal of the public school which the child would be required to attend	Establish and operate a home school	180 days per year, 4 hours per day

Home School Laws of the United States

Subjects Required	Teacher Qualifications and Testing Requirements	Notice Required	Recordkeeping Required
Reading, writing, math, science, and social studies; also composition and literature in grades 7–12	High school diploma or GED or a baccalaureate degree to teach Testing: must articipate in the annual statewide testing program and the Basic Skills Assessment Program	None	Maintain evidence of regular instruction including a record of subjects taught, activities in which the student and parent engage, a portfolio of the child's work, and a record of academic evaluations, with a semiannual progress report
Reading, writing, math, science, and social studies; also composition and literature in grades 7–12	High school diploma or GED to teach No testing	None	None
Reading, writing, math, science, and social studies; also composition and literature in grades 7–12	High school diploma or GED to teach No testing	None	Maintain evidence of regular instruction including a record of subjects taught, activities in which the student and parent engage, and a portfolio of the child's work, with a semiannual progress report
Language arts and math	No teacher certification Testing: must administer a standardized test to children in the same grade levels tested under the state testing program (grades 4, 8, and 11)	Submit a notarized application to the local superintendent using the standard form provided by state department of education	None
For grades K–8: None *For grades 9–12:* English, mathematics, science, social studies, and wellness; also must take college preparation subjects according to declared path—foreign language and fine arts for University path; focus area for Tech path	*For grades K–8:* High school diploma or GED *For grades 9–12:* College degree (or an exemption granted by the commissioner of education) Testing: must administer a standardized test in grades 5, 7, and 9; must be given by commissioner of education, his designee, or a professional testing service approved by the local school district	Submit a notice of intent to the local superintendent by August 1 of each school year	Maintain attendance records; must be kept available for inspection and submitted to the local superintendent at the end of the school year

Home School Laws of the United States

	Compulsory School Age	Legal Options to Home School	Attendance Required
Tennessee (Con't.)		Establish and operate a home school in association with a church-related school	As prescribed by the church-related school
		Operate as a satellite campus of a church-related school	As prescribed by the church-related school
		Operate as a satellite campus of a non-recognized religious school, based upon an assertion that the church-related school option unconstitutionally excludes certain religions	As prescribed by the religious school
Texas	"as much as six years of age, or who is less than seven years of age and has previously been enrolled in first grade, and who has not completed the academic year in which his 17th birthday occurred"	Establish and operate a home school as a private school	None
Utah	"between six and 18 years of age"	Establish and operate a home school as approved by the local school board	Same as the public schools
		Establish a group of home school families as a regular private school	None
Vermont	"between the ages of seven and sixteen years"	Establish and operate a home school	175 days per year

Home School Laws of the United States

Subjects Required	Teacher Qualifications and Testing Requirements	Notice Required	Recordkeeping Required
As prescribed by the church-related school	*For grades K–8:* None *For grades 9–12:* High school diploma or GED Testing: must administer the same annual standardized achievement test or Sanders Model assessment used by the local school district for grades 9–12	*For grades K–8:* None *For grades 9–12:* Register with the local school district each year	None
As prescribed by the church-related school	No teacher certification Testing: as prescribed by the church-related school	None	None
As prescribed by the religious school	No teacher certification Testing: as prescribed by the religious school	None	None
Reading, spelling, grammar, math, good citizenship	None	None	None
Language arts, math, science, social studies, arts, health, computer literacy, and vocational education	None specified; however, the local school board can consider the basic educative ability of the teacher No testing	A de facto part of the approval process	None
None	None	None	None
Reading, writing, math, citizenship, history, U.S. and Vermont government, physical education, health, English, science, and fine arts	None Testing: must submit an annual assessment from: (1) a certified (or approved Vermont independent school) teacher, or (2) a report from a commercial curriculum publisher together with a portfolio, or (3) results of an acceptably administered standardized test	File a written notice of enrollment with the commissioner of education any time after March 1 for the subsequent year	None

Home School Laws of the United States

	Compulsory School Age	Legal Options to Home School	Attendance Required
Virginia	"have reached the fifth birthday on or before… September 30…and who has not passed the eighteenth birthday"; 5-year-olds can be excused	Establish and operate a home school	Same as the public schools; generally 180 days per year
		Operate a home school under the religious exemption statute	None
		Use a private tutor	None
Washington	"eight years of age and under eighteen years of age"	Establish and operate a home school	Equivalent to: 2,700 total hours in grades 1–3; 2,970 total hours in grades 4–6; 1,980 total hours in grades 7–8; 4,320 total hours in grades 9–12
		Operate a home school as an extension of an approved private school	180 days per year or equivalent to: 2,700 total hours in grades 1–3; 2,970 total hours in grades 4–6; 1,980 total hours in grades 7–8; 4,320 total hours in grades 9–12

Home School Laws of the United States

Subjects Required	Teacher Qualifications and Testing Requirements	Notice Required	Recordkeeping Required
Reading, writing, math, spelling, history, government and citizenship	Either: (1) possess a baccalaureate degree, or (2) be a certified teacher, or (3) use an approved correspondence course, or (4) submit acceptable curriculum and prove the parent can teach	Teaching: must file an annual notice of intent with local superintendent by August 31 (August 15 beginning in year 2000), or as soon as practicable if starting mid-year Testing: must administer a standardized test or have child otherwise evaluated every year (for those six years or older on September 30 of the school year); submit results to local superintendent by August 1	None
None	None	Submit a notice of intent to local school board to teach No testing	None
None	Teacher certification	File a notice of intent with the local superintendent to teach No testing	None
Occupational education, science, math, language, social studies, history, health, reading, writing, spelling, music and art appreciation, U.S. and Washington constitutions	Either: (1) be supervised by a certified teacher, or (2) have 45 college quarter credit hours or completed a course in home education, or (3) be deemed qualified by the local superintendent	File an annual notice of intent with the local (or applicable nonresident) superintendent by September 15 or within two weeks of the start of any public school quarter to teach Testing: must annually, administer and retain a state-approved standardized test by a qualified person or have the child evaluated by a certified teacher currently working in the field of education	Maintain standardized testscores, academic progress assessments, and immunization records
Occupational education, science, math, language, social studies, history, health, reading, writing, spelling, music and art appreciation, U.S. and Washington constitutions	Must be under the supervision of a certified teacher employed by approved private school	None	None

Home School Laws of the United States

	Compulsory School Age	Legal Options to Home School	Attendance Required
West Virginia	"compulsory school attendance shall begin with the school year in which the sixth birthday is reached prior to the First day of September of such year or upon enrolling in a publicly supported kindergarten program and continue to the sixteenth birthday"	Seek local school board approval to operate a home school	Same as the public schools; generally 180 days per year
		Establish and operate a home school	None
Wisconsin	"between the ages of 6 [by September 1] and 18 years"	Establish and operate a "home-based private educational program"	Must provide "at least 875 hours of instruction each year"
Wyoming	"whose seventh birthday falls before September 15 of any year and who has not yet attained his sixteenth birthday or completed the tenth grade"	Establish and operate a home school	175 days per year

Note: Copyright 2000 Home School Legal Defense Association, reprinted by permission. Last revised January 13, 2000.
Source: Home School Legal Defense Association.

Home School Laws of the United States

Subjects Required	Teacher Qualifications and Testing Requirements	Notice Required	Recordkeeping Required
English, grammar, reading, social studies, and math	Be deemed qualified to teach by the local superintendent and school board	Teacher certification: A de facto part of the approval process Testing: As prescribed during the approval process	As prescribed during the approval process
English, grammar, reading, social studies, and math	High school diploma and formal education at least four years higher than the most academically advanced child to be taught	File a notice of intent with the local superintendent two weeks prior to starting to home school Testing: must annually, either: (1) administer an acceptable standardized test, or (2) be evaluated by a certified teacher, or (3) assess progress by another agreeable means	None
Must provide "a sequentially progressive curriculum of fundamental instruction" in reading, language arts, math, social studies, science, and health; such curriculum need not "conflict with the program's religious doctrines"	None	File a statement of enrollment with the state department of education by October 15 each year to teach No testing	None
A "basic academic educational program" that provides a sequentially progressive curriculum of fundamental instruction in reading, writing, math, civics, history, literature, and science	None	To teach, must annually submit to the local school board a curriculum showing that a "basic academic educational program" is being provided No testing	None